THE
KINGDOM
OF GOD IS
AT HAND

THE
KINGDOM
OF GOD IS
AT HAND

✦ ✦ ✦

THE CHRISTIAN
COMMONWEALTH
IN GEORGIA,
1896–1901

✦ ✦ ✦

THEODORE KALLMAN

THE UNIVERSITY OF
GEORGIA PRESS
ATHENS

Designed by Kaelin Chappell Broaddus
Set in 9.5/13.5 Bunyan Pro Regular
by Kaelin Chappell Broaddus

Most University of Georgia Press titles are
available from popular e-book vendors.

Printed digitally

Library of Congress Cataloging-in-Publication Data
Names: Kallman, Theodore, author.
Title: The kingdom of God is at hand : the Christian Commonwealth
    in Georgia, 1896–1901 / Theodore Kallman.
Description: Athens : The University of Georgia Press, 2021. |
    Includes bibliographical references and index.
Identifiers: LCCN 2020041089 | ISBN 9780820358680 (hardback) |
    ISBN 9780820358673 (paperback) | ISBN 9780820358666 (ebook)
Subjects: LCSH: Christian Commonwealth. | Collective settlements—
    Georgia—History—19th century. | Socialism—United States—
    History—19th century.
Classification: LCC HX656.C47 K35 2021 | DDC 307.7709758/473—dc23
LC record available at https://lccn.loc.gov/2020041089

TO
DEBBIE
AND TO
THE MEMORY OF
LEO BILANCIO
AND
LARRY FINFER

CONTENTS

✦ ✦ ✦

PREFACE

✦ ✦ ✦

The Christian Commonwealth was a small, obscure social experiment in the woods of central Georgia in the late nineteenth century. Inspired by primitive Christianity, postmillennial optimism, and American democracy, its courageous, yet naïve, members labored for over four years to achieve their goal, the Kingdom of God on earth.

Their experiment was unique, but they were joining thousands of disgruntled Americans who sought to challenge the unfettered capitalism of the Gilded Age. It had produced unprecedented growth and development, but at a hefty price of poverty and privation, political corruption, self-serving individualism, excessive materialism, xenophobia, and imperialism.

Radical by some perspectives, Commonwealth was emulating two great traditions: the apostolic Christianity of the followers of Christ and the Puritan desire to found a "city upon the hill."

They did not realize their hope for social salvation, but, for many, personal regeneration brought on by love and sacrifice led them to further endeavors in pursuit of a more humane world.

ACKNOWLEDGMENTS

✦ ✦ ✦

I want to thank several people whose roles in making this work possible were critical. Ron Zboray guided me through some of my earliest writing. W. Fitzhugh Brundage commented positively on an original paper and, later, loaned me microfilm of the *Coming Nation*. Charlotte Alston assisted me in finding translations of Leo Tolstoy's letters to Commonwealth leaders. Ginger Davis and Sue Berkenbush provided me with a massive amount of primary source material on Ralph Albertson and the Christian Commonwealth.

Mary Linnemann at the Hargrett Library at the University of Georgia and the librarians at Georgia State University, the Schlesinger Library at Radcliffe, Yale University, the University of California, Berkeley, the University of the Pacific, and the University of Georgia helped in a multitude of ways.

Thanks to Patrick Allen and Nathaniel Holly, editors at the University of Georgia Press, and the early reviewers for their insights and advice.

Finally, my wife, Debbie, gave me the support and encouragement that allowed me to finish this project.

THE
KINGDOM
OF GOD IS
AT HAND

PART
ONE

GENESIS

CHAPTER I

✦ ✦ ✦

Awakened and Inspired
"The Fathers"

To the Editor of *The Kingdom*:
I have a proposition to make to those who love Christ. . . .
Why not come together and put all that we have, little or much, into a common fund, buy a tract of cheap land, and go there to live and work all good works in Christ's name? Let us deed our land to Christ . . . make it a holy land, a home for all who love Christ. All things that we need, food and raiment and houses, our own labor will supply. We cannot suffer. All things will be done in love. Life will be one. Christ will be our partner. Let us make his laws our laws, his will our will. Let us keep our doors open that whosoever loves him may enter,—nothing laid on them but that they acknowledge Christ as Master and promise to obey him and that they add their possessions to ours that we may have all things in common.

—John Chipman, the *Kingdom*

ON NOVEMBER 29, 1895, John Chipman, a Florida engineer and businessman, sent the above "Proposition" to the editor of the *Kingdom*, a Minneapolis-based newspaper of "applied Christianity." Founded as a mouthpiece for the Reverend George Herron, a radical Christian Socialist activist, the paper blended midwestern Populist discontent with the views of radical clergy. In the late nineteenth century, it was the most popular journal in the United States promoting the Social Gospel. A postmillennial religious movement, the Social Gospel preached that Christ would not return until humanity had eased the plight of the poor and oppressed. Thus, through churches and missionary societies, the movement set out to eradicate urban America's poverty, illiteracy, hunger, and homelessness.[1]

3

Chipman was an orthodox Episcopalian, influenced by Frederick Maurice and Charles Kingsley, two English Christian Socialists. He believed it was impossible to live a Christian life in a competitive society filled with "trouble, discontent, and unfaithfulness." Capitalism violated Christianity's message of unselfishness, cooperation, nonresistance, and brotherly love. Following Christian ideals in a capitalistic society would "involve the sacrifice of the means of life." Calling for a rejection of capitalism, he espoused faith in the Social Gospel and believed love could transform society into "a glorious Kingdom of God." He proposed that families combine their assets to buy land "in west Georgia or east Tennessee...and set up a farm with a small sawmill, a small cotton goods factory, and livestock." The colonists would "work hard, raise cotton and spin it, cut logs and saw them, raise grain and vegetables, and become independent of the world." However, Chipman insisted that evangelical responsibilities—the conversion of others, not economic gain—must be the priority, and the colony must remain "open to all who would come." He believed its evangelical work and example would convince the world of the advantages of moral living. At least, it would "make one little corner...into a glorious Kingdom of God."

Chipman found authorization for his colony in Acts 4:32: "Them that believed were of one heart and of one soul: neither said any of them that aught of the things which he possessed was his own; but that they had all things common." He believed this statement defined communism as the proper Christian method for solving economic problems.[2]

Despite being an orthodox churchman, Chipman criticized the mainstream churches. "What is the duty of the Holy Church," he asked, to burn incense or "to raise mankind to life?" He asked the church to "lead mankind out of the desert" but if it could not, to at least help form the Christian Commonwealth.[3]

Chipman's proposition attracted many responses, favorable and critical, and started a debate in the *Kingdom* and private correspondence between many interested parties. Most critics opposed the separatism of communitarianism. A Wisconsin minister replied that Chipman's New Testament source was only an ideal and communism was impractical because it surrendered individuality. He noted that no community, other than those with "abnormal" family relations, like Oneida and the Shakers, had succeeded after abandoning individual property. Nevertheless, he asked Chipman for more details. Chipman responded that Christians were obligated to "follow

Christ's commands wherever they lead us." They had led Christians to break with Rome and the Puritans to immigrate to America, and now they were awakening the church.

Other communities "based on folly"—Oneida, the Shakers, the Mormons—had succeeded. How could it be impossible for a community founded on obedience to Christ, open doors, communal property, and labor for all not to succeed? J. H. Arnold from South Dakota agreed that Amana fulfilled Chipman's desire for the "Christ life" and a visible Kingdom of God on earth. However, it was a "dull, insensible sort of happiness, such as an ox experiences." From Georgia, W. Harper argued that to withdraw from one's neighbor was hardly "loving him as thyself" as commanded by the Gospel.[4]

George Herron challenged Chipman's critics with a different example. He asserted that the Catholic monastery was organized Christian Socialism and demonstrated communism's practicality. Everyone in the monastery performed at their best and had their needs fulfilled. Herron dismissed Protestant accusations of Catholic corruption and viewed the monastery as a primary force in advancing valuable components of Western civilization—agriculture, industry, education, and the arts.[5]

Chipman's proposition evoked positive responses from many who were dissatisfied with Gilded Age America and believed it necessary to separate from it. Three men, George Howard Gibson, William C. Damon, and Ralph Albertson, all with loyal followers, found Chipman's proposition inviting. Gibson had established the Christian Corporation, a cooperative colony in Nebraska, while Albertson and Damon were starting the Willard Cooperative Colony in North Carolina.[6]

Gibson was a Populist newspaper editor in Lincoln, Nebraska, whose ideas were a blend of agrarian radicalism, Christian Socialism, Tolstoyan anarchism, and the Social Gospel. He had a passion for personal and social righteousness and believed that if people saved their souls through unselfishness in their social relations, the world would follow suit.[7]

In 1887, the ideas of Edward Bellamy's *Looking Backward* intrigued Gibson. In it, he saw that applying Christ's "golden rule" to material production would result in abundance for everyone. In his Lincoln newspaper, the *New Republic*, Gibson commented on the growth of Bellamy's Nationalism and expressed interest in cooperative colonies. He was not alone. Many Americans in the late nineteenth century were reading the utopian literature of Bellamy, Henry George, and Laurence Gronlund. They saw communalism and cooperatives as a potential solution to economic instability and social problems. That perspective produced the most communal activity in America since before the Civil War.[8]

Gibson viewed Gronlund as a courageous advocate of socialism but disagreed with some of his proposals. To his dismay, Gronlund limited the application of socialism to capital: "All matters of consumption, enjoyment, and personal use will remain private property." He believed this was necessary to avoid revolution. In contrast, Gibson held that unequal private wealth would preserve social inequality and stimulate bitter competition, class conflict, and revolution.[9]

In addition to cooperative communities, Gibson's editorials showed interest in the reform efforts of the Farmer's Alliance, the Social Gospel movement, and Christian Socialism. He often quoted the *Dawn*, the organ of the Society of Christian Socialists, calling it "a teacher of pure primitive Christianity." Edited by W. D. P. Bliss, an Episcopalian priest and key figure in Christian Socialism, the *Dawn* introduced Gibson to liberal theology and many spokespersons for the Social Gospel, whose arguments he analyzed in his editorials.[10]

Gibson unsparingly criticized Social Darwinism's sanction of competition and survival of the fittest. In a letter to the *Alliance-Independent*, the Populist Party's newspaper in Lincoln, he condemned competition in American society: "There are tens of thousands in [Chicago] all the time out of work, fighting for positions and the low wages which enable capitalists to rake off dividends for idle and scheming stockholders." Later he wrote to Henry Demarest Lloyd with an alternative: "We must put together our property, labor, economic wisdom, knowledge, varying talents, Christianizing or democratizing what we have and are.... We feel that it is wrong to continue the selfish struggle, even with charitable or philanthropic intent."[11]

Gibson believed that the piecemeal reforms advocated by social reformers were futile and became almost vitriolic when talking about settlement houses. He did not believe that a class of voluntary, professional, charity-dispensing, and charity-supporting saviors could reform a society that accepted individualism and private property as its chief "goods." Almsgiving wounded the manhood and womanhood of all whom it did not degrade, and as long as there are class differences, we cannot establish Christian love. He observed, "Uplifting the masses is all right, but it would be much better to put a stop to the beastly struggle that crowds them down."[12]

Gibson left the *New Republic* and became editor of the *Alliance-Independent*, which he renamed the *Wealth Makers* to express his belief that workers, both rural and urban, were the creators of wealth and to create solidarity between them. Gibson editorialized that the profit system was selfish and inequitable. It produced a society in which "commercially organized, selfishly ruled circles of production and distribution" poured wealth into the pockets of the few and undermined the manhood and Christianity of the many. The solution was to promote "the Christianity of Brotherhood" and replace "single-handed competition with many-sided cooperation."[13]

When the Populist Party created its Omaha platform in 1892, Gibson viewed it in Christian Socialist terms, believing that Populism and Christian principles were mainly the same. He tried to incorporate Christian Socialism into the Populist Party's political platform, arguing that "God's priceless abundant gifts must not be used for purposes of oppression and robbery. Society owes as much help to one individual as to another. Monopolists are . . . kings, despots, robbers, slaveowners and they must with such be classed. In the degree that I love liberty, I hate monopoly." He believed a Christian life demanded communism because the "each-for-himself system of production and distribution could not be Christianized."[14]

Gibson wanted to introduce the Social Gospel and Tolstoy's ideas to the Populist movement. He derived his economics from Tolstoy's Christian anarchist perspective. Later, in the *Social Gospel*, he wrote regular columns on "the economics of love." The commercial system is evil, and its "trusts, monopolies and corporation combines are a legitimate offspring and part of selfish, struggling individualism" that is "worse than chattel slavery." A Christian could not practice love in a marketplace governed by an anti-Christian, competitive, each-for-himself business rule. The strife created divided men's hearts, prevented love between families, made some rich and many poor, and brought evil to humanity. However, Gibson doubted that the each-for-himself world could be Christianized and instead turned to communitarianism because it was impossible to live in the competitive world "without partaking of its sins and plagues." The way to live was to practice love and Christlike unselfishness through labor in a community "without money and without price."[15]

George Herron's book, *The New Redemption: A Call to the Church to Reconstruct Society According to the Gospel of Christ*, became a significant influence on Gibson. Herron argued that "the duty of man to man" must take priority over the individual rights of capital and labor and must emulate Christ's crucifixion to bring a new redemption through sacrifice. Herron frequently spoke at midwestern Populist meetings and in 1894 delivered the commencement address at Nebraska's state university. He proposed a socialist theocracy to destroy the "domination of organized, cunning capitalists," eliminate economic competition, and organize the state according to Christian doctrine. According to Herron, the state could survive only by accepting "Christ as the supreme authority in law, politics, and society." The Marxist critique of capitalism and class influenced Herron and Gibson, but Gibson rejected Marx's belief in class conflict as the hope for the future. Only brotherhood and cooperation would melt down class differences and bring peace on earth.[16]

Herron, while advocating state socialism, cautiously supported cooperative and communal enterprises. Henry Demarest Lloyd, a wealthy Chicago radical, agreed, and the two men prodded Gibson in that direction. "Rightly initiated," they believed, a community could be "one key to the situation." Gibson's interest in organizing society and communal enterprises around a common interest, "industrial democracy which is organized Christianity," sounded like a paraphrase of Herron.[17]

Populism and Christian Socialism proved to be incompatible. Silver-minded Populists were not socialistic levelers. Gibson's radicalism generated such hostility that he lost the Populist endorsement and editorship and was left politically isolated and disillusioned. In response, he became captivated by the idea of a self-sufficient cooperative community as a path to reform.[18]

In 1894, Gibson warned Lloyd that the Populist leaders meeting in St. Louis would try "to eliminate, or shelve, the socialistic planks in our party and to recommend as leaders that we make free silver and government paper money—simply paid out—the issue, or the dominant question, with us."[19]

After seeing Herron at that meeting, Gibson called for a conference of Christian cooperators in Lincoln, which led to the formation of the Christian Corporation. The corporation purchased the *Wealth Makers* and operated it according to Christian principles as a "common property brotherhood organization." They also acquired land around Lincoln to establish "a farming, stock-raising, fruit-growing, manufacturing and love-educating paradise."[20]

The Christian Corporation based its philosophy on a simple statement of faith: "We believe in God our infinite father; in Christ our perfect brother; and in the law of equalizing love expressed in the command, 'Thou shalt love thy neighbor as thyself.'" Reflecting Thomas Jefferson and Henry George, the corporation held certain "self-evident" truths: all men had the right to share equally in the earth's abundant natural resources. The earth is "by a common inheritance, for use only, and not for speculation." Later, when Gibson expressed this philosophy in the *Social Gospel*, he added a quote from Jefferson to the end: "The earth is given as common stock for man to labor on.... Whenever there are in any country uncultivated lands and unemployed poor, it is clear that the laws of property have been so far extended as to violate natural rights."[21]

In less than a year, the Christian Corporation consisted of ninety-nine members in twenty-three families. It owned 1,360 acres of land and had assets of thirty thousand dollars. Gibson called it a "democratic industrial equality, communal organization and an association of Christian Communes to equalize conditions and allow none to lack."[22]

When John Chipman's "proposition" appeared, Gibson's Christian Corporation had been functioning successfully. However, his radical political views had caused a decline in the circulation of *Wealth Makers*, which put financial stress on the paper and the corporation. After reading Chipman's "proposition," Gibson became attracted to his proposed self-sufficient cooperative community, and perhaps needing financial resources, he left the Populist Party on the verge of being "wiped out" by fusion, sold the *Wealth Makers*, and joined the dialogue in the *Kingdom*.[23]

In response to Chipman's critics, Gibson argued that colonies, such as Brook Farm, had failed because they were imperfectly Christian, and "no undertaking ruled by Christ has or can come to naught." Promoting his version of a Christianized world, Gibson thought the mainstream church was the greatest obstacle to the practice of true Christianity. "The chief obstruction," wrote Gibson, "has been the ... worldly standard of the churches and the churches' sanction of selfish business codes and practices." It accepted the "respectable selfishness" of the business community, partook of its wealth, and created "pleasing worldly standards" for its congregation. He was not sure that a cooperative community could lead to the Kingdom of God but believed that if its members demonstrated an "allegiance to Christ," a "Christ-filled" society could be established.[24]

When asked about church charities, Gibson, like many in the Social Gospel movement, rejected them as the solution to social problems because they degraded the poor. Gibson believed that work was vital to the attainment of the Kingdom of Heaven for all. "God worked, the angels worked, why," Gibson asked, "shouldn't men, the children of God, also work. Our work was to complete the creation of God through labor, sacrifice, and cost so that we may serve and be served to the utmost." Reverend William Thurston Brown, later an associate editor of the *Social Gospel*, agreed that "charity is foolish and immoral." People wanted justice and access to a means of living, not charity.[25]

Social Gospelers asked how the charitable had acquired their wealth. Noting the contribution of fifty thousand dollars by a wealthy Chicagoan for the feeding and clothing of waifs and newsboys, they asked if those dollars had been "forcibly subtracted from the earnings of living men, likely from many of the poor fathers of future destitute newsboys." Brown, bitterly, referred to the "blood-stained money" and "stolen wealth" wrung from the hearts of the workers. The wealthy families then engaged in some charitable work for their victims, work that had become both a fad and a sign of status in the "best society."[26]

As the debate in the *Kingdom* wore on, Gibson announced that he was ready to "reach out glad, loving, fraternal hands to Mr. Chipman." Speaking for himself and members of the Christian Corporation, Gibson stated, "We are ready, as fast as our scattered property can be sold, to take hold of this plan, which has for ten months been our plan, and will locate with him in the best place to serve one another and the world."[27]

Herron followed this exchange and asked Lloyd for moral and financial support for Chipman's enterprise. He would "make almost any sacrifice . . . to start this movement rightly. It seems to me very important." He and Gibson began formulating a plan for what would become the Christian Commonwealth, while Lloyd provided moral support: "I am following your efforts with the sincerest sympathy and admiration. Nothing could be better than the spirit in which you are moving." Although skeptical of its ideology, which he believed was narrow and limiting because it adhered rigidly to Tolstoy's doctrine of nonresistance, Lloyd admitted a temptation to settle in such a community. He had come to believe that communitarianism was "the most religious manifestation of our day" and could play a civilizing role to prevent the anarchy that he feared was coming. Despite the temptation, he remained in his "place" in reform circles.[28]

In January 1896, Gibson and Chipman agreed to form a Christian Socialist community. They announced the birth of the Christian Commonwealth Colony in a circular and began to discuss sites in Alabama, Tennessee, Florida, and Georgia. Their circular read, "We have accepted . . . the teaching . . . that led Christ and his disciples to have 'all things in common.'"[29]

At the Willard Colony in North Carolina, Chipman's "Proposition" and the subsequent debate in the *Kingdom* attracted the attention of William Damon and Ralph Albertson. Damon, a University of Wisconsin graduate, had been, for nineteen years, a Methodist preacher in California and a professor at Napa Collegiate Institute. Revolting against the formal church but clinging to his Christian theology, he came east to teach at the American Temperance University in the town of Harriman, Tennessee.[30]

In 1895, Damon, desiring to "find a better environment than capitalism in which to raise his children," had organized, with the blessings of Frances Willard, leader of the Woman's Christian Temperance Union, the Willard Cooperative Colony, a community with about fifty committed prohibitionists. Temperance was the centerpiece of Damon's colonization scheme, but he also advocated socialism or communism to provide the framework for a brotherhood community. Lacking local support in Harriman, his group moved to Andrews in Cherokee County, North Carolina. Damon had no formal plan for his colony, but after Albertson's arrival, he agreed to adopt the Sermon on the Mount as the fundamental principle that would lead to equality of labor, ownership, and social relations. They sent out a call to brotherhood in which everyone would "give all, forgive all."[31]

Albertson had grown up on Long Island, where, influenced by articles written by George Kennan, he developed a deep interest in Russia and read some of Leo Tolstoy's work. It became the foundation of his most radical intellectual perspectives. At Oberlin Theological Seminary, George Herron's sermon "Message of Jesus to the Men of Wealth," which condemned the self-interest, immorality, and injustice in Gilded Age America, deeply influenced Albertson. Herron thought a "rich Christian" was a contradiction in terms. One could be rich and good, just and generous, but "to have while others have not was anti-Christ." Even worse, men got rich by making other men poor. Herron believed that to be a Christian was to "stand for the things and the life that Jesus stood for," and not all "Christians" were truly Christian, nor did their churches follow Jesus's teachings. With Saint Francis of Assisi as his model, he advocated "the recovery of Jesus from Christianity." Herron's economic views came from Europe, where economists understood Christ's communism. He viewed surplus value from which profit is supposed to spring as pure fiction. Profit was the forcible appropriation of the product of the labor of others. Herron used Henry George's belief that Christ was the ultimate authority on political economy to bolster his argument and paraphrased Marx: a man should "share according to the need of each—

give according to his ability." His emphasis on cooperation inspired Albertson, while at Oberlin, to unify the Protestant denominations of several Ohio communities into "union" churches.[32]

Albertson grew shocked by capitalism's brutal competitiveness and the violence surrounding the labor movement. Self-centered industrial and class warfare would solve nothing. The world needed to know God and learn that conflict and violence were not Christ's way. He turned to Tolstoyan nonresistance and philosophical anarchism to overcome evil with good and "build the new order of peace and brotherhood."[33]

As he approached graduation, Albertson, influenced by the notion of "muscular Christianity" and his manhood, joined the Student Volunteers for Foreign Missions, believing it the path to the "hardest" and most heroic job available. James Fairchild, the president of the seminary, convinced him that an Ohio working-class church would give Albertson a sufficient "cross" to bear, so after graduation in 1891, he became the minister at the Lagonda Avenue Congregational Church in Springfield, Ohio. He quickly energized the congregation by creating an institutional church that served all their needs, social, educational, professional, and theological. Later, at Commonwealth, Albertson stressed that the world was waiting "for the men and women who shall severely test every detail of their lives by the social law of service."[34]

Albertson contacted Washington Gladden and adopted some of his views of the Social Gospel. Like many Social Gospelers, Albertson was frustrated by most churches' inequities and preoccupation with individual salvation, their alliance with big business, and their avoidance of social issues. To address these concerns, in late 1894 he invited George Herron to speak to his Springfield congregation. Albertson admired Herron's synthesis of Christianity and sociology and his "virile plea for a Christian economics" and began to give sermons on cooperation in the Kingdom of God and the socialism of Christianity. In response, the Springfield business community severely criticized him, which may have hastened his departure from Lagonda. Herron's creed became Albertson's and made him realize that the church and ministry had failed him and would not be his path to service.[35]

His experience in Springfield reinforced a growing perception of Gilded Age America as a land of the "discontented, the disinherited, the insolvent debtor class." He had faith in these "social outcasts," and it was they, not the churches, who were the "future and success of the Christian religion." If they could be gathered together in brotherhood, they would find emancipation.[36]

While in Springfield, Albertson visited Chicago frequently and met many prominent reformers and radicals, among them Jane Addams, Eugene Debs, Graham Taylor, S. H. Comings, John Gavit, John Altgeld, Florence Kelley, Walter Thomas Mills, Louis Post, and Clarence Darrow. Inspired by Henry Demarest Lloyd's *Wealth against Commonwealth*, they discussed the social problems of the day, and the Chicago reformers expressed sympathy for the "colony idea" but did not convince Albertson that they would follow through.

Like Gibson, he was discouraged by piecemeal political and social reforms and became increasingly fearful of industrial and class warfare. For him, "Hull House does not go far enough. The new Socialist Party does not go far enough. Trade Unions and single tax and cooperation and charity and education all fall short or go astray. I believe that nothing will cure industrial inequity short of the life of Jesus here and now."[37]

Settlement work was too slow, politics was corrupt, and violence and revolution violated his belief in Christian nonresistance. He thought "poverty and ignorance and crime and degradation . . . would increase around Jane Addams and Graham Taylor faster than they could eliminate them. The only hope . . . was in separation and segregation." Changing society's institutions to regulate selfishness was insufficient. Rigid, deterministic systems such as those of Marx and Fourier could not perfect society's institutions.[38]

Albertson represented a perspective that drove many people into Christian Socialism and utopian communities. He was disturbed by labor leaders, who used agitation, conflict, and violence seeking bread and clothes rather than the Kingdom of God. Their methods and goals offended many sympathetic people and impeded reform's progress. His view attracted support from William Thurston Brown, who believed that many socialists pursued self-interest rather than the brotherhood of all.[39]

Albertson claimed that the New Testament made him a communist. He viewed Jesus, the Sermon on the Mount, and Saint Francis of Assisi as communistic. For a society to be Christian, its "distribution can only be communistic," and social peace could occur only in a "communistic or communal organization of society." Such ideas led Albertson to the Christian Commonwealth, despite Herron's skepticism about its possible success. In return, Herron's position frustrated Albertson because he was satisfied to be a voice in the wilderness rather than an active participant.[40]

Albertson approved Bellamy's application of the "golden rule" to industrial production, but Bellamy's centralized state and strictly ordered society lacked appeal to a man enamored of Tolstoy's anarchism. Socialist communities held great charm for Albertson because of their fellowship and sense of security, but some lacked appeal for other reasons. He laughed at the Brook Farm intellectuals for their amateurish attempts at farming and others who had wholly isolated themselves from the outside world. Albertson read Tolstoy with delight, but Marx irritated him. The social schemes of Marx, Fourier, and George were too mechanical, inflexible, and infallible. By excluding other truths, they created unnatural uniformity and conformity. Despite dissatisfaction aroused by observations of other utopian theories and experiments, Albertson maintained his irrepressible postmillennial urge. At Commonwealth, Albertson stood for communism and nonresistance but did not expect indiscriminate obedience. Commitment to service and love was more necessary than obedience to laws or theories.[41]

He believed that "the root of social wrong is selfishness and the chief bulwark of selfishness is the institution of private property" because "it sets every man against his neighbor as an aggressor to get from, and a defender to keep from others all that is possible." As a step toward founding a community based on Christian love, Albertson began corresponding with Damon. In the fall of 1895, he went to see him in Andrews. Both men believed in a connection between individual and social salvation and that a socialist, "Christ-filled" society could bring about the Kingdom of God. Inspired by that vision and embracing Christian Socialism and Tolstoyan ideas, Albertson, on October 27, 1895, preached a "Farewell Sermon" at Lagonda Avenue Congregational Church and left for North Carolina. By abandoning the ministry, he began his rise to a leadership position to bring about Christian Socialism in the United States through the revival of the communitarian ideal.[42]

Damon, an experienced educator, and Albertson decided to base their community on the "People's University." Although the school was never organized, its promotional circular expressed their philosophy: "We believe that the political economy taught and lived by Jesus Christ is practicable, that the love and brotherhood of the Kingdom of Heaven may be realized on earth. We believe in the possibility and practicability of unselfishness, and we want to provide for the education of young people in an atmosphere free from greed. We pray 'Thy Kingdom come' and we propose to live in that Kingdom on Earth ourselves and teach others so."

While Albertson and Damon were incubating socialism and education in North Carolina, they followed the debate on colonies occurring in the *Kingdom*, and by early 1896 Chipman, Albertson, and Gibson were exchanging ideas on Christian Socialism. They reinforced each other's enthusiasm for their shared ideals and goals and convinced themselves that they could achieve their objective. Chipman was the most encouraging and determined supporter and offered to finance a colony's founding. His offer appealed to Gibson because it promised to provide a communal experiment with the financial security that he did not have in his Nebraska corporation.[43]

By early 1896, Damon and Albertson were making progress at Willard. They had constructed a building that housed four family apartments, a dormitory and bachelor's quarters, a schoolroom, and storage for groceries. In March, a fire in their barn and gristmill killed a dozen horses and mules and destroyed eight hundred bushels of corn. The losses totaled several thousand dollars and put Willard in an untenable financial situation, which made Chipman's offer to finance a new community one that they could not refuse.[44]

The men decided to combine their movements and issued another call for a community. Sent out in June 1896, the plea appealed to all who were "ready to turn away from self-seeking" and desired that the "earth become like heaven." It was time to acknowledge the "power of love" and abandon "the each-for-himself rule, now followed by the industrial and commercial world, from which all evil flows."

> We plan for the visible Kingdom of God on earth, for a holy land, to be redeemed by purchase out of the hands of the selfish and given to the meek. We plan to build Christian factories, mills, machine shops, etc., that all who come to us may have permanent places to labor. . . . We plan for the life-long education of our children and ourselves, so that we may have perfect bodies, skillful hands, intellects furnished with the most advanced knowledge of the forces of nature, of discovery and invention. . . .
>
> We recognize one God over all, one law, of love, labor, outpouring; one perfect example of right living—Christ. But dead divisive dogmas, intellectual opinions regarding infinite, incomprehensible, or unrevealed mysteries we shall not require assent to. Intellect differences shall not debar from membership any who are prepared to do the will of God. The one simple duty is to love and labor for one another.[45]

In July, Albertson attended the National Cooperative Congress in St. Louis, where he helped organize and became a director of the American Cooperative Union along with N. O. Nelson, Alonzo Wardell, and Henry Demarest Lloyd. On his return, he began a series of essays in the *Kingdom* on democracy, socialism, property, and the relationship of Christianity to social problems. He synthesized his notions of Christianity and democracy and challenged critics who called communitarian socialism selfish by dismissing "selfish socialism as logically impossible." He did not believe that the Gospel of Jesus could be practiced fully by individuals. A Christ-filled society could save the world by replacing private property with common property and distributing goods according to need. Nevertheless, he warned against "that so-called socialism which is organized . . . to get and gain for itself and its members only." A colony that "hates the rich but loves their riches . . . falls short of true socialism and true Christianity." Colonies must practice self-sacrifice and nonresistance. Colonists must form "unselfish socialism [that] will find its life in the giving up of . . . things." A colony must "set a pattern for the Christian state" to come. He appealed for a community based on "the standard of Christ, the teaching of the same spirit that led Christ and his disciples to have all things in common."[46]

As the discussion continued, Albertson invoked Herron's belief that social salvation could come only through sacrifice as symbolized by Christ on the cross. He wrote in the *Kingdom*, "The meaning of the cross to the industrial and commercial world is the crucifixion of selfishness, which means the renunciation of private property, which is the path we must take to 'bear away' the social sins of the world."[47]

Albertson agreed with Gibson about the churches, noting that men's lives contradicted their Sunday prayers. Outside the church, men "raised high barriers of 'mine and thine' between themselves . . . and strengthened these barriers with laws and prejudices and bullets and every form of force." He told the churches to "take down the ideal of His Kingdom of Heaven from the dusty shelves of primitive Christianity and embrace it to their hearts."[48]

By mid-1896, these four men, with almost no face-to-face contact, agreed through the medium of print to form "an educational and religious society whose purpose is to obey the teachings of Jesus Christ in all matters of life and labor and the use of property." Its atmosphere would be untainted by capitalism's institutionalized selfishness, nonresistance would flourish, and their labor would be "the free expression and measurement of love" for humanity. They would rely on the knowledge and spirit of love and reject any use of coercion or force.[49]

Their covenant condemned capitalism and committed them to a cooperative brotherhood. It urged all to join in "rejecting as folly and fearful sin the each-for-himself industrial and commercial struggle and the pursuit of private property." They would demonstrate the power of love and harmony as working principles by building a moral society that lived up to Christianity's rhetoric, and the colony would welcome anyone who gave up the "the treasure that divides us."[50]

Thus, Chipman's "Proposition" inspired the establishment of the Christian Commonwealth, and the *Kingdom* was the vehicle for its formation. The key leaders came out of the Social Gospel, Populist, and temperance movements. They believed that the church's and the world's unbelief in the economic wisdom of love and the safety of complete self-surrender was delaying the establishment of the Kingdom of Heaven on earth. To accelerate that, their community would apply the Social Gospel to all aspects of life. Jesus Christ and his apostles were the sources of their social vision. They wanted to reduce Christianity to the practice of "following Jesus" by emphasizing his original message of compassion and evangelism and emulating his example of generosity, service, love, and nonresistance. Brotherhood, the law of love, and communism, as expressed by the Sermon on the Mount and book of Acts, were the means to realize the Kingdom of God. They advised readers to sell their possessions, give the proceeds to an organization of "industry and mutualism of service," and "to avoid being utterly sacrificed," come to the Christian Commonwealth, which they organized to make that possible. Finally, they wanted to model their community on the socialism of primitive apostolic Christianity. They adopted Saint John's vision of what one needed to do to enter the Kingdom of Heaven: equal distribution of goods to meet all needs and equalization of conditions under the law of love. To achieve that, the cause of Christ deserved every bit of their time, money, and blood; the possibilities of divine humanity were great if one took the sacrificed Christ of love as an inspiring example.[51]

The Christian Commonwealth's organizers believed that selfishness was sin and the source of struggle for property and power, which was the cause of the world's evils, but they did not want to be mere dreamers, theorists, or idealists. They sought to preach and practice love and show men how to be saved. In the individualistic, strife-filled world, that was impossible because individuals, trying to meet their family's needs, felt no mutual care or neighbor love. By forming a society in which people "love as Christ loved, serve as Christ served and suffer as he suffered," they could make the sacrifice for social world redemption.[52]

The decision to locate in the South was pragmatic and a matter of convenience. Albertson, Damon, and their followers were already in North Carolina, and Chipman, the primary financial contributor in Florida, insisted on a location no farther north than Tennessee or, preferably, Georgia.

The South offered many advantages to the colony movement. Imogene Fales, a Populist turned socialist, noted that the colony movement was distinctively American, and the lands of the South and West called for cooperative communities that would educate for a new civilization. Ruskin Cooperative Association actively advertised the appeal of the South: abundant, affordable land and building materials, a hunger for capital to alleviate poverty, improved transportation links, and a pleasant climate. Investors and other communitarians found the conditions attractive. Rare in the antebellum South, utopian socialism was surprisingly common in the post–Civil War era. Several communities were established, among them the Shakers in Florida and Georgia, socialists at Ruskin in Tennessee and, later, Georgia, single taxers in Fairhope, Alabama, and a community of sanctified women in Texas. In Fitzgerald, Georgia, a community for the reconciliation of Civil War veterans was established and became the largest colony in Georgia.[53]

Although "mission" was not their primary motivation, there was missionary zeal in their decision to locate in the South. They saw themselves as restoring a region that had once been "more nearly a paradise." They believed that cotton's dominance was the leading cause of the region's poverty, a realization that southerners would not recognize for several more decades. They noted that local farmers raised sweet potatoes, sugar cane, corn, cowpeas, peanuts, melons, and garden vegetables, but "cotton is king." On the other hand, few orchards or vineyards existed in central Georgia, which was a natural home for peaches, plums, and grapes. Flowers too could be successfully cultivated where they grew wild in rich profusion.[54]

Chipman made a preliminary trip and sent Albertson a list of available Georgia plantations. In October 1896, Albertson and T. C. McKenzie, an Atlanta grocer, set out in his horse-drawn delivery wagon to search for a suitable location. They were looking for one thousand acres adjacent to land that could be purchased if they needed to expand. They covered three hundred miles crisscrossing Georgia and Florida south to Apalachicola, before returning to Columbus, Georgia. Captain A. G. Grant showed them several tracts of land in Muscogee County. A 935-acre antebellum plantation owned by A. S. Dozier, twelve miles east of Columbus on the road to Macon, drew their attention.

Dozier Creek, a small stream, flowed through the property. The creek bed had a hard granite outcropping, which they could use to build foundations, and the clay would make excellent bricks. The land needed fertilizer and rehabilitation with forage growths. It had plenty of pine trees and some poplar and oak. The buildings included the plantation house under a grove of elms, a dilapidated barn, and a half dozen cabins that had been slave quarters and were now inhabited by African American sharecroppers. There were no other improvements and, except for the timber, only two hundred acres under cultivation.[55]

Somewhat removed from mainstream America, it straddled the Central of Georgia Railway line midway between Columbus and Upatoi. After a pleasant year in the mountains of North Carolina, Albertson thought the Georgia site was inferior. Nevertheless, he noted the land's "Divine beauty" and believed they were "providentially led to locate here." He reflected later that the location had seemed promising: "the climate, the soil, the transportation, power, labor, the scarcity of capital, local conditions of neglect—all spelled opportunity and advantages for enterprise and hard work." Albertson's optimism ignored that it was a failed plantation of half rolling upland that was worn-out cotton acreage. The soil was suitable for fruit but not for subsistence agriculture. The swampy bottomlands of heavy loam and dark black clay were fertile but challenging to cultivate. Nevertheless, he and his companions' optimism was grounded in the Kingdom of God movement and its goal of creating a Christian Commonwealth to establish God's kingdom on earth.[56]

The men met with Dozier, paid a bonus, and began the legal transfer of titles. On November 1, 1896, John Chipman purchased the plantation for four thousand dollars. He put up the first thousand in cash and wanted the land deeded to Jesus Christ. Albertson objected because Christ would not pay the taxes. The community assumed the remaining debt of three thousand dollars at 8 percent interest payable in three annual installments. Dozier and other Columbus men who dealt with the newcomers were "highly delighted with them" and believed they would be "good and valuable citizens."[57]

Albertson immediately sent for the Damons, his family, and the other Andrews colonists. On the day before Thanksgiving, he, McKenzie, and Reverend J. Franklin Browne welcomed the first eighteen settlers arriving from North Carolina. The people of Columbus took notice, and the local newspaper wrote, "Quite a number of people arrived yesterday from the northern and western states and will settle in the new colony twelve miles from Columbus. These people have come to make Georgia their home."[58]

The first arrivals attracted much attention from the local population. The locals called the colony "Agapolis," or "City of Love." The community never used that name, but it showed that Columbus residents were aware of a critical component of Commonwealth's ideology: Love your brother. In late December, the colonists agreed on "Christian Commonwealth" as their colony's name. They chose it because it had a strong moral flavor and embodied the aspirations of common people living a common life.

Others followed from all over the country: Nebraska, Florida, Washington, Massachusetts, Ohio, and California. Some brought teams and tools and a supply of flour, corn, and potatoes. A few had money, but most had only themselves. They immediately began to transform the physical and social landscape. In the first weeks, they cleaned up the property, cut timber for fuel, and began to erect a sawmill. Meanwhile, carpenters renovated the sixty-year-old plantation house to provide shelter for the first colonists and planned cottages for the families that would follow.[59]

Although the colonists did not have a detailed plan, they were clear about their intentions. A Columbus reporter described their socialism without passing judgment: "To a certain degree everything is in common. Every man is a worker; there are no drones.... No man shall be allowed to depend on others for his support, but every man shall contribute the surplus of his labor to the general or common fund.... The larger the surplus, the better off the colonists will be." Another observer stated that Commonwealth wanted "to show the world, that the practical religion, taught by Christ, is something to live by," in a "system under which brotherly love would be the ruling influence."[60]

The first colonists planted as much as the winter season would allow. They rejected cotton and corn, the South's staple crops, but the property, despite its neglect, was well adapted to fruit, so they planted several acres of strawberries and young fruit trees. Thus, fruit and truck farming became their primary agricultural activity.

They put together a poultry stock and planned a large dairy farm. Small factories and other industrial pursuits would follow agriculture. The first colonists impressed outsiders with how quickly and diligently they worked. The energetic activity attracted visitors from Columbus, and William Damon, the first president, welcomed them warmly and showed them around.[61]

Despite the workload, the colonists did not neglect social affairs. They held their first wedding in December. Freda Schauploch and Christian Boad, a young couple from Canton, Ohio, married in the drawing room of the plantation house. Ralph Albertson presided, aided by Damon and Browne, who had migrated from Goshen, Massachusetts. The wife of Columbus professor A. G. Grant played the wedding march. After the wedding, the community served an elegant supper to its members and several Columbus guests.

The following week, twenty colonists, including many children, arrived from Nebraska by rail. From Columbus, they had taken a train out to Midland, which was the rail stop nearest to Commonwealth. The group included Gibson's family and members of the Christian Corporation in Lincoln and others from Spokane, Washington, and Genoa, Nebraska.

Sheffield, a Nebraska farmer, accompanied by his family of eight, led the party. He told a Columbus reporter how drought and cold weather had thwarted his efforts to farm in Nebraska and optimistically described Commonwealth's plan. They would build houses, churches, and schools and start raising celery, corn, and strawberries. He admitted that progress would be slow, but he expected things to improve quickly and noted that more Nebraskans were on their way. Eventually, they would produce goods native to the locale and others the region imported. He expected that if they were successful more farmers from outside the South would follow.

The sawmill machinery, which they had bought in Ohio, arrived and was set up. The sawmill had a twenty-five-horsepower steam engine connected to an edger, a cut-off saw, a saw gummer, a feed mill, and a shingle machine. It could produce six to ten thousand feet of lumber and ten thousand shingles each day and allowed Commonwealth to obtain all of its lumber from its land. The shingles were used for community buildings or sold in Columbus. The colonists also erected a storehouse for materials purchased in Columbus.[62]

About a week later, a freight train from Genoa, Nebraska, brought several carloads of household furnishings, tools, equipment, and machinery that belonged to families already there. The freight included horses, livestock, and farm implements from Washington that came to Nebraska by wagon. Several men, whose wives and children were already at Commonwealth, accompanied one car to feed and water the animals.

By late December, forty-five people lived at Commonwealth, many strangers to one another, and they expected to have sixty before long. Another twenty families were waiting in Nebraska until housing was available. After preaching his first sermon, "What Is the Kingdom?," in January 1897, Albertson told reporters that three hundred families were determined to join as soon as possible.[63]

To facilitate commerce and contact with the outside world, Commonwealth asked the Central of Georgia Railway to build a depot and warehouse on its property. Railroad officials came to confer with the leaders and expressed interest in building up the community. They established a flag stop and mail catch on colony land but never provided the colony with a station or agent, which was a disappointment and an inconvenience. They finally promised to build a depot named Commonwealth at Garrett's Switch about a mile away. The colonists would have to send and receive all freight from there. The railroad also clarified the settlement's location on the railroad line and set passenger rates from everywhere in the United States. Tickets read Columbus to Midland, which was closer but still a flag station and not listed in the railroad guide. Despite that, ticket sales were brisk.[64]

Columbus residents were filled with curiosity but gave the first colonists a cordial welcome and were extremely positive about the community. An *Enquirer-Sun* reporter visited Commonwealth and called it "one of the most interesting social experiments ever made in the United States." Impressed by the members' refinement and intelligence, he concluded that they were "far above average." He noted that the population included ministers, editors, and professors. He saw no evidence of poverty and noted that the colonists must have money for they had brought or purchased a significant amount of machinery and supplies. The reporter concluded that Commonwealth would quickly become one of the most prosperous communities in the South. A reporter commended Albertson as a gentleman and for his business acumen and wrote that there was every reason to believe they would be successful. Another visitor noted that they were "making great headway towards building the town."

Interest in Commonwealth spread rapidly throughout the country. In the first month, the founders corresponded with over three hundred applicants. They encouraged artisans to relocate so that they would have skilled workers to perform the construction and operation of factories. To appeal to families, they announced the immediate construction of a school building and planned to establish a college.

During the summer of 1897, the remainder of the Gibson group, sixteen families, replicated in reverse America's great westward movement. Looking for opportunity, they made a three-month journey from Nebraska to Georgia in prairie schooners loaded with household furniture and farm implements. They encountered some of the same dangers and hardships as earlier westward migrations. In July in Kentucky, they were struck by sickness—the men with chills and fever and children with measles—and considered giving up. After leaving Memphis, they lost a child and some horses to disease. Pressing on, they reached Nashville and expected to be in Commonwealth by early August. But even that short trip was delayed, and they did not reach

Commonwealth until late August. Their arrival considerably increased the population and capital of the colony.[65]

Almost immediately, there was an outbreak of malaria. Most of those who came from Nebraska and other western states succumbed to it. There were about twenty cases that resulted in long, tedious, and expensive recoveries. Fortunately, a doctor lived four miles from the colony, and once acclimated, the colonists experienced no severe illness until the decimating outbreak of typhoid fever a few years later.[66]

There are no existing population records, but it is clear that Commonwealth grew steadily. Arrivals in 1897 raised the membership to nearly one hundred. Community leaders were pleased with the growth and confident about the future but feared that rapid growth would overwhelm their resources and organization. They sought to remain self-supporting and free from idlers and thus planned to bring in people gradually as work and housing were available. They hoped to have several thousand inhabitants within a few years and become one of the largest and most important colonies in Georgia, comparable to the American Tribune Soldiers' Colony Company, a community of reconciliation for Civil War veterans in Fitzgerald. But their optimism was misplaced. Over its existence, Commonwealth rarely averaged more than one hundred members.[67]

In October 1897, the community announced that it would publish a monthly journal to promote the colony and proselytize its tenets and principles. The journal was originally called the *Social Christ*, but the leadership changed its name to the *Social Gospel* before the first issue. Charles Howard Hopkins, a historian of the Social Gospel movement in the Progressive era, implied that the Christian Commonwealth coined the term "social gospel," but the name did not originate at Commonwealth. George Herron, the Kingdom movement, and others had used it in the early 1890s. Albertson may have picked it up when Herron lectured at his church in Springfield. Commonwealth's *Social Gospel* did help popularize the phrase and make it the accepted name of the entire movement, displacing such precursors as "applied Christianity" and "social Christianity."[68]

The first year everyone engaged in manual labor—farming, gardening, grubbing, building fences, preparing fuel, logging, building and running the sawmill, carpentering, and working in the orchard and nursery. Meager incomes forced constant self-denial. Food was "limited in variety and as monotonously unpalatable as the bread of the Moses-led Israelites." To survive,

Commonwealth had to rely on a variety of often anonymous "heaven-sent" sources of supplies.[69]

Yet survive it did. The year 1898 saw more formal political and economic organization, construction, agricultural progress, and the first issue of the *Social Gospel*. The colonists had laid the foundation for a thriving, prosperous community in the American Deep South based on love and Christian Socialism.

CHAPTER 2

✦ ✦ ✦

The Law of Love

Love thy neighbor as thyself.
—Matthew 22:39

IN THE FIRST MONTHS, Albertson wrote, "Our organic and permanent constitution is the Law of Love.... We love not only with our hearts but with all our property and all our labor."[1] Members drew up a simple document that stated, "The recognized unalterable organic law of the Christian Commonwealth shall be: Thou shalt love the Lord thy God with all thy heart, and thy neighbor as thyself. Membership in this body shall be open to all and never be denied to any who come to us in the spirit of love, unselfishness, and true fellowship."[2]

It was their Christian faith that made the "open-door" policy a founding principle: "We cannot turn aside, nor exclude, the least of his brethren. To our feast, we must call the halt, the maimed, the lame and blind, the prejudiced, the ignorant, the criminal and the poor. As Christ called them and loved them, so must we."[3] How the policy worked initially is not clear, but despite having to give one's property to the community, four hundred people expressed a desire to come but were told to wait until accommodations were available.[4]

It was morally obligatory to love without reservation. They offered a universal welcome to every human being—tramps, the poor, and outcasts—to come, share, and live as they did. Consistency to this ideal was essential, but ultimately they rejected irrational devotion to any theory, even the open-door policy, nonresistance, and communism.[5]

The Christian Commonwealth never shut its doors to anyone and welcomed everyone regardless of religious beliefs, wealth, age, and health. It offered membership to everyone who signed its covenant. Its property was for the use of God's poor. Doctrinal differences were irrelevant. There was no intellectual opinion test. "Deeds, not creeds" were required, and loving by serving and working was the substance of their religion. Whether a "beggar" or a "professor," anyone willing to bear the cross to benefit humankind was welcome.[6]

There were no financial requirements or membership fees that would exclude the neediest. "Anyone can come without a dollar, even ragged and dirty, and be received into full brotherhood." The requirements were a commitment to unselfishness and a willingness to follow Christ and the religious principles of the community.

Occasionally newcomers, to facilitate their acceptance, produced letters of recommendation from ministers, lawyers, bankers, or merchants. Few at Commonwealth took them seriously. As Albertson said, "I believe in every man that comes here—at least so far that no amount of documentary palaver would help their case a bit."[7]

Later, some blamed open membership for Commonwealth's problems, but in the beginning it did not seem to be an issue. Gibson, concerned about laziness, crime, and exploitation, raised the question occasionally. He, Albertson, and Damon agreed that the Sermon on the Mount was their guiding principle and that exclusionary policies such as those at other communities were unacceptable. A Columbus observer noted that Commonwealth "is not made up of calamity howlers and men who have made a financial failure in life, but is composed of men, many of whom, who have left good-paying positions, in order to show to the world, that the practical religion, taught by Christ, is something to live by; and that in order to live the life which Christ intended for us to live, required that we live under a system, under which brotherly love would be the ruling influence."[8]

Those at Commonwealth believed that the age was coming when men would abandon the Gilded Age's coarse, vulgar, selfish business interpretation of life and embrace the higher, sweeter significance of life as taught by Christ.

We have been drawn together by a common passion for individual and social righteousness and for what we conceive to be the Kingdom of God. It is the purpose of our lives . . . to join ourselves to one another and to Christ in bearing away the sins of the world. We make straight the way

for the surely coming reform of the twentieth-century, which will be a reform of propertyism and industrialism.

> The incarnation is the gospel message of the New Testament. It is the
> coming of God into human flesh and human life.... They receiving him
> into their social life, are to become the Kingdom of God.[9]

In its first issue, the *Social Gospel* announced that the Christian Commonwealth was a manifestation of the "brotherhood of man and fatherhood of
God." With its motto, "The Kingdom of Heaven is at hand," the journal pro-
claimed that its purpose was "to inspire faith in the economic teachings of
Jesus." The *Social Gospel* "is the proclamation of the kingdom of heaven, a di-
vinely ordered society, to be realized on earth. It is the application of the
Golden Rule and the Law of Love to all the business and affairs of life." If
you asked most people why they went to Commonwealth, their response
would have been the "pursuit of Universal Brotherhood." It was not a term
that Ralph Albertson favored, but it was a favorite expression and was regularly used, even showing up as graffiti on community buildings.[10]

Commonwealth entertained a range of political and religious views, but
members were united in opposing capitalism and the existing economic order. "We believe that the competitive system of individualistic warfare, bearing the fruits of bitterness and oppression, is a great evil from which all who
love must free the world and themselves as far as they are able."[11]

Albertson viewed capitalism as warfare: "While we do not hold that all sin
is necessarily the product of property selfishness, we do hold that property
selfishness is fundamentally and directly responsible for the prevailing conditions in human life in which are cultivated the deepest and darkest pas-
sions of all men, both ... putting every man at necessary warfare with all
other competitors for life-crushing down tens of thousands of weak ones
while the 'fittest survive.'"[12]

James Kelley, of Greenwich, Connecticut, an associate editor of the *Social
Gospel*, agreed and exposed another flaw in the competitive system: waste.
What was the point of parallel railroads, parallel churches, and parallel agen-
cies doing the same work or working at cross-purposes? Under a system of
socialism or cooperation, institutions and infrastructure could be rational-
ized and made more efficient to everyone's benefit. Despite opposition to
the "competitive system," Commonwealth was never able to move far outside
of it. They needed money and trade for interest, taxes, and goods that they
could not produce themselves.[13]

Everyone was committed to some degree of socialism or communism, but the details of their ideology are vague. The Social Gospel, the Kingdom movement, and the Sermon on the Mount guided them, but more than any theoretical ideology or "ism," "the purpose common to us all was to demonstrate the practicability of the law of love in industrial life."[14] Albertson said they were devoted to "a mongrel mixture of Christianity and democracy." As postmillennialists, they believed they could implement the Kingdom of God on earth through the law of love and not wait for it in heaven.[15]

Chipman, Albertson, and Gibson all condemned capitalism and believed, like Marx, in a classless society, but Albertson chose Saint Francis over Marx as his authority on socialism. "Francis teaches it in one of the sublimest lives in history. Marx wrote a book." When Albertson wanted to pay his cofounders the highest compliment, he said that Damon, Chipman, and Gibson "were prepared to live up to their most radical convictions. They were made of Francis of Assizi [sic] metal."[16]

Albertson was not alone in admiring Francis. In the late nineteenth century, the medieval friar had become America's most popular saint, even among Protestants. Social reformers viewed Francis's life as the embodiment of the Sermon on the Mount. He demonstrated that religious beliefs must be lived and enacted to challenge corruption in the churches.[17]

At Commonwealth, Sue Fay Hinckley often quoted Saint Francis in her diary. One passage, which reflected Commonwealth's philosophy, stated, "The Bishop of Assisi said to Francis one day: 'Your way of living without owning anything seems to me very harsh and difficult. My Lord, replied he, if we possessed property we should have need of arms for its defense, for it is the source of quarrels and lawsuits, and the love of God and one's neighbor usually finds many obstacles therein; this is why we do not desire temporal goods.'" A life of Francis's "gospel poverty" and simplicity was not Commonwealth's long-term vision. Members had not taken a vow of poverty but initially had to accept its reality.[18]

Commonwealth saw simplicity as a virtue but not a solution. Members were not slaves to material goods and realized that worldly things contributed to order in their lives if they avoided being enslaved by them. "We have … this advantage over Francis of Assisi. We live in an industrial age. We have machinery. We have group production, organization, modern science. And our objective is primarily social. Otherwise his faith and his life are for us to follow. To preach a social gospel, however, we must have land and industrial equipment."[19]

The most tangible manifestation of Commonwealth's classless society was the abolition of differences in wealth. Whatever else there might be in their Kingdom of God on earth, one thing that would not exist was rich and poor. Universal brotherhood meant the leveling of property and its privileges. Christ's cross symbolized the crucifixion of selfishness and the renunciation of private property. "In colony life, the question of individual property-holding rights and personal privileges vanishes like mist.... Our main problems are as to how we may house more homeless, and feed more hungry, and provide industry for more labor, and bind up more broken-hearted, and inspire more faith and courage, and minister to more need and contribute to more happiness."[20]

Members believed in an equality that went beyond abstractions but challenged those who thought that equality meant elimination of individuality. Sue Fay expressed it best. To her, there was equality of all as children of God, but beyond that there were natural differences. All should have an equal opportunity to make the most of their ability. That did not mean that they would have identical opportunities. A world of complete sameness would be "monotonous, stupid, and insufferable." She wrote, "It is more righteous to be real than apparently uniform: to cultivate our God-given tastes and instincts, than to stunt and dwarf them. Let us rejoice in variety and welcome all expressions of identity as gifts of God to His world."[21]

Commonwealth was determined to nourish individuality and foster everyone's unique characteristics. In contrast to communities like the Shakers, Oneida, and Fruitlands, they created a society that supported variety in everything: diet, dress, amusements, recreation, study, and work. Sue encouraged everyone to rejoice in variety and cherish individuality, even in friendships. She cautioned everyone not to misjudge expressions of individuality as selfishness, nor did special bonds negate the equal fellowship of communal life. Commonwealth expected the same respect toward everyone. Anyone who put out her best effort deserved respect, no matter the endeavor or outcome.[22]

Outsiders viewed Commonwealth as socialist. They were communist in the sense that each member put all they had into the common treasury and all property was communal. "If any man becomes a member of the colony he must add what he can to the commonwealth of the place, whether it be much or little. If it be much, it gives him no higher standing than if it is little, for it for the common good and he reaps the benefit either way. The common interest is the concern of all and is shared alike by all."[23]

Opinions diverged about how far communal ownership should extend in practice. All community members believed in some degree of socialism, but their views were so diverse that it is difficult to define a specific ideology. Chipman and Gibson were ardent theoretical communists, but neither of their wives gave all of their possessions to the community. On the other hand, Damon and Albertson were not communists but contributed their possessions, yet their wives insisted on having eggs to eat even when there were not enough to go around. To Albertson, Commonwealth was a social and industrial experiment that had elements of communism. Some members had private pocketbooks and others had watches. Most had something that others did not have. There were four organs in the community, and the general feeling was that things that were needed and used individually could be held separately. But when the *Social Gospel* mentioned "Mrs. Albertson's piano," it pained Ralph. The comment caused some rumblings in the community, even though she gave lessons to members and often played at ice cream socials, musical and literary programs, and evening services.[24]

Albertson defended private ownership of clothing for pragmatic reasons of fit but qualified it, referring to the community's generosity. "Personal wearing apparel was privately owned but it as well as the houses we had to live in was freely given to anybody who needed it, regardless of any theory of communism. I must say that through the entire history of the enterprise, there was the most unselfishness exhibited that I have ever known or heard about." Almost everyone used the communal laundry, so each family or individual had a private mark on their clothes.

Other than some apparel and a few personal possessions, Commonwealth's members kept little private property, and they gave of that freely to anyone in need. There were instances of tension and conflict over ownership, but for the most part common property served as a unifying force. People were careful of community property and quick to check both abundance and waste. The collective consciousness of shared public property prevented destructive actions toward it.[25]

Even their Christian religion defied categorical classification. To them, no two persons had the same interpretation of Jesus. There was no need for absolute Christianity. What was needed was "better Christianity" than what churches preached.[26]

Gibson and Albertson were united in their Christian values and their condemnation of mainstream churches. In the *Social Gospel*, Gibson wrote, "The Laodicean church with its Sunday talk about saving souls and its six days' race after wealth and power, leaves the persons of the masses of mankind at the mercy of 'the great men of earth.'" A "great majority in church and the world has lost all faith ... in right living and believe in the good of gain above God." Churches had adopted a worldly standard and sanctioned a selfish business code. To overcome the evils of the self-seeking world, Gibson believed the church had to return to its origin as a loving society of brothers with a defined purpose to redeem the world.[27]

Many ministers preached love and the Gospel, but they did not always practice it. Instead, they pursued salary and material comforts. Observers thought highly of Commonwealth for practicing what it preached. An admirer commended members for being obedient to the heavenly vision in their economic brotherhood and willingness to sacrifice "within hearing of the market" and in the "sordid din of the competitive order."[28]

Several prominent followers supported Gibson's condemnation of mainstream churches. Vida Scudder, a Wellesley College professor, "sympathized with its spirit." Samuel Zane Batten, a founder of the Brotherhood of the Kingdom, was "in completest accord." Another brother, Frank Irving Wheat, was in "cordial sympathy" and praised the Christian Commonwealth as "a holier and more radiant cross heralding the coming of the Son of Man than any possible flaming herald in the clouds." Reverend Carl Thompson, a socialist evangelist and member of J. Stitt Wilson's Social Crusade, thought Gibson was right—that the church lacked "moral heroism." Katherine Lente Stevenson, president of the Massachusetts Woman's Christian Temperance Union and a board member of the Right Relationship League, gave her "unqualified endorsement" but suggested Gibson did not go far enough in his criticism. E. Talmadge Root, secretary of the Massachusetts Federation of Churches, "heartily agreed."[29]

In their critique of the church and belief in brotherhood and "industrial Christianity," they were rational believers in justice:

> The message of Commonwealth ... is a message of courage and good cheer to those who are capable of an earnest and faithful and cool-headed obedience to a high social ideal.
>
> The message that humanity needs to hear is: "The Kingdom of Heaven is at hand." ... We hope to convince men of the truth of these oft repeated words. We attempt to ... show that the truth is workable and livable and rational and feasible and possible of realization to common men and women.[30]

Gibson and Albertson also viewed philanthropy as misguided. "The pagan charities of a Croesus or a Vanderbilt and the cold-blooded, clean skirted beneficence of a Lady Bountiful may represent the activities of the Church, but they are by no means distinctively Christian.... The call of Christ is the call to live the Vicarious life—the life that pours out itself for other life—the life that is lovingly immersed in the life of the world—the life that is individually lost and socially found."[31]

For Albertson, the path to reform was the personal regeneration of all men and women, but they could not do it as individuals. He never liked the description of Commonwealth as a "reform colony." It was "simply a group of people who are trying to find for themselves and others the natural and right way of life and social organization." "The greatest need of the world is its need of Love," he noted. "We need social reforms, but ... love is the only redemptive force to count on.... There are some, ... who, when reason and revelation both call, will lovingly lay all upon the altar of the new social sacrifice which shall awaken social conscience in a disorganized humanity and lay the foundation of the divine social system of brotherhood and love—the Kingdom of God."[32] There "must be a body of men and women who socially unite" to "bring social and industrial salvation." Every one shared this responsibility and believed that it would bring redemption and social regeneration. In their passion, they were willing to suffer to bring about the Kingdom of Heaven. They must be "so given up to the passion for social righteousness that they would gladly die for it, must pass through the passion week of social reconstruction and suffer on the cross of commercial hatred, before the Kingdom in largeness can come." This society would "be a Kingdom of God on earth" and would teach others to think new thoughts and do away with selfishness. This regeneration must take place in a community that had separated itself from the world's evils.[33]

Albertson desired to merge democracy with Christianity, but given the lack of agreement on communism or the community's purpose, he tried to be open minded. Gibson, more of a theorist than Albertson, felt the same way. At Commonwealth, he wrote, "we find our lives by losing them in service. And this because love begets, and service wins service." He added, "We are not seeking to gain one of another, as they do in the world. We are supplementary parts of one another, each contributing what power of service he has, each served and cared for by all. In such relations, we have peace of mind; we have delightful fellowship; we are surely working toward the ideal conditions, which depend on brotherhood labor."[34]

In the pioneer conditions, Albertson found the sense of fraternity and unselfishness unparalleled:

> I think it amounts simply to a feeling of nearness to other people. I did not
> necessarily like them all. Many, I am sure, I should not have cared a snap
> for under the ordinary circumstances of life. Some of them, as a matter of
> fact, I did not like very much. I am inclined to think that it is only in a life
> organized something like ours was that a true, keen happiness can come
> from contact with people one does not like. And as for those one does
> like, and I liked many of the people who were at Commonwealth, there
> is something indescribably beautiful that comes among such as the direct
> result of the abolition of property. . . . We plunged into the woods with
> axes and into ditches with spades and into fields and hedges and wherever
> labor was needed and worked ourselves into unutterable weariness day af-
> ter day, and month after month, in that exquisite new joy of comradeship
> and the hope of an honest world. Brotherhood was better than philan-
> thropy, which often failed to make people happy.[35]

Despite the sense of fraternity, by Commonwealth's second year, it was estimated that 25 percent of the people who came left after a short time. Their
reasons for leaving varied. "Colony 'hardtack,' monotonous manna, majority rule, just or unjust criticism, the real or fancied faults of others"—each
caused some to leave. One stated he "would not work for another man's children." Others lacked the grace to be "high privates." Some who thought they
would be their "own boss" and free from accountability did not fit. Others
found the pioneer conditions tough and "could not endure hardness as good
soldiers of Jesus Christ." Still others left because of outside pressure. One accused the colony of too much frivolity: "As Mr. Maginnis departed, he did us
much good by saying his objection to Commonwealth was that there was too
much frivolity and not enough serious conversation. Now we have been accused of almost every failing under the sun save this one . . . too sober, grave,
sedate—even extremely dull—and under the weight of daily burdens our
consciences seemed to say 'amen.' . . . But frivolous! We had such a laugh over
it that our dinners digested rapidly. Sure proof that the criticism was true."
Ultimately, many just "loved the world and the things that are in the world"
and did not find them at Commonwealth. On the other hand, the power of
sacrifice raised others to become brave, faithful brothers and sisters.[36]

The *Social Gospel*, while optimistic, never hid the colony's hardships or
deprivation. The editors sent letters to prospective members informing them
of the circumstances in detail and warned of poverty, debt, sickness, and pi-

oneer conditions. Gnats, mosquitoes, chiggers, ants, cockroaches, and flies were the norm. Crickets destroyed one's clothes. Rough board-and-batten houses meant dampness, cold, and mildew. The women had a meager supply of furnishings and utensils. Commonwealth wanted men, women, and children who could subdue these conditions to realize the Kingdom of God. They asked people to consider "carefully and prayerfully" whether it was their duty to do so. They discouraged anyone who could not "endure severe hardship cheerfully, gladly suffering for the cause of God's kingdom."[37]

In one 1899 case, the colony had ample correspondence with J. B. Hays of Ohio and took pains to explain the conditions under which they were living. Hays showed up with six other persons. He thought things at Commonwealth were as represented, but the younger people were dissatisfied. They left and found work in Columbus. There were no hard feelings, but the community was disappointed at the turn of events. In the *Social Gospel*, Commonwealth reiterated its warnings: "Don't come to Commonwealth until you are ready for the sacrifice of brotherhood. Don't urge or permit others to come with you who are not ready, nor willing to be made ready."[38]

The myriad reasons for leaving suggest that many who came ignored the community's conditions. Or one could argue that many were pushed to Commonwealth by even greater hardships that existed in the late nineteenth-century world of the Gilded Age.

Letters of inquiry often ignored the warnings to the point of absurdity. One prospective colonist wrote, "Suppose I should want to take a trip to Europe, or go home to see mother, or want to dress better than my neighbors, or want to send my daughter to Europe to study art in Paris; How should I get the money to do it with?" Commonwealth claimed to have received over a hundred letters along these lines. The leadership's response was always the same—they would provide for legitimate needs as best they could, but they would not bestow luxuries on anyone while some were suffering.

In the future, socialism would provide luxuries, necessities, and generous blessings freely for all, but "at present the call of Christ was to give up needless luxuries and worldliness and mammonism and selfishness and bear the cross of social redemption. Commonwealth . . . is an organ of social sacrifice wherein the disciples of Jesus practice the law of love and find abundant life—with tribulations." To make that sacrifice and practice love, members of Commonwealth organized to serve each other and the world.[39]

PART
TWO

SOJOURN

CHAPTER 3

✦ ✦ ✦

How We Organize

Organize life according to the Christian ideal.
—James P. Kelley, the *Social Gospel*

BEFORE THE *Social Gospel* began publishing in February 1898, existing historical sources for the Christian Commonwealth are rare. It was a time devoted to pioneering and survival, and few records were created or preserved. We know little about the early leadership, other than that Damon and Gibson served as presidents. The community held elections, but the outcomes are unknown. Nevertheless, the colony appeared to function relatively smoothly without a constitution, formal institutional structure, or adequate capital, and it survived.[1]

The first families at Commonwealth were diverse but unified by a commitment to brotherhood life. Their leaders were preachers, writers, teachers, and "thoughtful mechanics and farmers." Jesus Christ was the source of their social vision. As postmillennialists, they wanted to create a Kingdom of God on earth, to produce conditions for the return of Christ. Brotherhood and the law of love were the means to realize that kingdom, and they would welcome all who accepted them, but they had no firm plan to achieve that goal. A shortage of housing limited the initial population to ten families, but the community had the horses, cows, hogs, chickens, and farm implements needed to get things going.[2]

Members wanted to escape the competitive system and instill humankind with the idea that God dwells in every human breast. They saw a constant struggle between God and selfishness, and selfishness was winning because it had become necessary to survive. But at Commonwealth one would not need to be selfish.

Even after a year, in response to requests for "our plan," they admitted to not having one. One principle guided them: the law of love. Other than that, their "plan" was evolving, not perfected. They could change, revise, or reconstruct it. One guide was the Marxist expression "From each according to his ability, to each according to his need." In carrying out their duties, they asked a question that has regained popularity recently but originated with Charles Sheldon, a Topeka minister, in 1886: "What would Jesus do about it?"[3]

They did not think that their "plan" was "the only society-saving formula." They encouraged unselfish cooperation everywhere. For cities, they advocated brotherhood organizations, social settlements with economic features, and cooperative stores and factories. They urged each believer in brotherhood "to gather about him a brotherhood band."[4]

Their cooperative spirit challenged America's fundamental belief in individualism. They saw individual selfishness and dishonesty as universal in the business world, in commercial and property relations, and in politics. To them, it was sinful, but contemporary religious institutions had not condemned it. In contrast, they preached repentance from the world's selfishness and saw brotherhood life as the way to salvation. One must immerse oneself in self-forgetful service. To be self-centered was the way of death; to be all-centered was the way of life.[5]

The challenge to each-for-himself individualism did not erase their desire for individual liberty. Their lack of a formal plan reflected a belief in an anarchistic vision that guaranteed personal freedom of choice. Within the colony, some members lived in private cottages that were not alike. Others chose community housing. Some members were satisfied with rough board-and-batten architecture; others desired shingles, porches, and other amenities. There is no early evidence of conflict or jealousy over different choices. Later, dissenters viewed the differences as a sign of favoritism in housing.

Some members planted personal gardens near their cottages, and others did not. One man, ambitious to demonstrate his agricultural theories, had a small "experiment farm" where he spent his spare time. There were no uniforms or peculiarities of dress. Clothing styles varied, but there may have been some pressure for modest dress to preserve a standard of equality. Sue Fay Hinckley described a "spring opening of hats," but each woman was limited to two hats.[6]

Except for the law of love, they had an amorphous ideology that did not lend itself to creating formal institutions. Gibson and Albertson, as devotees of Tolstoy, were not enthusiastic about inflexible rules or formal political organization, and initially the colony had no law code. They placed "no reliance on force, or on anything but the knowledge of love and the spirit of love." The only law was "Thou shalt love thy neighbor as thyself." The community rejected centralized leadership and operated informally and loosely. Members expected leadership to emerge out of inspiration and service. Members whose service, "sacrifice," and devotion to duty "inspired the greatest love" would guide the community.[7]

With no constitution, their covenant, a "bond of organic union," was their fundamental document. Every member signed it:

> I accept as the Law of my Life Christ's Law, that I shall love my neighbor as myself. I will use, hold or dispose of all my property, my labor and my income, according to the dictates of love, for the happiness of all who need. . . . As quickly as I may be able to, I will withdraw myself from the selfish competitive strife and devote myself to the co-operative life and labor of a local Christian Commonwealth. As a member . . . I will work according to my ability in labor together with God for the production of goods for human happiness.[8]

It was a commitment to religious life, not a commercial arrangement. Unlike Ruskin, Commonwealth placed character above money as a condition of membership. Other colonies had failed because "money, not manhood, entrance fees, not love" were more important. Applicants took "consecration test" to prove their willingness to give all, both labor and property, to the community. "The leading inducement to enter a society of brothers must be made nothing material to get or to tempt the selfish beyond to-day's bread and this must be labored for when strength to labor is possessed." Once understood, they received full membership.[9]

One did not have to reside at Commonwealth to become a member. Those who were unable or unwilling to transplant were "urged to preach the gospel ... until they have gathered a band of converts about them with whom they can join hands, hearts, and property in the uplifting redemptive work of our leader, Christ." As a statement of faith, they printed their covenant in the *Social Gospel* and other publications and attracted worldwide interest. By mid-1898, about one hundred families in twenty-three states and nations had signed the document and become members. The numbers grew so fast that Albertson began to speak of it as a "movement," not merely a communal experiment. He encouraged new members to embrace "common property," but, if they were not ready, they needed to demonstrate only their love of Christ.[10]

The resident population fluctuated because of high turnover but was never large. No records exist, but it probably averaged between seventy-five and one hundred people. Estimates of total residents over the colony's life range from three to five hundred. Alexander Kent set the number at five hundred based on a statement from the colony president. Later, Albertson put the total at three hundred. The issue is complicated because some residents were not members of the community, and it is not clear whether the evidence refers to members or nonmembers. At times, the number of nonmember residents exceeded 50 percent. A close examination of arrivals, departures, and activities mentioned in the *Social Gospel* and the Columbus newspapers from November 1896 until the community disbanded turned up about 230 distinct names, but the records did not make a clear distinction among members, residents, visitors, and tourists.[11]

One can create a reasonably accurate list of residents from the *Social Gospel*'s accounts, but no formal record exists. With few exceptions, Commonwealth residents left no accounts of their experiences there or their lives before and after Commonwealth. Fire destroyed critical 1890 census data. General descriptions of individuals or the membership as a whole are informative but superficial. Throughout the community's existence, men were the majority, and single men outnumbered single women and usually outnumbered married men. Pioneering under frontier conditions did not have a great appeal for most women.[12]

Despite Commonwealth's founding by outsiders, roughly one-quarter of its residents were southerners. They made up a larger contingent than similar communities. Fairhope, in Alabama, founded by twenty-eight Iowans, and Newllano, founded in Louisiana by Californians, did not have nearly as many southern members.[13]

Day-to-day survival consumed the minds of early members. They had arrived late in 1896 and, through sacrifice inspired by brotherhood, cleaned up the old plantation, built fences, planted fields and orchards, and constructed needed buildings. Though they were poor, their commitment to cooperation, not competition, allowed them to find joy and pleasure in everything.

As noted in the *Social Gospel*, "Infinite Love speaks to them in every voice, is written upon every flower and shower, and shines in unmistakable and lasting beauty through the faces of our fellow workers." It was "the Master sending forth heavenly harmony."[14]

Organization and supervision of labor were difficult, but members accomplished much through hard work and frugal living. The law of love meant work, without exception, by everyone. Every man, woman, and child contributed their share. The adults thought it beautiful that even young people accepted work as a matter of course and were willing to labor for public welfare and not private gain. "Preachers, professors, and poets ... worked side by side with farmers and mechanics, shrinking from nothing." As a result, both physical structures and cultivated land grew sizably in the first year and a half.[15]

By early 1898, the colony had grown and appeared to be on the verge of flourishing. Members seemed pleased with their progress, and there was optimism within and outside the community that it would become "one of the largest and most important colonies located in the South."

In February, members held their second election of "official servants," and the women completed their own "industrial organization." They elected Rebecca Brown as president and Isadore Gibson, George's wife, as secretary. Brown was also the superintendent of the General Housekeeping Department. Bertine Croyle took charge of the plantation house and oversight of the sick. Sadie Pease became the chief cook. Lucy Fay headed up the dressmaking and sewing, and Dora Hall superintended the communal laundry and poultry department. Louise Merce from Berzelia, Georgia, a woman who probably had some experience, was given charge of the poultry yards. Despite having a separate organization, women experienced some gender equality in the broader community. They were elected to high offices and participated in critical decision making. On the other hand, family and most domestic work remained organized along traditional gender lines.[16]

By late spring of 1898, the colony's affairs had become more complex, and open membership was creating some problems. From the beginning, there had been virtually no restrictions on the acceptance of members, either nonresident or resident. Nonresident members offered moral and minor financial support but had little influence on colony life.[17]

It became clear that the colony's growth required rules on newcomers and nonresident members. To clarify, the Commonwealth leadership wrote a contract that everyone working at the community had to sign:

I, _____, do hereby contract, bargain, and agree with The Christian Commonwealth, that for such board and other benefits as the said Christian Commonwealth shall voluntarily give me I will work faithfully at the labor I may be assigned to, and my board is and shall be accepted by me as payment in full for the labor I perform, and I hereby relinquish all claims whatsoever to any wages. . . . And I furthermore agree to peacefully and promptly leave the premises of The Christian Commonwealth whenever I may be officially requested to do so.[18]

Newcomers served a brief probationary period and could apply for membership within three months of arrival. Beyond that, resident nonmembers received the same treatment as members. Early on, a verbal understanding had been sufficient, but disagreements arose. This policy and the contract became part of the official bylaws when Commonwealth wrote a formal constitution.[19]

The community's faith in the transformative power of love committed them to "open their hearts and arms to embrace all who would be loved." Their brotherhood would put a new purpose and spirit of life into anyone, even the "tramp" and the "loafer." Unfortunately, some new arrivals never adopted the founding members' commitment to love, sacrifice, and egalitarianism.

Others accepted the founding ideology but saw gaps in the leadership's adherence to it. They felt excluded by the founding members' power and privileges and began to criticize and challenge them over alleged favoritism and mismanagement. To protect themselves and clarify community affairs and operation, the leaders decided to formalize and document their commitment to majority rule.

In May 1898, John Chipman transferred Commonwealth's deed to a group of fifteen trustees who were longtime members of the community. The deed stated that the trustees were to administer the Christian Commonwealth as "agents for Christ" devoted to obeying Christ's teachings and laws and that "the majority of members of the 'Christian Commonwealth' shall be the sole interpreter of these laws" and have the power to rule. Reflecting its anti-institutional, nonresistant, and anarchist sensibilities, the colony had rejected any need for government sanction and had not incorporated after almost two years of existence. In late spring 1898, members finally began to discuss writing a constitution and bylaws, formalizing the organizational structure, and incorporating under the laws of the state of Georgia.[20]

In response to this development, Albertson published "A General Letter to the Members of the Christian Commonwealth" in the May *Social Gospel*. In the letter, expressing his faith and anarchistic tendencies, he reasserted his opposition to institutionalization. "We need no presidents," he wrote, "no by-laws, no votes, no fees. The time has not come for officers and paper constitutions. Perhaps it never will. I feel quite sure we don't want a machine to save the world with. The Christian Commonwealth is not so much an organization as it is a movement. We must have leaders ... but they shall be naturally the men and women who serve most and inspire to greatest love."[21]

Albertson's assertion proved wrong, and despite his opposition, a majority at Commonwealth agreed that they needed a constitution, formal institutions, and elections. In August 1898, thirty-four members petitioned the Muscogee County Superior Court for a charter, which it granted in November. It contained details on the legal aspects of the colony but barely changed its daily practices. The same day, they received an Order of Incorporation from the court.[22]

They then wrote a formal constitution based on the "law (not made, but recognized) of supreme love to God and equalizing love to our neighbor" and which vested "all powers ... in a majority of the resident members." It called for obedience to the teachings of Jesus Christ and rejected any membership fee or test other than coming "in the spirit of love, unselfishness, and true fellowship" and consecration of their labor and property to the service of Christ. The written constitution formalized most of the practices and procedures that they had developed over a year and a half.[23]

The constitution formalized the policy and process for membership. New members had to fulfill three conditions: (1) "They are to come to us in the spirit of love, unselfishness, and true fellowship"; (2) "They had to accept the constitution and ... authority of Commonwealth as expressed by a majority"; and (3) they had to "consecrate all their labor and property, without reserve, to the service and obedience of Christ." The bylaws prescribed the manner of accepting new members. They had to sign the community's covenant. The three-month requirement for formal application remained. Those who failed to apply had to leave the colony. The membership board examined the applications and made recommendations at the business meetings. It would also inventory the accepted applicants' contributions and "act as a peacemaker" between members. The specific mention of the peacemaker role in the constitution implies the existence of conflicts that needed resolution, but few details became public.

Despite its commitment to "open membership" and faith in the ability of "love" to transform newcomers into good members, Commonwealth realized by 1898 it needed a method to deal with those not changed and created a termination process. After "an open trial by a special committee of five," a report would be submitted to the members for a vote. A majority vote would annul all rights and privileges.[24]

Commonwealth expelled only three members during its existence. One circulated a lewd and immoral manuscript. A second was persistently and incurably lazy. And a third had lied about being an unmarried widower when his wife was still living. In each case, the colony delayed expulsion until those members had demonstrated their unfitness or lack of sympathy for the brotherhood movement.[25]

The constitution stated that Commonwealth held all property in common, and it could not be "alienated, encumbered or disposed of" without a two-thirds vote of the members. The colony continued to send out literature inviting "whosoever will" to join them and, in joining, become equal owners of the community property. Their goal was absolute equality, and they expected that whoever came would surrender their possessions, as the first members had done, to the common treasury. "All who brought ... some property and some money, literally and legally had not a whit more than the tramp who had crawled out of a freight car for a drink of water, and found himself an equal owner in the Kingdom of God," but this was never rigidly enforced. Nevertheless, any contributions of funds or property were "absolute and irrevocable gifts" and not investments from which contributors could expect personal returns. Members withdrawing or expelled had "no legal claim to reimbursement."[26]

Residents did not use money within the community, and most cash received by members went into a common fund. For their labor, each member received nothing more than shelter, clothes, food, medical care, and education. No one received wages for services rendered. It was completely communistic where "each worked for all and all for each." Anyone willing to accept those conditions was welcome to join. Departing members did not have any claims when leaving the community.[27]

Attitudes toward the constitution varied. Several members entirely rejected any government and thought that there should be no community attempt to control labor, which should be a spontaneous expression of love. Albertson was among those who held this exalted conception of labor under communism. But despite his feelings, he ultimately accepted an organization with formal management and delegated responsibilities. It caused some grief to the purists who held faithfully to their simplistic solution. Chipman, with a literally inspired Bible and perfected church in his soul, felt that the constitution, once adopted, was inviolable and must not be changed one iota. Albertson, on the other hand, felt that the people who wrote it and were governed by it could modify it as necessary. Ironically, they never formally changed the constitution, although they violated it on occasion.[28]

Once members accepted the need for formal organization, Commonwealth created a traditional organizational structure that worked smoothly. Community politics were completely democratic. Women had all franchise rights and privileges and exercised them regularly. Reflecting both the suffrage movement and progressive thought, every member, male or female, over age eighteen could run for office and vote. Following their faith in the Kingdom of God, "there is neither male nor female class, there are no sex distinctions of superiority and inferiority." "Mothers, wives and sisters should be reckoned distinct human entities and have equal rights with their brothers at the Commonwealth ballot box." Everyone voted on election day and elected nine women among the thirty-six leadership positions.[29]

Elections would be held annually or, if necessary, more often. Every adult member chose the "official servants," all officers and department superintendents. The elected officials did not make laws. An Executive Board made up of officers and department superintendents met weekly or at special meetings called by the president to discuss colony business. The meetings were open to the entire community, and every adult member had an opportunity to speak and vote directly on all laws and rules of action. The Executive Board then met "to arrange for carrying out the instructions of the society." At any time, 5 percent of the resident members could appeal any delegated power, ruling, authority, or board decision and call for a referendum vote by the entire membership.[30]

Whether inspired by New England town meetings or a reflection of progressive advocacy for direct legislation, Commonwealth members met regularly to resolve such questions as "For what family should we build the next house? Shall we build a sorghum mill? Must all members eat in the common dining room? Shall a man who has a government pension be permitted to live in the community? Shall the Head of Farming or Horticulture have his choice of men and teams? How do we solve the cooking problem? Shall 'Negroes' be taken into the community?"[31]

The first elections under the charter and new constitution occurred in December 1898. To "give voters the utmost freedom of choice," the bylaws forbid making nominations. Moreover, members thought anyone seeking or campaigning for office was not a "true brother" and distrusted them. Those elected by the "voice of the people" would feel a moral obligation to provide the best service in the "Christ spirit."

The week before the election, members received a blank "Christian Commonwealth Ballot." Members consulted "with one another as to who were the best men and women for the various places of leadership and special or extra responsibility." The officials to be elected included president, vice-president, secretary, treasurer, labor director, health officer, and three members for each board: Agriculture, Mechanics, Horticulture, Extension, Education, Women's Work, Business, Textile Fabrics Manufacturing, Religious and Social Meetings, and Membership. If no one received a majority, members would hold a runoff of the top two vote getters on the same day. "Official servants" were elected for one year but could be changed sooner if necessary.[32]

The community elected William Damon as president. Of the founding four, Damon wrote and spoke less but led quietly and by example. He was active in the community but not interested in being a dominant figure. His role was merely to "preside" over the weekly meetings, not to make executive decisions. His leadership was welcome, and he served as president longer than anyone. Albertson, with his religious background, was the best speaker and had presented weekly sermons for the first year and a half. Gibson viewed him as the leader and the dominant voice. In turn, Albertson saw Gibson as the "spiritual leader who was loved and respected by everyone" and "always true to his own high-minded ideals." He was also the most "thorough-going Tolstoyan" of the group. Neither seemed charismatic compared to John Humphrey Noyes at his Oneida community or Mother Ann Lee, the founder of the Shakers. Still, both had loyal followers who had been with them in previous cooperative experiments. John Chipman, tied to business interests all over northern Florida—Rockwell, Fernandina, Dunnellon—did not relocate immediately, although he influenced events from afar.[33]

Outsiders referred to Albertson as the "most prominent member" of the community, and most sources see him as the prime mover. Because most of the manuscript sources are Albertson's, he might have given himself a larger role than he deserved, but he did command a presence. In 1994 I spoke with a woman in West Newbury, Massachusetts, where, after Commonwealth's demise, Albertson had a farm where he entertained Harvard students on the weekends in a Brook Farm–type of environment. She raved about the dynamism of his personality and how he had a charismatic presence when he entered a room.[34]

The community chose Sue Fay Hinckley as vice-president. Albertson later paid homage to her, one of his congregants from Springfield, who was "one of the strongest characters and leaders of the community." She had been an Ohio schoolteacher who followed Albertson, first to North Carolina and then to Commonwealth. Her Christian spirit, attitude, and ideology were completely in tune with Albertson's. She was influential among the women and probably contributed more than any other member to the harmony and overall success of daily life. She was also highly creative in writing, drawing, and painting, which she engaged in to recuperate from the burdens of her daily responsibilities.[35]

She was an original member of Commonwealth and met Daniel Hinckley there. Albertson married them in October 1898, in what was one of the "prettiest affairs" in the colony. The members decorated the community's largest room with bamboo vines, palmettos, and a profusion of decorative plants that grew on the grounds. With one exception, everyone in the community and friends from Georgia and Alabama attended. Four little girls strewed flowers along the path as the bride in her white dress approached the altar. Soft piano music played throughout the ceremony as both old and young entered into the festivities. The couple received many gifts, and the community prepared and decorated a comfortable home for them. Perhaps the best news was that they would remain at Commonwealth, where they became "foundation stones" and powerful, influential voices.[36]

Jule Talmadge became recording secretary. A semi-invalid, he was barely capable of living a pioneer existence. He served as secretary from beginning to end and was responsible for the colony records. He also served as librarian, wrote poetry, and reviewed books for the *Social Gospel*. For manual labor, he folded the *Social Gospel* for mailing. Talmadge drew a government pension that he kept, although he contributed to the common fund and paid board. With personal funds, he acquired tobacco and other small luxuries more frequently than some more hardworking members. His mother, Lydia, had been connected to a cooperative society when young and was attracted to Commonwealth. She came from Nebraska in January 1899 for a visit. Everyone thought that she would stay, but she returned to Nebraska in April.[37]

Jacob Troth, a Virginia Quaker who had arrived in October 1898, became treasurer. Albertson described him as "toothless, tall, slender, nearly seventy years old, a vegetarian and gourmand." He was a deep thinker who had been president of the Virginia Peace Society. With boundless devotion, he lived at Commonwealth until the end. He was, by nature as well as by birth, a simple Quaker who told Commonwealth's members that they were "Quakerish" in their principles and limitations. He delivered mail, ran errands, and joined the print shop staff in late 1898. He brought in quite a few subscribers among his Quaker friends who sympathized with the *Social Gospel*'s message.[38]

Founding members dominated the elected leadership, and many held multiple positions. Damon was president most of the time and did a good job. Gibson served a term as president. Albertson resisted holding that office, but at times, in addition to his *Social Gospel* work, he served as both business manager and commissary agent, two vital jobs concerned with the economics and the food supply. Despite his lack of high office, Albertson often emerged as the leading voice in the community. In most debates, he got a majority on his side of the question. Some members perceived this as undemocratic, but Albertson's views on Christianity, socialism, and democracy were more in line with the majority, and he was persuasive in espousing them.[39]

After the founding four, Daniel Hinckley was one of the most important members. A native of Roxbury, Massachusetts, Hinckley graduated from Harvard University with a degree in agricultural science and became farm superintendent of the Bussey Institution at Harvard. Before coming to Commonwealth, he had "homesteaded in North Dakota, traveled to Washington and Oregon, and spent five years at intensive farming back in Massachusetts. Neither discontented nor disturbed by the drift of American society, Hinckley was attracted to Commonwealth by the Christian literature that they sent out." He spent most of his time as director of labor, where he did an excellent job but was also known for indulging in "the reveries of a bachelor" before his marriage to Sue Fay.[40]

As director of labor, a position he held from the earliest informal organization, Hinckley had an important job. He monitored all work, "keeping labor and tools in touch and properly adjusted." He kept himself "posted as to the need for laborers in the various departments by frequent observation and consultation with the boards of management." Each morning, he assigned workers to the departments where they were needed. Finally, he evaluated work quality and reported any deficiencies at the business meetings. Not everyone was pleased with the subjectivity of the process, and they rejected some of the proposed time checks on the labor force. Many of the critics left, and the community retained its simple system, which relied on

its belief in brotherhood and individual responsibility. There were no production quotas. To the extent that productivity was a problem, it was caused
more by faulty equipment than by lax workers, but Commonwealth was confident that it could become self-supporting and produce a plentiful surplus.[41]

He also served on the Board of Agriculture with Henry Croyle and George
McDermott. They had broad responsibilities. The board had charge of all
farm and garden work and livestock. It maintained the roads and bridges,
cleared land, cut timber, and built fences. Finally, it provided fire protection.
George and his wife Ida came to Commonwealth from Nebraska. They were
both idealistic, hardworking, and committed to the purposes and principles of the community. George did much of the plowing. Ida had an aggressive personality—argumentative, energetic, a little dogmatic, but positive and
faithful to the community's ideals.[42]

The community elected W. L. Carman and two recent arrivals, James
Brower from Kansas and Sam Byerly of Virginia, to the Board of Mechanics.
With the aid of William McHenry of Mississippi and John G. Steffes of Illinois, they made bricks, supervised blacksmithing, and built and maintained
the buildings, houses, and wagons. They also determined locations and made
plans for new residences and public buildings.[43]

The Board of Horticulture consisted of William Damon, his wife Amelia,
and George Hartman, a recent arrival from Chicago. Aided by C. W. Minor,
from New York, they had charge of the orchard and nursery, vineyard, and all
other fruit raising. Damon, as superintendent, played a critical role in establishing the orchard and nursery. He loved the outdoors and worked there all
day long. Damon's expertise in horticulture and fruit cultivation made him
valuable, and his orchard and nursery demonstrated Commonwealth's ambition and its "best work."[44]

Damon and Talmadge joined Sue Fay Hinckley, the school superintendent, on the Board of Education. They were in charge of the Commonwealth
school and served as intermediaries with the Muscogee County school system. They were also responsible for the kindergarten, night school, proposed
industrial school, and library.

Albertson, Brower, and Carman led the Board of Business. They took responsibility for purchasing, storing, and distributing supplies to the community and the sale of products from the other departments. They also supervised the post office and had ambitious plans for a restaurant, store, and
cannery.

The Board of Textile Manufacturing included F. J. Loiselle, his wife Maggie,

and John Steffes. Its name spoke for itself, although they were not yet manufacturing textiles. They would also respond to requests from the business
department for specific textile products.

Sue Fay Hinckley, George Howard Gibson, and Charles Cook made up
the Board of Membership. Their responsibilities included examining applications of prospective members, taking an inventory of new members' contributions, and mediating disputes among the membership.[45]

The Board of Women's Work consisted of Lucy Fay, Ida McDermott, and
Sadie Pease. They were responsible for the laundry and clothing care, dressmaking, and chamber work. Lucy, Sue Fay's sister, emerged as a leader in this
area. She had neither the intellect nor the leadership qualities of her sister, but in many ways she was more helpful and more useful. She handled
most of the issues surrounding housekeeping and the domestic economy, an
area that often undermined communal success. Not married, she was freed
from domestic responsibilities to take on the more significant housekeeping
problems. Sue Fay Hinckley and Lucy Fay were sisters whose contributions
to Commonwealth, both spiritually and physically, were unmatched.[46]

Albertson, Gibson, and Cook made up the Board of Extension, which they
regarded as "the most important department of all" since it "kept the community in the world, but not of it." They handled all "propaganda work, general correspondence, publishing ventures, off-site meetings, and the organization of any proposed new colonies."[47]

Through their department, Gibson and Albertson thought that by con-
necting with the outside world they could expand its brotherhood efforts
and alleviate the hard conditions and economic burden at Commonwealth.
Opportunities for business investment would be "for the Lord." Investment
in Commonwealth, new branches, or entirely new societies of Christian cooperation would "lay up treasures in Heaven" for the investors.[48]

Commonwealth's covenant implied a desire to start new communities,
and their charter gave them the power to do so. To Gibson, the articles of incorporation created an "unselfish or Christian corporation," which could establish businesses and start branches anywhere. He defined a Christian corporation as "a love-ruled fraternal, non-profit-seeking body, . . . which is not
merely unselfish within itself . . . but disposed to run its economic power
unselfishly to serve the world." Taking as his example the selfish cooperation that had created ninety-two new trusts in Gilded Age America, Gibson
thought unselfish men could do better. They should pool their capital and
establish a Brotherhood Trust motivated by more than profits and force the

profit seekers out of the markets. He appealed for businessmen who were morally sick of brutal competition to join with Commonwealth in this pursuit.[49]

By the fall of 1898, encouraged by a huge worldwide circulation and wanting Commonwealth to be a "city upon the hill," the *Social Gospel* hoped to spread its vision and give recognition to worldwide leaders in Christian reform. Commonwealth's members planned to organize "branch societies" to advance their educational and evangelical work. They wanted to locate one on the Gulf Coast and build a steamer to connect the colonies and transport raw materials and food supplies on the Chattahoochee River.[50]

When they circulated their covenant by mail, hundreds of copies were signed and returned. Many included offers of land, machinery, and equipment for use at Commonwealth or to establish new colonies. Individual members made more than a dozen proposals for colonies in Virginia, Tennessee, Colorado, and Florida. In August 1898, Damon visited an orchard west of Macon, Georgia, whose owners, Dr. and Mrs. Breese, wanted to make it the basis for a branch Christian Commonwealth. The week before, he and Samuel Comings had visited Mrs. A. G. Helmer near Atlanta. Active in the suffrage movement and school, library, and civic affairs, she wanted to start a colony and school on her plantation. There is no evidence that Commonwealth helped her, but eight months later, with the aid of some Atlanta people, she and her family started a colony based on John Ruskin's plan in Milner's Grove, Georgia.[51]

In August 1898, John Chipman, still in Florida, proposed a new community on the Gulf Coast. He issued a call for ten or twenty families to join him. His motives were not obvious. Did he not want to move to Georgia? Did proximity to his business interests take precedence? Or was he so optimistic as to think that another community could thrive despite Commonwealth's ongoing struggles? Chipman was conflicted. A successful businessman, he preached that the material world had enslaved men and quoted Christ: "Whosoever... renounceth not all that he hath, he cannot be my disciple."[52]

Commonwealth gave Chipman's plan its approval, in contrast to other proposals. It was ambitious but would "add much strength to the work" they were doing. Chipman held an option on three hundred acres of land on Florida's west coast. Part of the land was on the coast and coastal islands in the Gulf of Mexico, fifteen miles from Cedar Key, a good trading point. Improvements included a few houses, a stable, cisterns, some fenced acreage, five hundred orange trees, and several acres of sugar cane. Chipman envisioned a health resort or a campground for fishermen and raved about the natural resources: fish, oysters, clams, crabs, turtles, deer, turkey, and a variety of heavy timber. The *Social Gospel* encouraged Commonwealth members in Florida and elsewhere to consider migrating to Chipman's proposed colony.[53]

Chipman received about twenty letters from people anxious to join, but only one offered financial help and sent a mere fifty dollars. Chipman feared that he would not be able to raise enough capital to start and considered locating closer to Commonwealth so that the colonies could share their resources, but ultimately nothing came of his proposal.[54]

Another proposal came from N. O. Nelson, a wealthy manufacturer of plumbing supplies. Inspired by Saint Francis and a visit to Commonwealth, he proposed a colony in Leclaire, Illinois. Nelson had created a cooperative village at his factory, where he housed, educated, and shared his profits with his workers. Now he saw an opportunity to expand his effort into a new Christian Commonwealth, and he sought support from the *Social Gospel*'s readers. He wanted men and women of heroism and faith who were willing to sacrifice and practice the gospel of brotherhood. He assured them that experienced communitarians from the Georgia colony would migrate north to assist them. There is no evidence of Commonwealth's reaction to Nelson's proposal, nor is there any evidence that he founded a colony resembling Commonwealth. A year later, Nelson wrote a glowing article for the *Social Gospel* about his Leclaire village, which was neither socialist nor formally organized like Commonwealth. In some ways it resembled Pullman, but Nelson based the village on the spirit of love, equality, and harmony.[55]

In early 1899, Albert Pease and Reverend Harry C. Vrooman, whose brother Hiram was a major donor to Commonwealth, proposed their colony plan for Florida's Gulf Coast. They controlled twenty-five hundred acres of debt-free land on Apalachicola Bay. The bay contained an abundant source of seafood, and the property consisted of hundreds of acres of fertile land and a large stand of timber that they could use to construct houses. Vrooman offered free land to people who would use it to advance Christian communism and planned to open a normal and industrial school as the basis for New Education. The *Social Gospel* announced the offer and encouraged people to contact Vrooman or Pease.[56]

Pease had been at Commonwealth for less than a year, and it is not clear why he left. He had tramped through Florida and the Southeast while recovering from illness and found something more appealing in Florida. Originally from Spokane, Washington, he had traveled to Lincoln, Nebraska, to join the caravan to Georgia. A religious man and a hard worker, he earned great respect in the short time he was at the colony. He became a trustee and acted in the community's best interests. During a visit to Macon, one resident described him as "the most interesting man from Commonwealth."[57]

The same year another community named Christian Commonwealth was organized and incorporated in New Westminster, British Columbia. The Georgia community corresponded with the enterprise, but there is no evidence of a formal connection. Nevertheless, its constitution, bylaws, and circulars expressed the same faith and purpose seen at Commonwealth, which expressed its confidence in and love for the Canadians and wished them success.

Around the same time, the Industrial Brotherhood, led by N. W. Lermond of Maine, was organizing a colony on Martha's Vineyard. Little is known about it, although there is some documentation suggesting that it still survived in 1906. Albertson praised Lermond for his scheme, despite its implausible vagueness, to bring a million men and a hundred million dollars to the cause of industrial socialism.[58]

In June, Mrs. G. M. Bacon of DeWitt, Georgia, who was studying cooperative life, visited Commonwealth. She was the cousin of Derrill Hope and the sister-in-law of Octavius Bacon, a U.S. senator from Georgia. Mrs. Bacon wanted to start a colony in DeWitt. Her husband had a large farm, highly improved, and near them were people interested in a cooperative life of love.[59]

Nothing came of most of these proposals, but they demonstrated that the Christian Commonwealth was having some impact on the nation's social landscape, although not assuming a direct role in these efforts. Most members felt that their first responsibility was to ensure the success of their colony before embarking on new enterprises. Later, when Commonwealth broke up, some members headed to the colonies in Florida and Illinois, seeking another opportunity to establish the Kingdom of God on earth.[60]

Despite their initial hesitation and the hardships they faced, Commonwealth's leaders remained hopeful that they could develop additional agricultural and manufacturing colonies on the brotherhood plan. They saw Commonwealth not as an end in itself but as "a costly but necessary organic brotherhood beginning." They hoped that if the colony was successful, significant numbers of those who had been ground down by poverty and those with sensitive social consciences would join the movement and work for economic readjustment and brotherhood organization.[61]

The archaeological remains of Commonwealth are vague and inconclusive, but it is clear that the leadership planned the site with function in mind. Despite their pioneer existence, colony members did not ignore aesthetics, although they were less committed to the merger of beauty and justice than were earlier utopians like Bellamy, Ruskin, and William Morris. They tried to locate public buildings and grounds to make getting together convenient. The long-term plan was to create a central village site with a large well to serve the surrounding cottages. The Gibson cottage was "the first to go up on the horseshoe curve, in the center of which commodious and convenient public or common buildings will be later built." Despite the rough nature of their board-and-batten structures, they landscaped them carefully. At the foot of the hill, where they built the community kitchen, they left standing "a pretty little grove of pines by the side of the creek." The Gibson cottage came to be known as "Rose Cottage" for its proliferation of exquisite crimson roses from several bushes. They also planted three holly trees and a cedar tree in the yard. In late 1898, it received some preferential treatment by being shingled on three sides to improve its warmth and appearance.[62]

After two years, Commonwealth had finally organized into a structured community that could look forward to the future. While it continued to suffer from shortages of labor and resources, much work had been getting done, and residents had made much progress. What remained to be seen was whether that small but dedicated labor force could move Commonwealth closer to the Kingdom of God.

CHAPTER 4

✦ ✦ ✦

Brotherhood Labor

Live and work all good works in Christ's name.
—John Chipman, the *Kingdom*

THE CHRISTIAN COMMONWEALTH's founders were neither ascetics nor materialists. Material things were good if rightly used, which was to supply everyone's needs equally. As Christian believers in the Kingdom of God, they were brothers to the poorest and willing to share their poverty as long as oppression existed. "All beauty and every luxury belong in the Kingdom of God—but so does every child of God belong in that kingdom—so does economic justice … therefore no one child of God can live in a palace while another lives in a hovel."[1]

Commonwealth was committed to hard work and service, but their standard of living remained low. They never advanced beyond the pioneer stage and remained impoverished throughout the colony's existence. Many members were urban "tenderfeet" who had never done manual labor, but their daily life consisted of hard, sweaty, physical labor.

Hardship, obstacles, and disadvantages filled Commonwealth's first year. As the first members arrived in November 1896, it was too late for them to plant a full crop in what turned out to be worn-out land. Malaria and the need to build housing then reduced labor available for agriculture. The shortage of capital made matters worse by hindering the ability of the head of the commissary, who was determined to avoid debt, to purchase more food, so rations remained scarce until the 1897 harvest. Until then, there was little food variety, and it was not always palatable. Despite members' hard work to become self-sufficient and produce a surplus for sale, they had to practice a "rigid economy."[2]

From the beginning, the colonists concentrated on growing fruits and vegetables. That was the foundation of the community and its hope for long-term success. Commonwealth's neighbors all raised cotton, but it was a crop the community, despite earlier assertions, chose to avoid. They believed that, with care, the soil and climate could produce fine crops, and such an enterprise would be pleasant and profitable.[3]

Food for members was a priority, and the first crops planted in the spring were corn, sweet potatoes, onions, cowpeas, peanuts, sugar cane, oats, rye, wheat, and garden vegetables. The exhausted land needed preparation, but the first year the commune had no money for fertilizer. Without it, they had a small corn crop. Nevertheless, cornmeal, prepared in various ways, became a staple. They raised a good peanut crop and converted it into peanut butter using a mill donated by an Ohio brother. Lacking coffee, they made cereal coffee but often did without sugar, tea, meat, and wheat bread. They used crude cottonseed oil as a substitute for lard. It was satisfactory and healthier. Later, a Pennsylvania brother sent them a barrel of refined cooking oil that was superior to cottonseed oil but would have cost twice as much. They supplemented their diet with wild fruit, especially the blackberries that, despite their prickles, were fun to pick in the early morning. Most members took shortages in stride, believing them temporary, but necessary, to achieve the kingdom. It was better to live on cowpeas, cornbread, sweet potatoes, and gravy where love is "than to dine at Delmonico's and compete with one another." Nevertheless, this hardship, more than any other, strained the faith of those without the larger vision of sacrifice that was necessary to achieve Commonwealth's goal.[4]

By mid-1897, several construction projects were under way. Workers started building a school, finished renovating the plantation house, and added a communal dining room. Anticipating the need for housing for newcomers, they finished the sawmill and planned its expansion. Members erected a print shop and furnished it with equipment to print the *Social Gospel*. They also built a flour mill, several cottages, carpentry and blacksmith shops, stables, and a new barn for eight horses, six cows, and fodder. They wanted to create a pleasant environment for those seeking an opportunity to escape economic turmoil and the cold, bleak competition of the outside world.[5]

Under Damon's direction, members removed hedges and briar patches, stopped water runoff, and laid out large tracts for planting. They fenced three hundred acres as pasture for cows and horses and another three hundred to cultivate. By late 1897, they had created a thirty-five-acre orchard and started a nursery and vineyard. In the nursery, Amelia Damon took charge of a wagonload of flower roots and shrubs that a Columbus woman donated and put together fine nursery stock for setting out the following spring. They planted two hundred grapevines and, in the orchard, set out five thousand peach trees, three hundred Japanese plum trees, twenty quince trees, and a thousand pear, cherry, and apple trees, plus figs, prunes, and apricots. In the nursery, they started another four thousand plum and one thousand peach trees.[6]

By the fall, Commonwealth was alive with enterprise. Prioritizing truck farming and market gardening was timely as some of their products had been coming from outside the region. Columbus got its onions from Bermuda, cabbages from Denmark, and turnips, chickens, and butter from all over the country. The colony planned to increase its crop diversity and sell its surplus in Columbus or ship it elsewhere.

By early 1898, many people had come and gone, but about one hundred remained. Members worked hard and lived frugally. A Columbus gentleman wrote, "They are men who are willing to live very economically, in order to make the work a success, in fact, nearly all the money they get is put into tools, implements, machinery, etc., in order to make their work more effective in the future." Trusting in love, they had "been comfortably provided for—no suffering, no hunger, no distress occasioned by loving too much." According to Albert Pease, they were happy and committed to the enterprise. "We have managed to live and find enough to eat.... A member of the colony would rather lie down in the road and die than return to the life under the old competitive system again." Living on less, they believed they could make their money go further to advance God's kingdom. Optimism prevailed as Albertson pledged that "this region of the country was once … a paradise" and "we are here to restore it."[7]

Commonwealth allocated work according to community needs and the workers' wishes. New members could choose the department in which they preferred to work. If there was no need in that department, they had to select another. Occasionally, superintendents, out of necessity, made assignments. Members who refused could appeal, and usually the superintendents could accommodate them within a reasonable time.

Work tended to follow traditional gender roles, although not exclusively. Women initially did much of the community work in the kitchen and dining room, but over time men played a more significant role. The young women did the housekeeping for the single men, and at least one romance developed as a result of a young lady making up a young man's bed every day.[8]

Initially, the residents had no washing machine. Some families washed their own clothes, and three men and four women laundered community laundry by hand. It was inefficient and laborious work. Nevertheless, they did it with "cheerful uncomplaining faithfulness and the hope that the unpleasantness would not last long." In early 1899, Pitt Whited of Tennessee gave Commonwealth money for a sizeable steam-powered washing machine and planned to come to the community to operate it. He arrived in April at the same time that the washer arrived from Chicago. They dug a well and built a new laundry close to the sawmill, where they could run both with the same steam engine. When Brother Whited did the first load of wash, it was "a red-letter day in our history." The machine reduced the amount of "clothes-pounding" by the women and "even the most skeptical of the ladies were converted to the 'new-fangled thing.'" Having the men take over most of the washing may have facilitated the women's conversion. On Tuesdays, the men tended the washing machine, while the women hung out the clothes, took them down, and sorted them. By 1900, all colony washing went to the laundry. Its capacity was greater than the community needed, so they planned to add more machinery and draw laundry work from Columbus. The new equipment also reduced the need for tailors by reducing the damage to clothing, and the combination of men and machinery eliminated many female backaches and domestic infelicities and moderated the stereotype of "women's work." Commonwealth saw that cooperation aided by modern equipment would do much to end household drudgery.[9]

From the start, rewards for diligent work and punishment for the lazy and indolent were issues never entirely resolved. However, Albertson thought they "came far nearer to its solution than New York City." Influenced by the application of love, almost "everybody—men, women, and children, found in the common good the only reward they were seeking, and in the displeasure of the community the greatest punishment possible." They did not implement rules or laws to eliminate inefficiencies. Still, most members gave according to their ability and received, as best the community could furnish it, according to their needs.[10]

Intellectual, rather than physical, activity in the print shop raised complaints about workloads. Some of the builders of the shingle mill did not think that the "literary aristocracy," who prepared the Social Gospel, worked hard enough. Sue Fay responded, "The effort which produces a strong editorial in classic English is worthy of the same respect of that which builds a shingle mill." The community's philosophy was clear. All work done for love's sake was equally honorable. The weak and physically frail would find blessed work with the lightest burdens. If those with intellectual gifts chose to do productive work outside the community, that too would be God's work. As they enlarged their business of publishing and Christian Socialist propaganda, they hoped that demand for intellectual workers would not exceed the supply.

This conflict was an ongoing problem because, a year later, the *Social Gospel* assured readers that "a man is a man here. One good worker is held in as much honor as another." The editors seemed to favor the farmers and mechanics whose "sweated shirt, engine-greased overalls and hardened hands are truly the insignia of nobility." The letter writer, bookkeeper, and editor needed to accomplish something tangible and apparent to retain respect and esteem.[11]

Despite Commonwealth's love, which had limits, and the social and moral compunction of its ideology, the community had lazy or inefficient workers. Some were unable to work as well as others, but others were freeloaders. The combination of open membership, noncoercion, and absolute sharing appealed to slackers. There was a "great deal of laziness" by those who believed in "the conservation of energy," mainly their own. Members viewed it as "the worst and meanest manifestation of selfishness." Members responded as best they could, gritting their teeth and working harder themselves "to inspire the brother to hustle," and overcome the conditions that contributed to their poverty. Everyone still received the same amount of the world's goods, although it is unlikely that the slackers enjoyed as much happiness at Commonwealth as the rest.[12]

Critics said Commonwealth ignored human nature when it came to work expectations. The leaders responded that shirking was the least of their troubles and that the lazy usually responded to the mild remedies of a Christian brotherhood organization. No labor problem became so severe as to compel expulsion from the community.[13]

Members' faith in "industrial love" was so strong that, initially, the leadership made no effort to track workers' time. As the community grew, its faith waned slightly, so they decided to keep records of members' labor and lost time. The director of labor and the department superintendents recorded all work performed and reported colonists "not performing faithful labor according to his or her ability." Superintendents also reported problems due to sickness or disability to the health officer. Knowledge of workers' illnesses led to medical care and community sympathy. Reports of individuals not performing faithful labor became public knowledge at business meetings, but there was no formal punishment. Their goal was to know members by their deeds, not their professions of love, which could not replace the need for labor. They hoped that shame over inadequate work would awaken individuals' sense of responsibility or lead them to withdraw.[14]

When the *Social Gospel* announced this system, it had a tone of failure and apology. Using coercion rather than brotherly methods was not living up to community ideals. Ultimately, the timekeeping system failed, and the colony returned to its original "free for all" gait. Nevertheless, Daniel Hinckley, as director of labor, kept a record of the work performed and made monthly reports on the various industries.[15]

Each workday found members scattered throughout the community. Everyone worked where needed and demonstrated a surprising amount of adaptability by taking on different tasks every day. Merchants and professionals took up new occupations. A tailor who had never chopped wood put in hours at the wood pile. Albertson's work varied among different tasks, including, to everyone's surprise, making corn dodgers. Other men hauled logs to the sawmill, where still others milled them into lumber. When the weather was good, Daniel Hinckley, George McDermott, and another dozen men worked on the farm. Meanwhile, Sue Fay taught school, while Damon worked in the orchard. Charles Cook, O. E. Barlow, and George Cushing set type and printed in the shop where Gibson worked at his editor's desk if he was not wielding an ax or hoe. At night, the men came in tired from the woods, workshops, fields, and orchards, but there was always a disposition to sing, be sociable, and make merry.[16]

As was common in communal experiments, the routine, mundane work often caused problems. At Commonwealth, it was cleaning the "earth closets," but the loving brethren never allowed this to become a major issue. For a time, Damon, Gibson, and Pease, despite their high positions, insisted on doing the chore to demonstrate equality and democracy. Albertson thought that was unnecessary and never partook. Charles Cook found it offensive and complained about it more than anyone, but, as a matter of conscience and principle, he insisted on doing his share. Over time, such unpleasant sanitary work lost its special virtue and became routine.[17]

Instead of sanitary work, Albertson took a position as an assistant cook to experience manual labor and demonstrate his modesty. He believed it was just as honorable as being a preacher, editor, or business manager, and the wages were the same—nothing. For Albertson, to labor for love's sake was a heavenly occupation, and most Commonwealth members agreed.[18]

In early 1898, they could afford fertilizer and expected a higher yield from their crops, but they also suffered from a serious drought, with rainfall reduced by 50 percent of the average for that period. By June, Commonwealth needed frequent showers just to save the crops and did not always get them. In July, the drought broke, and rain greatly benefited the crops.[19]

Besides lack of rain, workers had to contend with root-knot, a nematode that killed young plants and reduced yields of older ones. First discovered in the peach trees, it spread to other nursery stock and to peas, tomatoes, melons, and garden plants. Nevertheless, Damon was pleased that the fruit trees were doing well despite the problems and thankful that there had been no other orchard pests.[20]

Despite these problems, workers enlarged the orchard and nursery throughout 1898. That fall, workers planted another 500 peach trees, 250 plum trees, and 100 apple trees in the thirty-five-acre orchard. It consisted of over 7,000 trees, mostly peaches, but including plums, pears, cherries, and apples. Fruit from the orchard looked good, but they still relied on some wild fruit. In the nursery they set 25,000 plum, 15,000 peach, 5,000 persimmon, and 2,500 apple stocks, most of which were coming up nicely. They also raised another 4,000 Japanese plum trees and budded 14,500 peach trees. By the end of the year, the orchards and vineyards looked good and food production was increasing.[21]

Optimism surrounded agricultural activities. The garden came up in late spring, and the members' diet thus improved. Some tomatoes were already blooming, and members set out the sweet potato plants. They had planted corn again and had high expectations because they had fertilizer. They had planted ten acres of millet and small fields of alfalfa and clover, all of which were coming up, while seventy-five chicks hatched in the brooder house.[22]

By midsummer, Commonwealth residents were picking blackberries and wild plums, strawberries were coming in, and the highly anticipated watermelon season began. Large clusters of grapes, including an acre of scuppernong, were bearing in the vineyard, and they had 500 pecan trees and 250 walnut trees in the nursery, which they transferred to the orchard and the community's avenues.[23]

Along with agriculture, housing construction dominated the early years, with the wood coming from community land. Logging was an arduous task.

S. W. Martin, Justin Cook, and Louis Heilman felled the trees. Henry Croyle and Albert Pease hauled the logs about a mile to the sawmill using two double teams on a logging truck. Will Carman ran the mill, and he, Pease, and Henry Staiff milled the logs into lumber for cottages. By the spring of 1898, workers were hauling fifteen logs a day and keeping three men busy at the sawmill full-time until they added an injector pump, which saved the labor of one man. That summer, carpenters completed an enlarged, covered sawmill building, seventy-five feet long. It made the millwork easier and more pleasant. Later, one of the mules died, which broke up a team and forced them to temporarily stop logging because they needed the other teams for farming. At the end of the year, they sent the big saw blade to Atlanta for truing and flattening, which shut down the mill and caused another work delay.[24]

Initially, housing was in short supply, and everyone crowded into the antebellum plantation house and the few tenant houses. To address the overcrowding, workers renovated the "big house" to hold as many people as possible. It became known as "the Retreat." Albertson and his family lived downstairs with another family while they waited for a cottage. They shared their accommodations with whoever showed up, with Albertson often sleeping on the floor. Upstairs, the unmarried men had "quarters" in two large rooms, but there were so many bachelors that they planned a dormitory-like structure for them. Ironically named "the Barracks" by the antimilitarists, the two-story building housed twenty-three single men at times. Later, some found lodging in separate houses, but all met in the dining room for meals, and their brotherly camaraderie made them far from lonesome.[25]

A "Maiden's Paradise," slightly less populated, was built for single women. Its use depended on the number of single women in the colony, for, in August 1899, it "reopened." The *Social Gospel* editor jokingly or erroneously referred to it as "the old maids' paradise."[26]

"The Growlery" became the name for another home for the "lonely and lorn" unmarried men, but after James Kelley's stay at the house, it became known as the Kelley Cottage. Later, workers added a room in the back and a porch in front to provide a home for the Hinckleys after they married.

Separate cottages for families were a priority, and in the first months, they planned to complete several. Costing a hundred dollars each, they were built quickly using rough board-and-batten construction and left unpainted. Construction slowed in the summer as food cultivation took precedence. As a result, by June 1898 only a few families had private cottages: the Damons, Gibsons, Albertsons, Cooks, Comings, and McDermotts. Meanwhile, the Pease, Croyle, Carman, Hall, and Staiff families lived in the Retreat. When the weather cooled and the harvests were completed, the colony returned to building houses. The Carmans had a large family and work on their house, "a three-room mansion of rough lumber," was completed in December. Located under the pines near the schoolhouse, it was adjacent to a little creek, which supplied water. After a prayer meeting, the entire colony had a "jolly time" at their housewarming despite having to sit on the floor. Mrs. Carman passed around a dish of salt as a gesture of hospitality, and they sang impromptu songs. When the Carmans moved in, a large room with a fireplace in the Retreat was freed up. A community vote transformed it into a sitting and reading room for the single men.[27]

Despite the need for more family housing, leaders' cottages often got special treatment. The community put a large porch on the Albertson house and justified it by its use for evening vesper services and ice cream socials. They also put a new roof, two new porches, and a summer kitchen on the Damon house and porches on the Comings and Cook houses. Given the summer heat in central Georgia, these porches seemed reasonable, but later, when dissent arose, what may have been favoritism became an issue.[28]

In its second year, Commonwealth acquired a new portable steam engine to increase its labor efficiency. Workers moved it around the community to run five machines: a cane mill, the printing press, a feed mill, a wood saw, and a feed cutter. Efficient labor in a small community improved their economic chances, and since labor meant love, increasing its efficiency increased their power of service.[29]

By the fall of 1898, Commonwealth's material assets had grown significantly. There were eight cottages, and colonists had two heavy logging trucks and four double teams, wagons and harnesses, farming equipment, poultry and incubator equipment, and furnished carpentry and blacksmith shops. Their farm stock included two mules, four horses, five cows, three pigs, and six young cattle. Later, they added four more horses, used for hauling wood, provisions, and fertilizer and performing general utility work. Louis Damon, William's son, cared for the cows and distributed weekly provisions to the community. Members rewarded him with pleasant smiles and hearty greetings despite the disadvantages of no scales, no measures, and no baskets. In their place were goodwill and the determination to do things well.[30]

Commonwealth made considerable progress in 1898. Farm production increased significantly and provided a greater variety of food. They had fine crops of Irish and sweet potatoes, sorghum, cowpeas, and garden vegetables such as tomatoes and cabbage. In October, workers harvested and husked a good crop of corn, picked eight loads of peanuts, and left even more in the ground. That fall, they planted, using two new turning plows, several different grains including nine acres of oats, eighteen acres of rye, four acres of wheat, and some barley. Members estimated that they had five times as much food as in the previous year, but not everyone thought the colony's diet had improved.[31]

Its gardens became extensive and profitable. John Thompson, the superintendent, supervised the planting, and Albertson and others hauled loads of tomatoes, watermelons, cantaloupes, onions, kale, and other produce to Columbus, where they sold it in the city market and hoped to open a cooperative store "on something near the Rochdale plan."[32]

Other crops and produce were also doing well. Over sixty fig trees were bearing. Thirteen Cydonian quince trees had loads of fruit, which made excellent sauce and preserves. Fifteen acres of sorghum grew well after the rains came and were a satisfactory substitute for the sugar cane roots that had failed to grow. The sorghum mill, driven by the new steam engine and maintained by Albert Pease, produced 225 gallons of syrup.[33]

Damon's concern was that peach trees took three years to bear fruit, so Commonwealth would have to wait for a financial return, but his expertise and planning seemed likely to pay off. Georgia was beginning to rival California as a peach-growing state, and in 1898 the crop was immense. East of Columbus, Fort Valley was shipping eight hundred carloads of peaches per season, and the South's railroads were hard-pressed to handle the demand for Georgia fruit. Commonwealth's location was in the peach belt, and Damon wanted a share of that market. He acquired the choicest seedlings, which were in high demand, and avoided low-quality July peaches while planting earlier varieties for the northern market and fall varieties for the South, which was dependent on California for its late peaches. After inspecting fruit on the young trees, Damon thought that Commonwealth could rival the huge orchards in Fort Valley. He expected that the colony would soon be shipping carloads of peaches.[34]

Damon had ambitious plans for the coming winter. He wanted to set out another 8,000 to 10,000 peach and plum trees. Most would be Japanese plums, but they would also plant Japanese persimmons and chestnuts, pecans, and other nut trees. In February, they expanded the orchard and nursery, as Damon and George Hartman set out one hundred acres of young fruit trees. In the vineyards, they trellised the scuppernong and young grapes. By

March, they added 20,000 plum cuttings to the nursery and set 1,500 young Japanese plum trees in the orchard. The *Social Gospel* advertised five varieties of Japanese plum trees for sale at ten cents each.[35]

The first frost of 1898 came in mid-October, weeks earlier than normal, and the early winter of 1898–99 was cold, but not cold enough to eliminate mosquitoes, which were an ongoing plague. There was no snow but considerable rain and frost. Many people caught serious colds and influenza, but by then the community had enough indoor work to be less vulnerable to the weather. The sawmill, cotton mill, print shop, and other shops kept operating on rainy days.[36]

Strawberries were one of Commonwealth's first plantings and remained a welcome luxury, but that winter workers set out five acres of strawberries that were destroyed by grub worms. In early 1899, Isaac Snedeker took over the strawberries, using hotbeds, which provided a favorable environment to grow cool-weather produce. By June, they were getting some strawberries, and that summer they set out 20,000 more strawberry plants.[37]

Cold, frost, and incessant thunderstorms curtailed much of the work in January. Farmers could not plant, so they turned to cutting and clearing forests. They hauled some lumber for the Loiselle family cottage, which they finished the following month, but most of the time the roads were too muddy for logging. A new cottage for the Staiff family was also nearing completion. It was finished that summer, just in time for the birth of their daughter, Marie. It included a twenty-five-foot-deep well, which provided high-quality water.[38]

By the end of the month, alder catkins had appeared, an indication that spring was near, and everyone prepared to plant their spring garden. Two weeks later, a severe storm hit. It brought three inches of snow, a bitter wind, and temperatures below zero, which caused considerable damage to the budding peaches and plums and other fruits, even the wild ones. Some had not yet opened their buds, so there was hope that they were safe, but it was too early to measure the losses. The oats and wildflowers also froze. Ever optimistic, the *Social Gospel* editors believed that the freeze killed off enough vermin to compensate for the losses. However, the freeze also killed a large garden of vegetables from which the colonists had hoped to derive significant revenue. They were used to hardships and not discouraged. Instead, many viewed the harsh winter as a reminder of the conditions in their former homes.

Warm weather returned before the end of February. Mockingbirds and migrating robins appeared, their spring songs competing with those of the frogs. Commonwealth was finally able to plant its gardens and see green appearing in the fields. Assessing the storm damage, residents saw that they had lost all of the plums and peaches that had buds. Another hard freeze hit in early March and put agricultural work farther behind. There was no new damage to the trees, but the cold damaged many garden crops and destroyed the blackberries and remaining peaches and wild plums. Corn, a critical commodity, was delayed, although some neighbors began to see corn stalks in mid-March.[39]

By April, despite the late start, the gardens looked promising, with radishes, green onions, and mustard greens all providing sustenance. The colonists rejoiced at the delightful weather and the glory of spring. "New-life gladness" came again in beauty and song, and members felt both "joys realized and joys prospective." Their optimism outpaced their reality, but because they believed they were "providentially led," they could not imagine a better place to begin their journey to the Kingdom of God.[40]

Another spring drought occurred, which resulted in only three rains in the four months before mid-July. Diners were pleasantly surprised that they still got some good beets, turnips, and cucumbers from the garden. The Irish potatoes were small in size and number but furnished good flavor. Even the field corn, planted in bottomland, seemed promising by the end of June. Despite the weather and their shortage of equipment, the farmers said that they were getting better cultivated crops than they had ever gotten in the competitive world. The dry season had reduced yields, but the quality was the best yet at Commonwealth.[41]

Future economic possibilities seemed endless. Some trees in the orchards were ready to bear fruit. A railroad stop and post office were in place. Steam engines eased the labor burden at the mills, the laundry, and the printing press. Workers had prepared a large amount of fertilizer, and using it with proper crops was making the land more productive. They were supplying themselves with grain and vegetables and were self-sufficient in wood for building materials, fuel, cooking, and heating. They built their own houses, buying only hardware, windows, and doors. Low taxes and no rent translated into cheap living. Among their proposed industries was a bookcase factory that they hoped to enlarge into a full-scale furniture factory. They planned for a retail store, a cotton gin, knitting machines, and tailoring, shoemaking, and brickmaking facilities. An industrial and intellectual school would support educators and producers.[42]

In early July, workers picked one hundred fifty watermelons and distributed two wagon loads to the surrounding community. They expected to consume about a thousand by the end of the month. "Free as water and not quite so thin," they were significantly better than northern-grown melons.[43]

When it came time to harvest other crops, the yield exceeded anything that the farmers had produced previously. Ears of corn were large and as well filled out as anything they had produced in Nebraska. The sorghum was well grown, juicier, and sweeter than the previous year. Wild grapes were plentiful, and workers picked and canned many quarts for later consumption. It was hard work, involving much tree climbing, but appropriating the free bounties of nature was a rewarding pleasure. On the other hand, the drought took its toll on the fall garden and on crops that had not fully matured. The nursery and orchard also had a good year in 1899. Commonwealth had set out nearly 30,000 fruit trees, and there were over 15,000 more in the nursery.[44]

By September, the weather had cooled off. It had been a year of weather extremes, with winter cold, summer heat, and a lack of rainfall, and it concluded with a rare snowstorm on New Year's Eve. Despite the weather, crop production had been decent. Members thought that the weather might have contributed to disease but also realized that typhoid had been present throughout the country—North as well as South.[45]

In the fall, workers gathered a large supply of peanuts, and the crop continued to produce. They were put to good use as nuts, butter, and fodder and were a welcome and healthy addition to the community diet. They also stored some vines, which they picked later and roasted, shelled, and ground the nuts. Nuts were easy to raise and a product with good revenue potential. Members hoped to begin the production of nut foods for the commercial market. The labor involved in manufacturing nut butter and other nut foods would more than pay for itself.[46]

Housing shortages remained a problem in 1899. There were only eleven residential dwellings in addition to the plantation house, which needed another renovation. New glass, paint, putty, whitewash, and wallpaper transformed the interior. Outside, carpenters tore away the rotten wood and built extensive porches to alleviate some of the crowding inside. Five months later, they made more improvements. Expediency and pragmatism continued to demand primitive, rough board construction. Once finished, the Albertson family moved back in to be joined by James Brower and his new wife, Lou Grobe.[47]

As the community grew, workers cut portions of the pine forest in every direction to allow everyone to see each other's homes. They left groups of trees, but the expansive vistas permitted them to see trains passing across the breadth of their plantation, and they expected the spring leaves and blooms to provide charming scenery. A side benefit was that they burned the brush in the evenings to provide an entertaining form of fireworks.[48]

Children added diversity to the kitchen staff. Organized into groups, they sang cheerfully while "doing the dishes":

> Corn bread for breakfast,
> Corn bread for dinner,
> Corn bread for supper,
> Way down on the colony farm.
> We won't go North anymore.[49]

There were no pretensions of equality in the communal kitchen. It was an example of socialism providing equality of opportunity but not eliminating inequality of position. Women initially undertook most of the work. The lack of proper equipment made it difficult, so men took over some kitchen labor. That did not eliminate overwork, which resulted in some sick days and disorder. Questions arose as to who was responsible for washing dishes if a regular worker was sick. The lack of formal organization created confusion and minor disputes, forcing the kitchen workers to adopt a new system, which reduced much friction and made everyone realize that they needed to adjust to changing situations, but they never completely eliminated the tension. After Albertson worked for a while as an assistant cook, he noted that "the kitchen, more than any place else, has been the grave of sensitive sweetness." Anxiety over pleasing the diners, annoyances created by limited equipment and provisions, and "amateur assistance" were all detrimental to a sense of serenity. Fortunately, there were workers who believed in God and Commonwealth and who, "bomb-proof" against the sourness, sang gospel songs all day long.[50]

In June 1898, the leaders appealed through the *Social Gospel* for a new cook, and two months later W. H. Dorchester, a dairyman and fruit farmer from Canada, arrived to a heartfelt welcome and took over the cooking. Clarence Hough aided him as an assistant cook and inspired everyone. He was the first in the kitchen in the morning and the last to leave at night. He cleaned the utensils and kept the kitchen orderly. He monitored water and milk supplies and made sure the "Maiden's Paradise" had sufficient logs for its fireplace. He also served as a steward in the pantry and the sexton of the church. A source of information and a lover of a good sermon, he did numerous other useful things daily. The kitchen could not have functioned without him.[51]

When it came to dining, most members favored a communal dining room as a matter of principle. The original dining room was not large enough to feed everyone simultaneously, but many new cottages had kitchens, so some families cooked for themselves. In March 1899, the Mechanical Board proposed dropping other construction projects to build a new community kitchen, larger dining room, and space for a restaurant. They had concluded that it was impossible to build private cottages with kitchens fast enough to meet demand and planned a thirty-by-seventy-foot structure, which would include a twenty-by-thirty-foot kitchen. It would be the largest building in Commonwealth and centrally located for everyone's convenience. Besides, eliminating cottage kitchens would allow greater occupancy in those residences and reduce the demand for new housing.[52]

Most people liked the plan and believed that a communal kitchen and dining hall would be more economical and less burdensome for women. However, there was some resistance to eating communally, so some families continued to cook for themselves. Gibson's aged mother-in-law refused to eat in the dining room, so he and his family, contrary to his preference, took meals in their cottage. The community did not pressure the private diners nor make them feel uncomfortable. Members who ate at home received the same rations as were provided to everyone else. Dining choices were an example of liberty of action taking precedence over any dogmatic, ideological attitude.[53]

Despite men being in the kitchen, the heaviest burden fell on women. It disturbed Albertson, who agreed with Charlotte Perkins Gilman that women "should be freed from their bondage to household drudgery." He thought that cooperative life would solve the problem, but it did not. When he saw "the breakdown of some faithful, hard-working women under the severe burden of cooking" unceasingly in the kitchen, he took an apprenticeship as an assistant cook. When he went into the kitchen, he was "Number Four." By then, Lucy Fay had become the chief cook, with Pitt Whited as her first assistant. Lucy was popular, and Albertson believed that she deserved her position, but the situation opened his eyes to the limits of equality. Instead, they had "rich and blessed diversity blended into harmony," but after several months, he also concluded that cooking was more properly man's work.[54]

As an assistant cook, Albertson noticed that even when there were minor issues with the food—sour bread, scorched mush—diners accepted it with cheerful smiles and a hearty appreciation for the cooks' efforts. Unstinted praise was not uncommon, as in one ten-day period when someone declared each day that the soup was "the best yet."[55]

With Lucy Fay's arrival, the kitchen staff was determined to provide quality meals and service despite their small means. They must have been successful, for about forty members who had been eating in their cottages returned to the communal dining room. It provided a huge boost in fellowship, esprit de corps, and economy.[56]

One of the most interesting members of the kitchen staff was John Karmen, a Chicago artist who came to Commonwealth to experience brotherhood life. Even though he was a sign painter, leadership placed him in the kitchen where he became a good cook. He sketched the kitchen as his artist's studio with its big range as the centerpiece and churned out sketches of the community between meals and while waiting for water to boil. He also made architectural drawings for inexpensive, well-planned communal buildings and cottages. Gibson thought they were better than the simple, rough-hewn construction that dominated Commonwealth's architecture. Karmen also interested a group of Chicago artist friends in the brotherhood ideal, in which they could combine their studies and creations. However, he did not stay long, in February 1900 returning to Chicago, where he organized the Oak Park Consumers' League. Unfortunately, there is no evidence that his Commonwealth art still exists.[57]

In 1898, Commonwealth created the position of sanitary commissioner, who was responsible for the general health of the community. Supervisors reported all cases of sickness or inability to work to him, and he, in turn, filed a weekly report to the membership. When leadership wrote the constitution, they changed the name to health officer and broadened the duties to include monitoring sewage drains and inspecting buildings for health and fire hazards.[58]

Except for an early outbreak of malaria brought by western migrants and the devastating typhoid epidemic of the summer of 1899, there was not much serious illness. No cases of malaria or "southern chills and fever" originated in the community. There was, however, some sickness and death.[59]

Samuel Comings's wife Hattie died in December 1898, a year after having a stroke. An earnest believer in temperance and the Social Gospel, intellectual and loving, she had devoted her life to caring for others but also had strict standards. When an admired clergyman took up tobacco, she refused to hear him preach. Damon conducted her funeral service, which was attended by all of Commonwealth.[60]

Ralph and Irene Albertson lost a son, Richard, who had been born at the colony and died at the age of seven months. Ralph thought he had starved to death or died from exposure, but the cause was never determined. The loss left a deep wound between Irene and Ralph that never healed and contributed to their divorce after the community disbanded. In early 1900, there were eight cases of measles. Irene Albertson was the only adult afflicted. Phyllis, her daughter, and six other children were also sick. All were better by the end of January.[61]

In January 1899, Leroy Henry and his wife Eora, both medical doctors, arrived, with their children, from Pacific Grove, California. Until they came, Commonwealth had employed a local physician in case of illness. The timing was perfect because the grippe (influenza) hit about twenty members shortly after their arrival. By late February, everyone had recovered, and Henry became known as "la grippe" man. Henry and Eora's medical knowledge became a valuable asset to the community, as did their material contributions. They donated a "love offering" of two hundred dollars to Commonwealth's common fund and provided money to erect a cottage for their family. The colony began construction in February, and the Henry family moved in by April 1. But one new house a month seemed to be the community's limit, and other longtime members continued to wait for their housing.[62]

Health officer reports no longer exist, but one April the *Social Gospel* published one showing the illnesses and the work time missed. In the preceding month, there had been six cases of illness, resulting in thirty-three days of lost time.

There were also two cases of chronic lung trouble and rheumatism, which the victims had contracted before they arrived. Nevertheless, those persons were working, as were others with minor chronic cases.

Considering the pioneer conditions and the workers' inexperience, Commonwealth remained remarkably free of serious accidents and injury. Lumbering and millwork were hard and dangerous, and bad luck hit when J. Bron, an engineer of the "teakettle" (steam engine), caught his wrist on the edger in the sawmill. He almost lost his hand but wound up with an ugly wound and was the only colony member to miss the Hinckley wedding. Austin Hall, a young boy, suffered a broken arm after being kicked by a mule. The colony had to call a Midland doctor to set the fracture. The boy recovered and be-

came more cautious around mules. Later, Henry Staiff suffered a serious an-
kle sprain when rolling logs at the mill caught his foot, and Bertine Croyle
fell and broke a bone in her wrist. By then, the Henrys and a doctor visiting
from California were on hand to set the bone for a full recovery.[63]

Commonwealth may have adopted a primitive form of Christianity, but
they were not backward-looking agrarians who rejected modern technology
and industry. Gibson called on Edison, Tesla, and other inventors to use their
abilities to serve the Kingdom of God. Machinery and motive power, if released from the monopoly of the selfish profit seekers, could be used to better serve the workers and the poor.[64]

Food production remained a priority, but members were determined to
develop industries, and their industrial organization and equipment grew
substantially. They accumulated a significant amount of machinery and made
constant improvements to the sawmill, adding a twenty-five-horsepower
engine and boiler and a steam wood saw. In other areas, they added a gristmill, several looms, two more steam boilers and engines, a steam-powered
washing machine, a cane mill, a feed mill, and an ample printing outfit. Workers started a machine shop with a twelve-foot lathe purchased in Columbus
for one-sixth its original cost.[65]

During the winter of 1899, Commonwealth received a vital gift from three
of its most prominent national backers, N. O. Nelson, Ernest Hammond, an
oilman from Corry, Pennsylvania, and Mayor Sam "Golden Rule" Jones of Toledo, Ohio. Nelson had visited the colony twice and, pleased by its progress
and confident of its success, sent regular donations. The three men pooled
their resources and sent Commonwealth a railroad carload of machinery.
Jones explained his support:[66] "I am a socialist. I believe in Brotherhood and
can only find peace in advocating those principles that will lead men to live
brotherly....What is called 'success in business' to-day will be commonly understood to be only another form of exploitation or plunder.... Profit getting according to present day methods is very largely robbery pure and simple; legal and respectable,... so would highway robbery and gambling be both
legal and respectable, if the highway robbers and gamblers made the laws as
the profit-getters do."[67] The machinery included another steam power plant
and the accessories and tools to operate it. It replaced the old boiler and engine running the sawmill and would run both the sawmill and the proposed
cotton mill. It was in position in February, and by July they had also hitched
it to the shingle machine, the gristmill, the cotton mill, and the large ma-

chine lathe. They gave the old boiler and engine the lighter job of running the laundry and the wood saw in the adjoining wood yard and possibly heating the Barracks. Leadership planned to open a large restaurant, and that same boiler would provide steam for heating and cooking. They hoped the restaurant would show the pleasantness of associational life and improve their finances. They planned to make it large enough to have room for the library instead of moving it to the schoolhouse. The technological improvements and physical expansion gave them joy at the realization that they were making progress toward their goals.[68]

Commonwealth never had enough power at its disposal. The colony moved the cane mill several times to access power and eventually set it up near the laundry and wood saw, where it shared a steam engine. They used it to convert their sorghum crop into molasses and milled cane for their neighbors on shares, which increased their supply of sugar.[69]

In early 1899, Commonwealth acquired a new steam-powered wood saw, which became a vital piece of machinery. It saved labor and allowed workers to cut enough firewood to supply thirty-four fireplaces and three wood-powered steam engines. They placed the saw next to the sawmill, where they had a central wood yard and a covered shed, which allowed the men to split wood on rainy days. Then they distributed it throughout the community.[70]

Commonwealth was making progress despite a shortage of skills. To attract skilled labor, the *Social Gospel* appealed for a shoemaker, doctor, brickmaker, laundryman, and other skilled workers. In response, A. O. Grote, a brick mason, arrived from the Indian Territory, and later Mr. and Mrs. H. Pawley arrived from Oklahoma. Before their arrival, the Pawleys had donated to the community. Mrs. Pawley showed up pregnant and gave birth in January 1899. Her husband worked as a gardener and, without training, became the part-time cobbler. He spent rainy days repairing shoes, and despite his rough work, people were pleased with it. They appreciated someone working for love, not money.[71]

In 1899, the shortage of artisans and skilled workers continued to hamper the colony. They needed a cook, shoemaker, tailor, printers, weavers, farmers, mechanics, and a man who understood the fruit-canning business. A year later, the *Social Gospel* appealed again for a weaver, shoemaker, and sawyer and noted that they had a blacksmith shop but no smith. The appeals always contained a cautionary note regarding conditions at Commonwealth:[72]

There are many useful occupations at which we need workers, as we wish to make our industrial organization as cosmopolitan as possible. But we request people not to come to us hastily as many have come here either without counting the cost or without clear knowledge of what they were coming to, and have afterwards gone away sorrowful. We would by all means prevent such as cannot be permanently happy here from coming at all. It is our glad privilege to welcome many to a brotherhood home without price. We particularly do not wish to have people come here who can be of greater value and effectiveness in the regeneration of society by staying where they are. This question must be left to the individual conscience and judgment to determine. We sacredly maintain the institution of the family. We have the ordinary religious meetings that are commonly held in Protestant churches. Our purpose is to obey the high social ideal, which is moving men everywhere, and to give organic expression to the social spirit, which is moving the world forward into the Kingdom of God.[73]

In October 1898, Commonwealth developed an elaborate rationale and planned to start a cotton mill and textile manufacturing industry. Members thought that "believers in Christ will believe in Christian business." Their corporation would be "a love-ruled, fraternal, non-profit seeking body, a body which is not merely unselfish within itself, or as regards the relation of members to one another, but disposed to run its economic power unselfishly to serve the world." Guided by love and brotherhood, they could compete successfully against selfish, profit-seeking corporations. By sharing gains equally among all members and not paying dividends, interest, or rent, they could sell goods at lower prices and drive selfish competitors out of the market. By rendering greater service to consumers, they would Christianize the industry and business of the whole world.

Colony leaders were enthusiastic about the plan and thought they had many advantages. They had a competent workforce of brotherhood cooperators guided by the law of love manifested chiefly by labor and service of the highest quality. They had low expenses in Georgia, where eighty people had been living on $2.50 per day or less for months. They could mill lumber from their woods, a free source of wood for fuel and construction, and they could make bricks for the factory. Although they had rejected the idea of growing cotton, they had enough land to do so if necessary. Otherwise, they could buy cotton directly from nearby plantations and were close to many well-established factories. They concluded that their "brotherhood organization of industry" would become "a shining success."[74]

One thing that they did not have was experience. To get that, they persuaded Felix Loiselle to relocate from Jamestown, New York, to start and operate the mill. When he and his family arrived in September 1898, Commonwealth crowded them and their household goods into a couple of spare rooms until the community could build them a cottage. Felix had skill and experience in cotton production, and Maggie, his wife, made a good first impression by giving each Commonwealth family beautiful towels that Felix had woven.[75]

The shortage of capital delayed the start of the mill and threatened Commonwealth's ability to pay its mortgage. They had managed to pay the November 1897 note of $1,000 plus $240 in interest. Fearing future problems, N. O. Nelson, in early 1898, set up a fund for outsiders to contribute to help pay off the mortgage, but it failed to raise sufficient funds, which forced Gibson and Albertson to travel to Chicago to seek money for the next payment.[76]

To raise capital, Commonwealth created the Cotton Mill Fund, for which the *Social Gospel* solicited financial aid. Noting the advantages listed above, they asked supporters to contribute a dollar per month as a charitable gift to the Christian reconstruction of society. After reading about the community's plan, a Philadelphia subscriber encouraged sympathetic readers to help purchase cotton mill machinery by setting aside money each month and forwarding it to the community on a specific day. Others had already made pledges to do the same thing, and money for the cotton mill came in from all over the country by early October. One donor was Grace B. Gidney, of Hyde Park, Massachusetts, who was a frequent contributor.[77]

Despite regular contributions and intermittent donations, the fund remained short of cash. In December, Commonwealth borrowed a hundred dollars from a Massachusetts man to buy looms, install doors and windows, and connect shafts to the sawmill's power. The progress boosted their confidence that Commonwealth Mills would shortly be weaving cloth and demonstrating the benefits of a brotherhood industry. A successful launch would be the strongest argument yet advanced for Christian Socialism, and they renewed their appeal to Christian Socialists across America for support to escape the exploitation from transporters and profit makers. In response, gifts, mostly ranging from one to five dollars, continued to come in from all over the country.[78]

Ultimately, the colony decided to weave towels. Loiselle and Albertson made visits to Columbus cotton mills and consulted with Brother Shuttleworth, who had extensive experience in cotton manufacturing. They located inexpensive secondhand looms and other machinery that they could buy cheaply. Determined to avoid antiquated equipment, they studied the latest improvements in cotton manufacturing machinery. They became convinced that, with their limited capital, they could start a profitable business and finally bought several used looms for five dollars each from Columbus mills. Some friends of the community thought buying used machinery was unwise, but Albertson disagreed, stating that new looms would have cost two hundred dollars each. He argued that they had been careful and were getting good machinery at a low price. He was wrong. The Columbus mill had replaced the looms for a reason, and Loiselle had to both buy and make attachments to rebuild the looms to work properly. Once he had the first loom weaving towels, he made a mold to have castings made for the others.[79]

Commonwealth began construction on a twenty-four-by-thirty-foot cotton mill and expected to be in operation by early 1899. They built a weaving room next to the sawmill so that they could use the same power. In January, anticipating completion, the *Social Gospel* began to advertise coarse nineteen-by-thirty-eight-inch "crash towels" for sale by mail.[80] Supporters sent in many advance orders, which were deeply appreciated, but the manufacturer of the loom attachments did not deliver them when expected. It took nearly two months, and a running correspondence urging delivery before they were shipped, and then they were at the mercy of the railroads. Advance orders for nearly a thousand towels accumulated, and the community was grateful for their customers' patience, but by late February the attachments still had not arrived. Finally, they arrived and appeared to work well. Loiselle had the "high honor and blessed privilege" of weaving the first "cloth of love," and the mill began to produce towels to fill the advance orders. Although they had advertised "crash towels," they were making Turkish bath towels, which were, theoretically, of finer quality. In February, the *Social Gospel* modified its advertisement and offered the towels for fifteen cents each or a dollar fifty per dozen. This was not a competitive price, as bath towels were selling in Atlanta for ten cents each. Ultimately, the price became moot. Although the first Commonwealth towels that shipped received praise, subsequent towels made on other looms that Loiselle had modified were of such poor quality that Albertson, as business manager, refused to ship them. The mill closed temporarily, and the *Social Gospel* apologized for the delays and thanked readers for their patience. Meanwhile, Loiselle worked to repair and improve the machinery. By April, the machines were still not operating properly.[81]

Colony management refused to allocate any more resources to the project, and in May 1899 the mill closed despite a large number of paid orders that it had not filled. Loiselle, angered by management's decision, later became a leader of the movement to disband the colony. When the dissenters lost in the courts, Loiselle and his family left Commonwealth. Without a superintendent, management put towel and cloth manufacturing on hold. They appealed for "a good loom-fixer and weaver" who possessed "in actual truth the spirit of Christ" and guaranteed him a permanent job. Meanwhile, they sent a circular to all advance purchasers explaining the situation and offering to refund their money. Only a small proportion requested a refund. They thanked the others for being patient and promised that they would fill their orders first when new looms were acquired and the mill was running.[82]

Commonwealth had spent $250 equipping the mill with secondhand looms that would not weave quality towels. The looms could produce other goods, but they needed another $250 investment to restart towel manufacturing. Demand indicated that the enterprise could be profitable and that better looms would contribute to Commonwealth's self-sufficiency. Lacking capital and the ability to borrow, leadership appealed to "interested friends" for help.

Commonwealth was thrilled that their appeal for "brotherhood capital" received a generous response. Contributors sent over five hundred dollars to re-equip and restart the mill. Contributions came from all over the world, the largest from Louise Burleigh Curtis, a New Englander married to an American art collector and a resident of Paris, who sent $250. George Herron, N. O. Nelson, and Grace Gidney added to the contributions they had already made. E. N. Potter, president of Hobart College, contributed. L. N. Freeman of Nebraska added a cotton mill fund donation to his earlier printing press donation. A. B. Ellis of Massachusetts, who later lived at the Burley community in Washington, donated.[83]

In November 1899, Commonwealth had enough money to prepare the building for new machinery. It would share a powerful engine with the sawmill and gristmill. They planned to restart production in February 1900 and expected it to be self-supporting. The *Social Gospel* advertised again for an experienced loom fixer and asked anyone with information to contact Ralph Albertson at his boyhood home in Greenport, New York, where he was recuperating from his bout with typhoid fever. While there, he visited cotton manufacturing cities in New England in a futile search for an experienced textile man, but despite everyone's efforts, the Commonwealth Cotton Mill never reopened.[84]

The print shop was Commonwealth's major source of revenue, but the colony's income provided a meager living for its members. The *Social Gospel* had over two thousand subscriptions at fifty cents a year, and the print shop did job work, turning out books, pamphlets, and custom printing. It repeatedly appealed to supporters to send them their print work. It boasted that their quality and prices would be competitive, and customers' contribution to the social evangelization of the world would offset the inconvenience of sending work to Commonwealth.[85]

The print shop published its first book, Ralph Albertson's *The Social Incarnation*, in December 1898. Thirty-six pages long, it sold for ten cents or twenty copies for a dollar and sold out by April. The printers immediately planned a second edition but were delayed because their type was tied up printing the *Social Gospel* on the large press. In September, they finally published a second edition in response to overwhelming demand.[86]

Written to help people better understand the basis and breadth of the Christian Commonwealth movement, *The Social Incarnation* contained reprints of articles that Albertson had written for the *Kingdom* and the *Social Gospel*. He refused to copyright it because "it belongs to the world," and he wanted to show the "distinctive truths" of Christian Socialist thought and the "voice of love" for which Commonwealth stood. In one chapter, Albertson explained how the community had applied love, brotherhood, and unselfishness to its social relations. Simultaneously, they published *Commonwealth Details*, a booklet filled with facts, illustrations, and general information about colony life, the place, and the people.[87]

As another source of income, the *Social Gospel* advertised and sold books by mail. It promoted books of interest to readers who were studying their work and the general movement of Christian Socialism and offered special deals or free books to purchasers. In mid-1898, George Herron had seven books on the list. James P. Kelley's *The Law of Service: A Study of Christian Altruism* was recommended by Herron and Josiah Strong as a book one "ought to read." They also sold John Thomas Codman's *Brook Farm: Historic and Personal Memoirs*, the story of a "great cooperative experiment" that all "students of the social movement should read."[88]

Whether to do so physically in the fields or mentally in the print shop, Albert Pease believed that to labor was to lead a religious life. "We work six days in the week, and in those six days we lead religious lives, and on the seventh we rest from our labors." Pease did not believe that any Christian devoted to brotherhood would have difficulty in the colony, despite the hardships. They would succeed and their children, raised outside of the competitive system, would derive even greater benefit from colony life.[89]

CHAPTER 5

✦ ✦ ✦

Brotherhood Life

To make universal the brotherhood life.
—John Chipman, the *Social Gospel*

DESPITE THE SELF-DENIAL, lack of personal comfort, hardships, and poverty, most members found joy in their daily lives. The cold nights and mornings made them "feel it is good to be alive." Singing birds turned the air into a "musical wave-beating ocean" as "infinite insect voices mixed and mingled with them." Their principle of sharing reinforced their sense of happiness. Sue Fay Hinckley wrote, "Here on my desk is a cup of sugar, from Ida McDermott. Mine is all gone and they are out at the house—but Ida uses hers so carefully that it never seems to give out; then she gives it out. Bless her!"[1]

A New York City visitor asked if they got lonely in the Georgia wilderness. The response was both ideological and pragmatic: "Where love is, is the heart of things, the heart of humanity.... They who love unreservedly are in the center of life's blessed activities." By contrast, the noise, rush, and confusion of the self-seeking world offered neither friends nor fellowship. One would be lonelier there than in the fields and woods.[2]

Food was a priority at Commonwealth, and despite shortages, the community's cuisine interested outsiders. In the first year, the diet was limited and bland. The dairy of seven cows did not meet the members' needs, and they often did without butter and milk. In 1898, a supporter asked what they needed. The answer was, "Cows, perhaps, more than anything else." In response, a Boston supporter sent the money to purchase a good cow.[3]

They had successful crops of cowpeas, sweet potatoes, sorghum, and pea-nuts, but their diet remained inadequate. When capital was available, they purchased pork, bushels of corn and white beans, and pounds of cracked rice, but they tried to keep spending to a minimum.[4]

To remove the dietary deficiencies, the *Social Gospel* appealed for as-sistance. In early 1898, the editors asked for breadstuffs and vegetables and other edibles while the large garden grew. Supporters donated a variety of food. Brother Shuttleworth of Columbus sent a quarter of beef, which the community thoroughly enjoyed. From Florida, Mr. and Mrs. J. W. Spencer sent fifteen Belgian hares. With Louis Damon caring for them, within a year they had about fifty rabbits weighing around eight pounds each and produc-ing quality meat. It is not clear how many the colony consumed, but they did bring in some income. They also raised the "fancy" rabbits as pets and planned to sell some when they were ready to ship.[5]

Later, in the 1899 court case, disaffected members complained of insuf-ficient food and unfair distribution. Commonwealth responded that major-ity rule determined dietary decisions and had prioritized other expenditures over elaborate diets. To keep everyone building cottages and to improve ag-riculture, they needed more tools, machinery, industrial equipment, and sup-plies.[6]

Members were aware that desire or need for food often exceeded the amount available. Eggs were a particular point of contention. Everyone de-sired eggs, which were always in short supply. The community collected only 1,446 eggs in the first six months of 1998. Nevertheless, Irene Albertson was determined to have eggs and got them even when others in the dining room did not. Some Chicago supporters criticized this inequity, but most Com-monwealth members appeared not to resent or criticize it.[7]

In early 1899, Commonwealth's diet improved with the addition of beans, onions, and lard. The farm stock grew to six mules, two new horses, eight cows, twenty pigs, a small flock of poultry, and a few hives of bees. Their food supply increased, but the weekly "rations," distributed every Saturday, were still limited. In March, members consumed mostly cornmeal, with some wheat flour, wheat middlings, and grits and small quantities of milk, eggs, pork, and fish. They had only cottonseed oil for cooking. They admitted that the food could have been better, but they were generally healthy and believed they were "in better physical condition than the mass of people who live on rich food and are guilty of much over-eating."[8]

Nevertheless, the harsh living conditions, sparse rations, bland diet, and limited funds kept the community on the verge of suffering. Albertson admitted later that their bill of fare was below their health needs, although the community's overall health had been good.[9]

In 1899, an increase in the supply of homegrown products, despite a spring drought, reduced food costs. No records exist, but the *Social Gospel* published a list that shows homegrown products consumed from January 1 to June 31, 1899. Milk and vegetable production had increased significantly. The only meat came from eighteen chickens, so they were either buying meat or temporarily embracing vegetarianism.

There are no records of meat consumption, but vegetables dominated. Many members and friends advocated vegetarianism. The community was flexible when it came to ironclad rules and saw the absence of dietary restrictions as a virtue. When the *Social Gospel* announced additions to Commonwealth's pigpen, it brought a storm of protest and disappointment from readers who sent anti-carnivore literature. There was some community sentiment against keeping pigs, and the high price of corn to feed them bolstered their argument. Ultimately, the colony sold some pigs in Columbus and used the proceeds to buy kerosene oil, which they had been without for weeks.

Nevertheless, it was the "force of circumstances" more than a widely held belief that led to periodic community vegetarianism. Producing sufficient meat was costly and difficult, and it was a rational decision, not principle or sentiment, that shifted Commonwealth to an occasionally meatless diet. Its absence led many members to care less about eating meat.[10]

James Kelley and Ernest Crosby argued vehemently in favor of vegetarianism, believing that a reasonable interpretation of Christ's teaching prohibited the abuse of animals. They pointed to the cruelty and wretchedness of cattle trains and ships, slaughterhouses, and pigpens. Noting the "right relations" desired by the *Social Gospel*'s readers, Crosby suggested that they should include "our dumb brethren." He concluded by describing his path to vegetarianism as gradual and easy. Nevertheless, meat remained part of the diet for those who preferred it.[11]

Commonwealth's interest in vegetarianism attracted the attention of food reformers worldwide. An Ontario vegetarian wrote that food reform was an essential part of social reform and encouraged the community to become an educational force for vegetarianism, an enterprise that would produce incalculable benefits to humanity.[12]

According to the *Social Gospel*, there was contention over the issue. "Some of us are confirmed vegetarians, while others are willing to kill the poor innocents to satisfy the wants of the inner man." Most members believed that vegetarianism was the highest point they could attain regarding what to eat, but then asked, "What difference if we are vegetarians or cannibals? 'Is not the life more than meat and the body more than raiment?'"[13]

Outsiders often asked how Commonwealth dealt with the "religious problem" created by its diversity. Despite the numerous denominations from which members had come, the community denied there was a problem. Devotion to "the religion of love in a brotherhood life" broke down the "wall" between sects. They differed in education and beliefs but agreed that loving one another all the time, in self-forgetful service, would prevent religious strife.[14]

There were no restrictions on religious discussions, and the law of love prevented any heated religious arguments. Most members preferred sincere, serious presentations of the message and viewed insincere histrionics and cheap effects as temptations of the devil. Love, service, and brotherhood were the religious questions of importance and discussions of them united members. Once a visiting preacher talked fifty-two minutes on the New Testament and "said little." Sadly, the "sermon tasters" had nothing to say, a devastating criticism of the preacher.[15]

Members said morning prayers in the dining room after breakfast and devoted Thursday evenings to prayer, readings, and discussions in fellowship meetings at the schoolhouse. They resembled family gatherings with "our Heavenly Father in the midst." The Bible got the most attention, but attendees also found inspiring secular materials. They discussed authors such as Tolstoy, Lloyd, Charlotte Perkins Gilman, Shakespeare, Victor Hugo, Richard Ely, and Ralph Waldo Emerson. Different members led the meetings and occasionally lectured on social problems. The meetings also provided opportunities to become acquainted with new members.[16]

Sunday prayer meetings were regular but unpredictable occurrences with no fixed program and occasional experimentation. Congregants had organ music and hymns, Bible studies, sermons, brotherhood discussions, and readings from works by George Herron, John Woolman, and James Kelley.[17]

William Damon often preached on Sunday mornings, but he retained so much orthodox theology "that his preaching was not as popular as he himself." He compared the Christian Commonwealth to the Israelites whom God had fed in the wilderness. He believed that despite hard times they must trust in the Lord. As long as they honored God with steady faith, he would provide for them. In "The Schools of the Prophets," he showed that the characteristics of the Old Testament communities resembled Christian Socialism in the 1890s. Those talks inspired many and led them to see their relation to the world and its movements for reform.[18]

In April 1899, Calvin Reasoner took over on Sunday mornings. He was an older man from Illinois who had been in the ministry and the diplomatic service. As he was too old to perform heavy physical labor, his usefulness to the community was limited to his work on the *Social Gospel*, where he played an important role as a book reviewer, writer, and philosopher. A recluse by nature, he was fond of the community women and established good relationships with Derrill Hope and Sue Fay. Albertson thought he was one of the most profound thinkers in the community and, like a true philosopher, had broken with his early beliefs. He was a passionless thinker who searched unceasingly for the ultimate truth and the unity of life but knew that it was unlikely he would find them. He had little tolerance for William Damon and his Methodist temperament or John Chipman and his Episcopalian orthodoxy. He and Albertson struck up a close friendship, with both making ideological concessions and the older Reasoner occasionally deferring to the younger Albertson.[19]

Reasoner's interests included the nature of God, the evolution of the cosmos, the purposes of creation, the need for free agency and temporary evil, and the uplifting of the finite into the infinite. He supported his conclusions with both scripture and philosophy, and his clarity and breadth of vision reinforced Commonwealth's founding ideology. He concluded that God is a social being and that the essential spirit or nature of God, as manifested in all creation, is communal. Through brotherhood relations, all Christ-born beings would be freely united in love and rise to inherit the infinite.[20]

Reasoner thought that Edward Carpenter's *Civilization, Its Cause and Cure, and Other Essays* was an intelligent book that celebrated democracy and Tolstoyan life. It contained many ideas that Commonwealth's members found appealing: private property as destructive to human unity, the desire for love, the reconciliation of the Spirit and body, evolution, and self-revelation.[21]

Gibson and Albertson shared Reasoner's admiration of Carpenter and his views on social problems. They agreed that the charity of the churches and the well-to-do was hypocrisy because it was their actions and greed that had contributed to the poverty of the working classes.[22]

In early 1900, Reasoner again intermittently addressed the Sunday meetings with his inspiring religious philosophy. On one Sunday, he analyzed the Sermon on the Mount. On another, he interpreted the views of P. T. Forsythe, a well-known critical theologian who developed a theodicy based on the cross, an idea that Albertson had nurtured for years. Reasoner's preaching was considered one of the rich blessings of Commonwealth life.[23]

Ralph Albertson had left Ohio tired of preaching but did more talking on Sundays than he wished. He hated the hypocrisy of the organized church and was happy that Commonwealth had starved it out. His point of view was popular and widely held. Members also enjoyed listening to Albert Pease, who was often enthusiastically esoteric. When Jacob Troth wanted a silent Quaker meeting, they had one. Essentially, they had space and time for everyone to present their ideas on Sunday mornings. Then, Sunday afternoons were a time for relaxation.[24]

Commonwealth saw no need to divide on sectarian grounds on Sunday mornings. Members encouraged both men and women to communicate all they had of truth and love. Everyone was free to express their beliefs, but no one tried to impose their ideas on others. Courtesy prevailed as fraternal brotherhood broadened hearts and minds.[25]

Anyone could lead these meetings. James Kelley was an important leader. He was a member of Phi Beta Kappa at Brown University who taught English literature at a Connecticut prep school. In 1898, he spent an extended summer vacation at the colony, during which he taught a Bible class and was the leading spirit in a large and popular Shakespeare club. Besides being an associate editor of the *Social Gospel*, Kelley contributed to the community's finances and was a frequent writer for the journal. For health reasons, he returned to New England in September, but while at the community, he contributed much to its courage and faith. He was a devout Christian who believed that a simple Christian philosophy was the only solid basis for solving social problems. He believed that incremental proposals were diversions from real solutions. The gist of the whole matter was whether a man who "hath the world's goods ... beholdeth his brother in need." Anything less was to disobey Christ, and Kelley, like many at Commonwealth, chastised mainstream ministers for not preaching that message.[26]

Kelley thought that many wealthy people believed they were a modern version of John Calvin's "elect": "They are elected to salvation in this world ... by the accident of birth, the favor of circumstances or the energy of their participation in the battle of competition." They devote their economic diligence to making their position secure, and after that they engage in half-hearted, amateurish benevolence.[27]

His critique of wealthy religious bodies and the "pious" rich who withheld their millions from spiritual uses and ignored "the heartbreaking need of this world for which Christ died" was biting. He noted that the Baptist Church–owned property was valued at eighty-two million dollars and a well-known member of that denomination (John D. Rockefeller) could buy up all of that property and still have a fortune left over. Kelley called for a crusade to rescue Christ's money from the hands of these infidels.[28]

On the other hand, Kelley was not sure that Commonwealth would survive or convinced that communism could remedy social ills. But the fact that the colony was communistic was not that significant. It was more than an economic experiment. Its importance lay in its determination to "take Christianity with thoroughgoing seriousness" in contrast to the indifference of the churches. The spirit of Christianity saturated the community, and in their daily life Commonwealth's members were practicing the true doctrine of Christ. He believed "that men are able most effectually and nobly to perfect themselves" in service to the world. In the long run, Commonwealth could be a great power for good through its self-renunciation and obedience to the law of love. In that way, the community could do its share to bring about social regeneration.[29]

After Kelley returned to Connecticut, he advocated a more pragmatic approach to reform. Acknowledging the ideals of Christianity, he suggested that Christ had done, and Christians can only do, what was best under the circumstances in which they found themselves. In a subtle critique of Commonwealth, he asserted that impoverishing oneself without enriching others was not a path to social justice. Perhaps self-serving, he thought he could accomplish more by holding on to the "good things of life which a vicious system has lodged in his hands."[30]

Sunday evenings, members held vesper services on the veranda of the Retreat or on Albertson's porch. They were usually about brotherhood and service but varied in character depending on who led them. Albertson often conducted these services and then, with Irene at the piano, led the group in community singing. One Sunday, the topic was biblical criticism with illustrations and explanations of both textual and Higher Criticism. On another Sunday, Derrill Hope preached. After the prayer meetings, the attendees discussed what brotherhood required. They tried to avoid convention and encouraged everyone, "sister and brother," to communicate all they knew about truth and love.[31]

Critics thought that Commonwealth's communism and lack of sectarianism rejected Christ in favor of secular humanism. The *Social Gospel* denied that notion, citing John 10:15 and its reference to the organic union between Christ and his followers. Liberty of conscience and freedom of thought led to diverse interpretations of Christianity, but in the community, conduct, not a creed, was the manifestation of Christianity. Their first and last loyalty was not to communism or any other "ism" but to Christ and his cross. For Albertson, the cross symbolized the "law of utmost service," and the "law of kindness" and communism was merely the kindness of the multitude. He believed that a selfish man in a communistic society would adapt to the conditions of kindliness around him.[32]

Most members felt discontent with mainstream churches for their failure to address modern social problems. To Commonwealth, the only solution was the

> altruism of Jesus and this solution is strictly and distinctively the business of the church. The church cannot be free of blood-guiltiness if she stands aside while the weak are oppressed and the innocent suffer.... If the existing church cannot or will not take upon herself ... the conservation of the common good in economic affairs, then we shall see a new church....
>
> The church ... takes it, rather, for granted that might is right, that shrewdness should crush weakness, and plays the charity part of a Red-Cross society while the horrid butchery goes on. Worse, she takes tribute of the victors!
>
> That which is built upon silk-cushions, and cut glass, gold plated service and mahogany furniture and pipe organs and high salaried ministry, while the poor suffer and the sick die of neglect, and all this money is wrung from the hands of poorly paid labor—is built upon the sand.
>
> Beauty and art and magnificence have taken the place of love.... There is a place for them ... but we may not enjoy them before our fellows have health, justice, cleanliness and fellowship.[33]

John Chipman brought a different religious perspective to the community. A High-Church Episcopalian, he could not think of leaving his church. He believed that "the church works," despite its flaws. Chipman thought the founders had organized the Christian Commonwealth with a plan to put Christianity into practice to correct those flaws and become a manifestation of the "real church." Chipman had the enthusiasm and passion of J. A. Wayland or George Herron. Still, he also had an ecclesiastic's philosophy that began and ended with the church. Advocating all to become the sons of God, he laced his writings with biblical quotations and calls for prayer.[34]

Despite his primary role in its founding, Chipman did not immediately come to Commonwealth. His influence came through correspondence and articles in the *Social Gospel*. He reiterated his belief that the community's purpose was to reveal the imminence of the Kingdom of Heaven. By repenting and returning to righteousness, one could enter that kingdom. In July 1898, he appealed for fifty more families to join Commonwealth's "army of the Lord" and be willing to die for it.[35]

Chipman continued to contribute financially to Commonwealth and finally relocated in June 1899. Before his arrival and reflecting his orthodox views, Chipman published what he proposed to do at Commonwealth in the May *Social Gospel*:

I. Ourselves to accept Christ as king, making every one of his commands our law, and living in love one with another.

II. To preach Christ to the world by showing that the life of obedience is not only possible but the only perfect life.

III. To organize or help organize those who are willing to accept his law—the law of obedience, sacrifice, and love.

IV. To join Christian to Christian, and organization to organization, till all be one, and to make this unity complete and eternal in the name of the Lord....

V. To redeem the land, acre by acre, and bless it and make it holy to God.

VI. To redeem all tools and property everywhere and make it all property of the Lord—blessed and fruitful for good work, impossible to use for evil work.

VII. To make universal the brotherhood life, with all that it means—unity, love, glad service, religion true and undefiled—till all people, tongues and nations, all land and all property will be holy, ... and universal love the law of the kingdom.

More formal than most of what Commonwealth published, this article reflected their views. Chipman emphasized the need for "the most thorough and perfect organization," but acknowledged that Commonwealth did not claim or expect to be that. But it was a "true branch of the great vine of

Christ's planting—a true part of his church, whose purpose is making visible the Kingdom of God on earth."[36]

He hesitated to come to Commonwealth because he did not think he could contribute any labor of value. However, everyone thought he, as a founder and leading spirit, would be an asset to the community. Albertson, knowing that Chipman had "considerable experience in business life," urged him to become the business manager, which would allow Albertson to contribute elsewhere. Chipman agreed, and the community approved. Everyone hoped his experience and efforts would improve their economic situation.[37]

One Sunday when Chipman attempted to preach and administer the sacrament, his congregation was indifferent. It shattered his hopes that Commonwealth would become a denominational church. Faced with a choice, the colony or the church, he remained loyal to the church and "gave us up for lost." After staying for several weeks, he and his family left in August 1899. He remained a member of the community but intended to carry on its work elsewhere.[38]

He moved to Augusta, Georgia, where he took charge of the Christ Church parish in the factory district. It was an unpromising situation. His church was in decline, disrupted by class divisions, labor strife, and poverty, but he had visionary plans—a cooperative wood yard, a store, house building, and industries. Still motivated by the power of love and duty toward God and one another, Chipman hoped the poor would accept the Christ spirit and join his cause. Appealing for support, he wrote to the *Social Gospel* to attract interest in his work. The outcome is unclear, but Chipman remained in the Episcopalian Church and eventually became a bishop.[39]

Commonwealth treated those who neither cared nor thought about religion with tolerance and respect. The criterion for acceptance was not religious orthodoxy but to be a good, kind, cheerful, uncomplaining worker. Daily selfless labor was worship and fellowship with man and God. The community recognized that there were members who were good workers who never voiced prayer or praise but who had more real religion than was found in "Sunday services." Regardless of their beliefs, good workers were good brothers, good lovers, and good Christians.[40]

The community did not separate life into secular and religious spheres. Their work was worship and fellowship because it was the activity of love for all. Members were Baptists, Congregationalists, Methodists, Presbyterians, Universalists, Episcopalians, Quakers, Trinitarians, and Unitarians, but most had broken with their churches. Their commitment to brotherhood in daily life carried over into their unified Sunday services, and sect divisions died out. Love raised them to a common ground above creeds, opinions, forms, and sacramental signs.[41]

Albertson was outspoken on this issue: "No man or body of men can make a creed for blind acceptance by any other man, and it should be done by men who love the fellowship rather than the stupid discipleship of inferior minds." For him, creeds signified intellectual laziness and a refusal to face the problems of life manfully. They diverted one from the most effective gospel preached, to follow and "imitate Christ" in the Sermon on the Mount. To do so was a measure of the depth of one's manhood.[42]

"Manhood" was a pervasive theme in late nineteenth-century America and one that had many meanings. Often associated with a "cult of strenu-osity" and the militarism of bourgeois Victorians like Theodore Roosevelt, it was also promoted by Christian youth leaders as a challenge to the "en-feebled Protestantism" of their elders. The *Social Gospel* praised Charles Sheldon's *In His Steps* for using its "masculine intellectual quality" and put-ting the "best manhood" into its readers' minds. Albertson and others saw manhood as imitating Christ, and his earlier desire at Oberlin to pursue "muscular Christianity" reflected this view. Later, he elaborated on "man-hood" and, for that matter, "womanhood," seeing both as characterized by "well-ballasted" moral earnestness. He viewed those who did not have those virtues as "cranks" for their narrow-mindedness and egotism. Spartan virtue and the hard life of experience were antidotes to the corruption and luxury of America at the turn of the century.[43]

James Kelley supported Albertson. He believed that man needed some-thing to do or bear to make life strenuous enough to be worth living. Devel-oping strong individual character and channeling it into aggressive altruism would bring out the best qualities of manhood. Kelley believed that contem-porary education "made life effeminate, weak, flabby, imitative, dull, stupid." In contrast, proper education would make life "virile and vigorous, intense, creative, interesting." The teacher was not there to please the pupil or any-body else, and student "success" was not his responsibility. In fact, "a few he-roic failures would be for the public good."[44]

Commonwealth's school sought to elicit the "embryonic manhood" of its boys and the "embryonic womanhood" of the girls. The community came to-gether to serve one another without money or price and hoped to "awaken the manhood in those who did not have enough love in their hearts." Even the "Old Gentleman," in a critique of an unnamed minister whom he had heard often, advised him to "teach New Testament doctrine, man fashion, and come right to the point with it."

On the other hand, Commonwealth's celebration of the manhood of citizen soldiers in the Spanish-American War seemed ambiguous for a nonresistant community. But it viewed aggressive, self-seeking, competitive capitalism and struggling to gain at the expense of others as degrading manhood.[45]

In contrast to its radical economics and politics, the Christian Commonwealth was traditional and conservative when it came to the home, the family, and, to a degree, gender relations. Members believed that the home was the basis of society and American homelessness was a path back to barbarism. They made the "home principle" a fundamental characteristic of the community.[46]

In the early days, daily life for women was hard. Their diet was poor, and some became sick. They had a limited supply of furnishings and utensils. Women who were not physically strong turned to Sue Fay for help. She was Irene Albertson's best friend and often cared for the entire Albertson family. Her physical energy and spiritual strength surpassed almost everyone's in the community.[47]

As the colony made incremental steps toward more gender equality and opportunity, the women organized and made most of the decisions in their sphere, but were concerned about women's working conditions. The community sought to relieve women "from the slavery of unnecessary domestic drudgery and place her upon the plane of equal and honored economic fellowship with man." Women had many opportunities outside the home. Occupations included schoolteacher, floriculturist, postmistress, dressmaker, printer, and laundry supervisor.

Nevertheless, patriarchy remained pervasive in many community affairs. Women took care of men's domestic needs, mended their clothes, and cared for the rooms in the Barracks but had less say in the broader aspects of community life and fewer opportunities on the *Social Gospel*. Until the end, men did most of the writing for the journal, and except for Albertson's writing, the language and vocabulary were male oriented. Albertson almost always referred to "men and women" in his articles. He often spoke of women's economic potential and expressed a willingness to share domestic duties to give women a chance. He thought that women in industrial occupations would be "sweeter and more womanly." The other writers rarely mentioned the opposite sex.[48]

Commonwealth had no unusual views regarding marriage. It was highly revered, and several weddings took place in the community. Despite the appearance and some examples of gender equality, married women still had "their natural duties of household and family to perform." In a *Social Gospel* book review, Albertson favorably quoted Andrea Hofer Proudfoot's *A Mother's Ideals*. She wrote that a mother's highest work was to "purify her sense of love" and to mother "the sons and the fathers of the race." Members welcomed and celebrated the birth of children. When the Pawleys had twins, a boy and a girl, in January 1899, it reinforced the sense that the colony was becoming "more like home and less a tenting place."[49]

The family was a "primal, sacred" institution. If Commonwealth was to survive, it had to preserve and give the marital home its "high and righteous place." The nuclear family remained intact, but the community "discouraged narrow family selfishness." Some families lived in private cottages, and others lived communally and cooked and ate together. Some did so on principle and others because of the shortage of housing. Shared facilities, such as the kitchen, laundry, and bakery, lessened the workload of the private sphere.[50]

One visitor correctly observed that all of Commonwealth was like a large family. Members referred to themselves as "a family of families" and believed that family was a divine institution. They had overcome selfishness because no one benefitted from it. Each worked for the interests of all and received, in return, life's necessities. Everyone's financial interest was the same. During times of plenty, they would receive in abundance. There would be no rich and no poor unless all were rich or all were poor. They practiced those relations outside the community by serving their neighbors with the same labor of love.[51]

Commonwealth's sexual relations were conventional. Members did not advocate celibacy or free love in theory or practice and dissociated themselves from communities that did. Regarding Oneida and other well-known communities, "The Christian Commonwealth is distinctly, fundamentally and essentially different in ideas and life. We are an economic-missionary organization." Calvin Reasoner was interested in human sexuality and wrote a brief, positive review of *Love's Coming of Age*, a series of essays on sexual relations by Carpenter, the English mystical poet. Familiar with many of his books, Reasoner agreed that sex was "the allegory of Love in the physical world" and could lead to the "absolute union of being." Union was the prime object, with reproduction being secondary. The romance and emotional yearning that sex produced led to a long-lasting openness of inter-change. There is no evidence that Commonwealth discussed this issue.

Later, a dissatisfied member, C. L. Brewer, in an attempt to discredit the leadership and disrupt the community by creating disfavor among its neigh-bors and supporters, wrote a manuscript that described Commonwealth as a "free love" society and accused several members of practicing free love. Someone exposed the manuscript in a community meeting, and members, aware of how that issue had aroused hostility to other communal societies and believing that it criminally and viciously libeled some members, voted almost unanimously against its publication. Nevertheless, Brewer insisted he would publish it. In response, the members requested that he withdraw from the community. When he refused, they expelled him, at which point he vowed to "destroy" Commonwealth. Later, he took the lead in filing a lawsuit that contributed to the community's demise. The community took pains to reassure everyone that they were not engaged in behavior associated with other communal societies. Nevertheless, there were rumors of sexual mis-behavior but no documented evidence of irregularities. Albertson implied that it might have occurred but was less common than in ordinary American towns and cities and later admitted that he had been less than moral in sex relations in Commonwealth.[52]

Despite promoting communism, Commonwealth members believed that the community could not replace the mother in the training and educa-tion of children. The community could not displace mother love, especially for girls. Children remained in their nuclear families, where their mothers taught them the principles of brotherhood, love, and equality, in contrast to what children learned in the outside world. Albertson cautioned against "personal motherhood," in which a mother selfishly limited her love to her children, in favor of "universal motherhood," in which everyone loved all children equally.[53]

Commonwealth expected children to be inclusive in their relationships, but the attempt to abolish natural divisions based on likes and dislikes cre-ated tension among children and adults. The more dogmatic felt it was a se-rious offense for children to make friends with some children and exclude others. Sue Fay used her spiritual energy to minimize this discrimination. Nevertheless, children had quarrels, which occasionally led to tensions. On one occasion, Faye Albertson, in a quarrel with other children, declared her father the "boss of this community." The incident caused Ralph great misery

as his actions became more closely scrutinized, and some accused him of being undemocratic and hypocritical.[54]

Outsiders were concerned about the children's happiness and worried
that they would become prematurely old or too serious. Commonwealth
members assured them that colony children had maintained their innocence
and were happy. The older children had become believers in brotherhood
life, and none were isolated from the outside world. Many remained in contact with "friends far away," even receiving Valentine's Day cards from them.[55]

In November 1898, Commonwealth's third mortgage payment of $1,000
plus $160 in interest was due. Chipman's Florida mining enterprises had run
into financial difficulties. When he realized that Commonwealth was not going to become the "real Church," which, in his mind, was Episcopalian, he was
looking for a way out. The *Social Gospel* publicized the community's financial difficulties and fear of foreclosure. If the community was to survive, it
needed to pay off or refinance its debt, and the journal appealed to friends
for help, which garnered little response. By October, Commonwealth had received no funds for the payment.[56]

The appeal caught the attention of a Chicago businessman, Edward Keyes,
who was purchasing agent for Associated Merchants, U.S.A. and editor of
Mixed Stocks: A Magazine for Storekeepers. The success of English cooperative
stores had inspired Keyes, who believed that merchants who adopted cooperative storekeeping could eliminate the waste of the individualistic system
and outsell their competitors. Commonwealth's cooperative nature, its ar-
dor for nonresistance, and the *Social Gospel* deeply moved Keyes. Graham
Taylor, the Chicago social worker, convinced him to found the Right Relationship League "to study, teach and promote cooperation and create a general publishing business to advance cooperation" and "support cooperative
trade and industry organized upon a Christian basis." The founders included
prominent reformers like Taylor, George Herron, John Gavit, and Dr. Bayard
Holmes. The impressive Board of Directors included Jane Addams, "Golden
Rule" Jones, N. O. Nelson, George Gates, president of Iowa College, and Mary
McDowell of the University of Chicago Settlement House. Other members
included Ernest Crosby, Vida Scudder, the Vrooman brothers, and Hazen
Pingree and Tom Johnson, mayors of Detroit and Cleveland, respectively.[57]

Keyes believed that "the law of competition was the antithesis of the law
of love." A businessman who practiced "social love" and managed his business
unselfishly would swallow up his competitors. He wanted to help retail merchants convert from private to cooperative ownership or organize new co-

operative stores and colonies, such as the Christian Commonwealth, believing that they would result in "less waste, less expense and greater power of serving."[58]

"Golden Rule" Jones, an avid reader of the *Social Gospel*, felt as strongly as Keyes about cooperation and believed that brotherhood was the manifest destiny of humanity. If practiced, it would provide every man his "right to work" and end the competitive system of social warfare, which created tramps and shot down peaceful protestors.[59]

In October, Keyes paid to have Gibson and Albertson come to Chicago to discuss raising money for Commonwealth. They impressed the Right Relationship League with their story of faith and determination and convinced the organization that they were neither an industrial nor an economic failure. They stated that they took in poor families without charge, which they believed was unparalleled. They were answering the call of God and appealed to the league's generosity, humanitarianism, religious purpose, and patriotism. Money was necessary, but what they were doing could not be expressed in commercial terms. Accepting the law of love and practicing the true gospel of brotherhood was worth more than monetary power could command. They convinced Keyes and the Right Relationship League to assume the remaining two-thousand-dollar mortgage on the community's property "to protect them." In return, the *Social Gospel* promoted both the league and its magazine, *Mixed Stocks*.[60]

Albertson and Gibson spent several weeks in Chicago spreading Commonwealth's message to potential supporters. With Taylor's assistance, Albertson lectured on cooperation at Hull House, the Chicago Theological Seminary, Northwestern University, the Chicago Commons, and Mary McDowell's University of Chicago settlement. He told his audiences that Commonwealth believed "Jesus meant what he said, and they proposed to give it a trial." He and Gibson reconnected with Henry Demarest Lloyd and met Aylmer Maude, Tolstoy's biographer and advocate for the Doukhobors, who had just formed a Tolstoyan colony in England. Maude and Albertson discussed settlement work and the obligation to reform industrial life. He and Gibson heard Herron lecture on the "social sacrifice of conscience" and were inspired by "the burning words of this great teacher." They explained that Commonwealth had "not put ourselves away from the world and its needs, but have taken it upon our hearts, and are pouring ourselves out to meet human needs." Their plan resonated with Herron, who believed that "it is in spiritual passion and action ... that human beings find themselves marching side by side in some great cause, their hearts beating to the same hope and harmony."[61]

The two men made an extraordinary impression on their Chicago contacts. Taylor compared their work at Commonwealth to that of Saint Francis of Assisi in his effort to save the Church from religious degeneracy, and Gavit praised them for "taking Jesus seriously." He saw them applying the "preposterous assertions of the Beatitudes to the social and economic relations of men in civilized society." For him, it was refreshing in "these sordid days of atheistic money-grabbing."[62]

Gibson and Albertson returned to Georgia with the necessary funds the day before the mortgage payment was due. The money came from different sources, but the Right Relationship League held the mortgage. Seven hundred dollars was without interest, and the community hoped the remainder would also become interest free.[63]

Albertson's experience confirmed his fundamental belief that love, the Kingdom of Heaven, brotherhood, and the millennium were "good things," and Commonwealth dared to pursue them. On the other hand, most men were too afraid or spiritually lazy or too attached to little "machine-made socialism" to pursue the complete socialism that Christ acknowledged as heaven's way.[64]

Food and shelter were Commonwealth's priorities, but education was not far behind. The colonists built a multiroom school building and worked with neighbors to establish a primary school to serve the children of the colony and surrounding county. The Muscogee County school commissioner interviewed Sue Fay and William Damon and pronounced them qualified to teach. Since Commonwealth paid taxes, the county paid their salaries, which they deposited into the common treasury. Sue Fay ran the school, where she was known to the children as "Aunt Sue." She considered each new Commonwealth child as "an acquisition, one more to lavish love upon, an angel on the block." Like a joyful "artist creating, she goes on loving and chiseling, and patiently perfecting the unfolding characters."[65]

Damon helped Sue conduct the school, while Derrill Hope was "the presiding genius" over the kindergarten. Called "Aunt Hope" or "Good Hope," she was a "sweet little love," highly revered by the three-year-olds. It was little wonder that on rainy mornings the children slipped away from home despite the rain to go to kindergarten. When William Edmonds, a newcomer, proved to be a good teacher, he took over from Damon, who then had more time for his orchard and nursery work. Commonwealth viewed their school as "a college of the new economy—a people's university and an ordinary American public school." The teachers taught both basic and advanced classes as well as lessons of brotherhood, which inspired a great deal of harmony, loyalty, and faith among the children.[66]

Commonwealth wanted educators to "train the imagination" to become excited about the observations and activities of daily life. They viewed society's endless demand for excitement and pleasure as unmanly and unwomanly and a path to evil behavior. "Learning 'by heart' the matchless poetry of the Bible" would provide inspiring truth, spiritual lessons, and beneficial excitement.[67]

Although not a permanent resident, James Kelley shared his educational views. He condemned the trends toward lower standards, the lack of discipline, and the emphasis on fun in American schools. During the war with Spain, Kelley commended America's victories as a triumph of discipline, while condemning the failures of the untrained and undisciplined. Discipline prepared one for worthy achievements, and it was time for the church and schools to instill this discipline in their youth manfully. In a community that amorphously believed that love and peer pressure were sufficient to uplift the weak and oppressed, Kelley brought a modern view to the source of progress. Given the flexibility of human nature, Kelley believed that a child reared and educated in a cooperative, altruistic environment would carry those values throughout his life. Like sheep that had gone astray, they would follow their natural leaders back to the fold if taught manfully.[68]

Georgia quickly recognized Commonwealth's school as one of the best in the state. The community was not modest about it. Students were taught self-reliance and self-respect through love, not punishment, and in one year the school had become better than the ordinary city school and had teachers who permitted students to do quality individual work. When the county schools reopened in January 1898, Commonwealth opened a "new four-room schoolhouse, the largest and best in Muscogee County outside of Columbus." Despite its primitive construction, the schoolhouse delighted the children and the teachers. They worked around homemade tables and had to be careful not to lose small items through cracks in the floor. Twenty-seven students attended regularly, and adults dropped in to study specific subjects.[69]

In May, the school's closing exercises attracted local attention but again exposed Commonwealth's ambiguity regarding the Spanish-American War. Held at Albertson's residence, the closing exercises provided both instruction and entertainment. Pupils recited their exercises, which confirmed the teaching abilities of Sue Fay and her assistants. Volney B. Cushing, a member of the Executive Board of the Prohibition Party and a nationally known temperance man from Maine, was the commencement speaker. His mother and sister were community members, and he had been one of the first subscribers to the *Social Gospel*. Afterward, Daniel Hinckley gave a humorous reading and Albertson sang while Irene played the piano.[70]

The climax was a duet sung by Ruth Damon and Elsie Pease. The war had broken out the previous month, and on May 1 George Dewey's naval squadron had destroyed the Spanish fleet in Manila Bay. Ruth and Elsie's song, "Yankee Dewey," sung to the tune of "Yankee Doodle," celebrated the event and probably raised some eyebrows about Commonwealth's commitment to Christian love, brotherhood, and Tolstoyan nonresistance.

> Yankee Dewee sailed his boats
> Down in Manila Bay, sir;
> He found the Spaniards on their floats,
> And blew them all away, sir
>
> Yankee Dewee, keep it up;
> O Dewee, you're a dandy!
> Yankee Dewee, keep it up;
> Yes, Dewee, you're a dandy!
>
> Then, Dewee sent us word,
> And this is what he said, sir:
> "We've sunk their gunboats, every one,
> And not a Yankee dead, sir!"[71]

That summer, Commonwealth began building a new school. It was a big job, and they lacked the workforce to meet the scheduled opening in October and postponed opening the new building until January. Instead, classes commenced in the old building with twenty-four students. Spring enrollment increased to twenty-nine, including five children from families outside the colony. School attendance varied but averaged twenty-five to thirty pupils, with the children, aged six to eighteen, grouped into six grades. In addition to the regular subjects, they had lessons in drawing, Latin, Greek, and logic. Physical exercise, a distinctive feature of the curriculum, was part of recess. In the new building, the regular school occupied the main room and the kindergarten another room, and leaders planned to move the library from the printing office into a third room.[72]

After dismissal from school, many young people took sewing classes from Mrs. Honens. They were popular for both girls and boys, and the boys' zeal amused many adults. Both genders competed for a prize offered to the most proficient in sewing after three months of classes.[73]

Commonwealth's school helped keep the community "in the world." Its teachers were involved with the Muscogee County School Board and participated in monthly meetings of the County Teachers' Association. Responding to their colleagues' interest, they invited the association to meet at Commonwealth. Many teachers were anxious to go. What made it even more appealing was the opportunity to "enjoy a day out in the woods" at a time when schools were expanding their nature study.

In June 1899, the three-county region held its "annual institute for white teachers" in Columbus. Sue Fay Hinckley and Hazel Albertson attended a pleasant and beneficial series of meetings. Sue Fay played a prominent role by giving a series of lectures and presentations on nature studies and exhibiting drawings and descriptions of leaves and flowers done by Commonwealth students. The high level of work done at Commonwealth's school impressed the county school commissioner and many teachers.[74]

Education was not limited to the classroom or children. The members believed in cultural and intellectual life for everyone. Only the "crying needs" of their community and world limited their cultivation of a taste for literature and art and training in their expression. Despite its importance, culture had to be incidental and helpful to service.[75]

At the schoolhouse, adults took literature and science courses three evenings a week and James Kelley led a Shakespeare class every other Friday evening. After his return to Connecticut, the class continued in the fall, first reading *A Comedy of Errors*. After spending his days in the nursery, William Damon taught Latin and Greek at night. William Edmonds designed courses on language and logic and lectured on them to a packed audience. A fluent and persuasive speaker, he gave an interesting address on the need and efficient way to study those subjects. Other members conducted classes in etymology, art, and music for adults and children. In response to requests, the Board of Education invited Albertson to teach a course in ethics. Meeting three evenings a week, it was lively, engaging, and well attended.[76]

From the beginning, Commonwealth planned to establish a college. Members criticized contemporary colleges and universities for neglecting vocational training, "the pursuit of serviceable knowledge." In North Carolina,

Damon and Albertson had opened a free school and had wanted education to be the foundation of their community. Now, they hoped to achieve that goal at Commonwealth:[77]

> We are planning also for a university, an industrial school, a brotherhood school, where all branches of useful knowledge, art, science, literature, mechanical skill, agriculture, etc., shall be taught, to the end that all individual talents and powers of service may be cultivated, trained, educated, perfected, so that utmost service of every sort may be rendered. In this university, not a part, but all our children are to be educated, in service, and the grace, dignity, divineness and love-creating power of free brotherhood labor of every sort, shall be upon all strongly impressed.[78]

A central goal of the postbellum South was the expansion of education for whites and African Americans, and Booker T. Washington's Tuskegee Normal and Industrial Institute in Alabama stood out as a highlight of that quest. Although black and white churches had separate Social Gospel movements, Commonwealth's commitment to the movement and interest in education drew it into a relationship with Tuskegee. It demonstrated Washington's influence on American social Christianity. To Commonwealth, Tuskegee was among the most important institutions in the country "for uplifting the colored race." Teaching both the hand and the brain, it "trained its students in the duties and ideals of noble manhood and womanhood." Following Tuskegee's lead, the community wanted to build its school along the lines of Washington's institution.[79]

There is no evidence of direct contact between Washington and colony members, but in early 1898 Samuel Comings and N. O. Nelson visited Tuskegee. They observed the teaching of technical skills, academic subjects, and "inspiring Christianity," which implanted in students both self-respect and self-reliance. They returned impressed by its "imposing exhibition of human progress" and saw it as "the true Archimedean lever for the elevation of a race." Nelson was so enthusiastic that he "lost sleep" over the possibility of opening a similar school for whites, with brotherly cooperation added to its curriculum. In return, a Tuskegee trustee, Reverend C. R. Bedford, visited Commonwealth and reviewed its plan for an industrial university. While there, he encouraged Comings and Albertson to attend the education conferences at Tuskegee.[80]

Meanwhile, Comings proposed a cooperative system of education for Commonwealth. He agreed with the community's critique of education that separated science and literature from practical skills and left graduates ill adapted for work in the world, having no "serviceable knowledge." Comings's curriculum would develop citizenship, general knowledge, and industrial skills. It would start in kindergarten and continue through college. Cultural and intellectual growth and learning the ideals of real brotherhood would be a focus, but because the community believed that "all should work," it also thought that all should become skilled.

In the *Social Gospel*, Comings proposed that Commonwealth raise twenty-five thousand dollars to open a "Cooperative University." It would be self-supporting and provide an education that would "remedy the ill effects of our factory system on the white race" and prepare students for a cooperative civilization. The community had the educators, preachers, editors, and skilled artisans necessary to carry out the plan. He asked for suggestions for a location and donations of land or money and received several plausible offers and many contributions. To inspire confidence in the donors and protect the enterprise, he proposed to create a trust to manage its assets. Moreover, by focusing on its educational nature, Comings thought they would receive better treatment from the courts and laws than would a cooperative association.[81]

In July 1898, Commonwealth, inspired by Comings and driven more by community enthusiasm than substantive preparation, announced a "Normal and Industrial Institute" to open in October. The curriculum would include four years of traditional academic work in an environment of applied Christianity. Each student would also have to pursue one industrial course, among them blacksmithing, horticulture, printing, steam engineering, and agricultural chemistry, with stenography and sewing for the female students. Each student would pay five dollars per month and perform "useful work" in Commonwealth for four hours per day. When implemented, the plan would benefit the community by providing labor and capital and benefit the students by turning them into skilled and productive men and women. The community needed capital to get the institute going and implied that they would welcome financial assistance.[82]

A Columbus newspaper offered praise: "Commonwealth seems capable of doing anything." The colony received many inquiries about the school, but their announcement was premature. The institute did not open in October, and three months later leaders announced that it was "indefinitely postponed," but stated that there was no reason to think it would not open the next year. They gave no reason for the postponement, but the community's ideals and ambitions often outstripped its capital and resources.[83]

Intellectual life at Commonwealth was fuller than most members would have had in the outside world. The "communized" library, supervised by Jule Talmadge, contained fourteen hundred volumes. They accumulated so many books that they had to move the library several times for lack of space. Every member and community neighbor had access to a wider range of reading material than most would have had otherwise.[84]

The colony formed several reading circles, precursors to today's book clubs. The books read often were associated with the community's ideology. In December 1898, for example, they read a new *Life of Tolstoy*, which produced an "interesting and profitable discussion." The reading circle merged with the Shakespeare class into one group called the Culture Club, which met on Fridays. Later, members formed another reading circle that met in the general parlor on Wednesday evenings. Often decorated with holly and other greens and blooms, the room had a large, cheerful fireplace, rocking chairs, a couch, and a table. The single men used it as a reading room when it was not used for meetings. One night an "animated discussion" took place over Bolton Hall's *Things as They Are*. Hall, an Irish immigrant, lawyer, anarchist, and disciple of Tolstoy, Henry George, and Ernest Howard Crosby, was an advocate of urban homesteading and had started a back-to-the-land movement in the United States. Readers concluded that it was a fine book.[85]

Guest speakers often appeared at community gatherings. Alice Gordon Gulick, the principal of an American school for Spanish girls in Spain and a translator for Spanish prisoners during the Spanish-American War, assured Commonwealth that Spanish people were friendly toward the United States. Volney B. Cushing gave an entertaining lecture on "The Lost Atlantis," which many members thought was a rare treat. Judge Cozart of the Recorder's Court in Columbus gave a semi-humorous lecture, laced with sarcasm and seriousness, that was one of the most enjoyable ever at Commonwealth. It kept the audience "exploding" with laughter the entire evening.[86]

Working as a group to survive dominated daily interaction at Commonwealth, but it did not preclude other social activities. Members engaged in harmless amusements but cautioned that, given their circumstances, pleasure must be subordinate to duty. They looked forward to the day when there would be less work and more play.[87]

Issues arose over recreation, which illustrated diverse views within the community. In one prayer meeting, the question of dancing and card playing came up. Some people were doing both, and others saw them as "dangerous" activities that might discourage "excellent people" from joining. The disagreement was not harsh, and the matter remained unresolved. The community was opposed to rules and not prepared to draw fine lines between right and wrong nor "force consciences by majority decrees."[88]

When a visitor expressed surprise that members used tobacco, the community responded that, other than being Christian Socialists, residents were not different from those of the outside world. Allowing tobacco showed their "live and let live" attitude. Gibson, stating that tobacco was a "filthy, expensive, and poisonous weed," acknowledged that some members were addicted. Still, the membership policy prevented driving the "tobacco slaves" away or patrolling the streets to prohibit the habit. On another occasion, swearing became an issue. It did not happen often, but the community revealed it "for the sake of people who have childishly silk-lined ideas about colony life." As a society of the sons of God, Commonwealth was not exclusive and felt obliged to invite "the bad and the good" to the feast of brotherhood.[89]

From the beginning, the Commonwealth women met regularly on weekday afternoons. Their gatherings were an opportunity for sociability, fellowship, and culture. They enjoyed light refreshments, read papers, and discussed matters of common interest. The meetings rotated among community homes, and occasionally the women gathered for supper at a member's cottage. Bertine Croyle hosted one in which she happily carried out her New Year's resolutions. What she resolved is unclear. Was it personal or an indication of social conflict?[90]

As in any close-knit social situation, there were occasional petty tensions. Sue Fay Hinckley described one in her diary:

> Went to call on Mrs. Colette this afternoon. She is an odd little woman full of prim ways and little precisenesses—giving me information about Karl Marx, Christine Nihilson, Emerson and the school of transcendentalists, as if every school girl didn't know perfectly well the facts she imparted. She also took me to task for not sufficiently softening a "C" in a French name. She carefully noted meanwhile, so that I could not help but be aware of it, the cut of my dress, taking pains to get around to see the back of it. It is the only place in Commonwealth where the dress would not have been frankly questioned about if any interest were felt.[91]

More often, the women paid homage to each other. In April 1899, at the Hinckleys, the women honored Derrill Hope. She was a white-haired native Georgian who had been a missionary in Latin America for nine years before joining the Topolobampo colony in Mexico. After its breakup, she remained devoted to communitarian ideals and joined Commonwealth, where she wrote for the *Social Gospel*, helped respond to the community's correspondence, and ran the kindergarten. She had a saintly influence on the community and remained one of Albertson's most pleasant memories.[92]

On another occasion, the women welcomed Amelia Damon home from a winter spent visiting the North. A week later, they returned to the Croyle home, where they met a woman who had just come from missionary activity among Appalachian whites in West Virginia. In new elections for their "industrial organization," the women elected Derrill Hope as president, Eora Henry as vice president, and Mary Gibson as secretary.[93]

Birthdays, wedding celebrations, holidays, and other social events, all with games for young people, occurred regularly and were well attended. Musical and literary talent, sometimes provided by visitors, accompanied the festivities. In June 1898, sixty-five people, almost everyone in the colony, attended an ice cream social that included such a program. Irene Albertson entertained on the piano, and the *Social Gospel*'s editors boasted that the affair cost almost nothing. The colony celebrated Sophie Smith's birthday with a candy pull for the children, and it came together to celebrate the twenty-first birthday of Justin Cook, offering him loving congratulations and good wishes. On Valentine's Day, the children had a party at the schoolhouse.[94]

Peanut parties were a regular Friday evening event, combining business with pleasure. Everyone spent a few hours shelling roasted peanuts, which they milled into peanut butter. Daniel Franks played his violin to enliven the labor, and there was singing, recitations, and readings by young people. They would read a book chapter or a selection from *Harper's* or *Current Literature* as they "bettered their brains, and buttered their stomachs."[95]

Members used any excuse for a picnic. The Fourth of July celebration in 1898 illustrated the range of amusements and festivities at such events. After a patriotic service, with speeches and singing on Sunday night, July 3, the entire colony "took to the woods" for a picnic the next morning. Albertson managed athletic contests for both "grown-ups" and the younger generation. There were foot races and sack races for the men and women, and the men raced wheelbarrows. Even the "Grandma of the Colony," Eunice Cushing, celebrating her seventy-eighth birthday on the Fourth, ran the women's race and had a great time. After dinner, there was lively music and serious speaking. Everyone enjoyed the funny songs and sober discourse. They followed that with a game of "base-ball" between fathers and sons, but the fathers' long-unused skills were no match for the boys. On another occasion, a "wood cutting picnic" became the site of a public reading of a Tolstoy letter. Sometimes, members picnicked outside the community. One outing to a park on the Chattahoochee River included a fishing party and picnic to send Sadie Pease and her daughters off to Apalachicola, where her husband, Albert, and Vrooman had started a community.[96]

Later that month, they emulated the Pilgrims' first Thanksgiving in the New England wilderness. It was a festive and religious occasion. The feast consisted of eighteen chickens and three turkeys, sweet potatoes, cornbread, peach and cranberry sauce, apples, and roasted peanuts. What was lacking may have indicated ongoing shortages. They had no pies, cake, wheat bread, butter, or sugar. Nevertheless, the entire colony enjoyed the dinner, recited the twenty-third Psalm, and sang the doxology. After dinner, many gave thanks for being at Commonwealth rather than in "the each-for-himself life of the world."[97]

The following year, Thanksgiving again resembled a New England feast. Everyone gathered at the schoolhouse for worship and then met in the dining room for a bountiful meal. They recalled a year of difficulties and trials but were thankful for the blessings of Providence that had come to them in every time of need. Frost, which had been so devastating earlier in the year, was now complimented for making the "frost-tinged foliage unusually beautiful." It was a positive view, even though early frosts had partly killed the flower garden and flowers and grasses in the fields.[98]

Christmas at Commonwealth was "not celebrated with solemn pomp" but was merry and rendered in "the beauty of holiness." Adults and children sang and performed Christmas anthems, solos, songs, and recitations accompanied by a talk on "the meaning of Christmas—God manifesting Himself in human life—in Christ, in us." Members and neighbors attended the celebration. Good music and song filled the air on Christmas Eve despite the absence of the best singers. The evening children's service included recitations and singing, including a Christmas song written by Derrill Hope. Six-year-old Ralph McDermott recited a poem expressing the colony's love for Grandma Cushing, who delighted in making rugs for the community. Written by Sue Hinckley, the poem honored "our precious, white haired Grandma, who makes so many rugs." Calvin Reasoner preached a powerful sermon from the book of John: "And I, if I be lifted up, will draw all men unto me." A visitor commented that it was worth coming a thousand miles to hear, and a recently arrived brother felt that "it was the truest worship he had attended in a long time." After the services, the adults retired to "the Elms," and the children decorated a beautiful Christmas tree in the corner of the dining hall, using ornaments sent by friends.[99]

On Christmas morning, the children awoke before dawn and assembled at the Elms. Irene Albertson accompanied them to greet each household with Christmas bells and carols. Afterward, everyone ate and prayed together in the dining room. Before the children could open their gifts, the adults told them about the great number of poor children who had no Christmas presents. Then, they exchanged homemade gifts, love tokens, and "fruits of the tree," and one year each child received a gift from Grace Gidney, who regularly sent gifts of love. A fellow Bostonian, Hannah Parker Kimball, the American poet, also sent gifts for the children, and Harvey Keyes sent books. Ernest Hammond sent the community a Rand-McNally atlas. Other gifts included two barrels of fine apples from Maine and a box of "good things" from W. A. Ross of Columbus. After the children received their gifts, the adults took them in a wagon to "distribute among the poor colored children of the neighborhood some very pretty picture books and other presents" that they had made. That evening a party for members, visitors, neighbors, and friends closed out the day's festivities. It was the happiest Christmas that Gibson could remember.[100]

The night after Christmas, members had another party with games and refreshments. There was a recitation of a Charlotte Perkins Gilman poem in which she painted a picture "of the year-long Christmas, for which the needy, sorrowing world waits." They had a stereopticon lecture by John Ward Stimson, a recent arrival, who had been the superintendent of art schools connected with the Metropolitan Museum of Art in New York City. Two days later, he conducted the evening prayer meeting, where he presented "something new and beautiful in the interpretation of nature."[101]

By New Year's Eve, quiet had returned to Commonwealth, so much so that when some enthusiastic young people rang the bell to usher in the new year, several members thought it was the fire alarm and started for the main building. They closed the school and kindergarten for the week, but most colonists went about their customary occupations on New Year's Day.[102]

Despite their privation, Commonwealth's members had a full and happy life. To tell the world, they reported their ideals and experiences in the monthly *Social Gospel*.

John Chipman, civil engineer, Rockwell, Fla. "Christian Commonwealth," *Commons*, Oct. 1898, 4.

George Howard Gibson, president of the Christian Commonwealth. "Christian Commonwealth," *Commons*, Oct. 1898, 3.

Prof. W. C. Damon, A. M., superintendent, Orchard and Gardening Department. "Christian Commonwealth," *Commons*, Oct. 1898, 4.

Rev. Ralph Albertson, superintendent, Department of Extension. "Christian Commonwealth," *Commons*, Oct. 1898, 7.

Old plantation house. "Christian Commonwealth," *Commons*, Oct. 1898, 5.

A carpenter. Courtesy of Hargrett Rare Book and Manuscript Library / University of Georgia Libraries.

"The Soul of Industry." Courtesy of Hargrett Rare Book and Manuscript Library / University of Georgia Libraries.

Sawmill in operation.
"Christian Commonwealth,"
Commons, Oct. 1898, 13.

Sawmill. Courtesy of
Hargrett Rare Book and
Manuscript Library /
University of Georgia
Libraries.

The big saw. Courtesy of
Hargrett Rare Book and
Manuscript Library /
University of Georgia
Libraries.

The Gibson House. Courtesy of Hargrett Rare Book and Manuscript Library / University of Georgia Libraries.

The Rose Cottage. Courtesy of Hargrett Rare Book and Manuscript Library / University of Georgia Libraries.

The Barracks. Courtesy of Hargrett Rare Book and Manuscript Library / University of Georgia Libraries.

The Elms. Courtesy of Hargrett Rare Book and Manuscript Library / University of Georgia Libraries.

Barns. Courtesy of Hargrett Rare Book and Manuscript Library / University of Georgia Libraries.

(L to R) Dan and Sue Fay Hinckley, Irene and Ralph Albertson. Courtesy of Hargrett Rare Book and Manuscript Library / University of Georgia Libraries.

The Damon family. Courtesy of Hargrett Rare Book and Manuscript Library /
University of Georgia Libraries.

Jules Talmadge. Courtesy of Hargrett Rare Book
and Manuscript Library / University of Georgia
Libraries.

Grandma Cushing. Courtesy of Hargrett Rare Book
and Manuscript Library / University of Georgia
Libraries.

John Croyle. Courtesy of Hargrett Rare Book and Manuscript Library /
University of Georgia Libraries.

The community. Courtesy of Hargrett Rare Book and Manuscript Library / University of Georgia Libraries.

Commonwealth school with teachers and scholars. "Christian Commonwealth,"
Commons, Oct. 1898, 11.

Group of young people.
Courtesy of Hargrett Rare
Book and Manuscript
Library / University of
Georgia Libraries.

Lassies of 1898. Courtesy of Hargrett Rare Book and Manuscript Library / University of Georgia Libraries.

Phyllis playing Irene's piano. Courtesy of Hargrett Rare Book and Manuscript Library / University of Georgia Libraries.

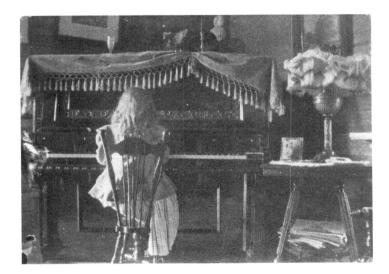

A tea party. Courtesy of Hargrett Rare Book and Manuscript Library / University of Georgia Libraries.

A picnic. Courtesy of
Hargrett Rare Book and
Manuscript Library /
University of Georgia
Libraries.

At a picnic. Courtesy of
Hargrett Rare Book and
Manuscript Library /
University of Georgia
Libraries.

Fourth of July picnic, 1899.
Courtesy of Hargrett Rare
Book and Manuscript
Library / University of
Georgia Libraries.

Women's foot race. Courtesy of Hargrett Rare Book and Manuscript Library /
University of Georgia Libraries.

Wheelbarrow race; President W. C. Damon on left.
Courtesy of Hargrett Rare Book and Manuscript
Library / University of Georgia Libraries.

Baseball game. Courtesy of Hargrett Rare Book
and Manuscript Library / University of Georgia
Libraries.

An old ex-slave. Courtesy
of Hargrett Rare Book
and Manuscript Library /
University of Georgia
Libraries.

Composing. Courtesy of
Hargrett Rare Book and
Manuscript Library /
University of Georgia
Libraries.

A letter to the old home.
Courtesy of Hargrett Rare
Book and Manuscript
Library / University of
Georgia Libraries.

CHAPTER 6

✦ ✦ ✦

The *Social Gospel*

The truth we had apprehended.

—Ralph Albertson, the *Social Gospel*

URING THE FIRST MONTHS, Commonwealth was preoccupied with starting the colony and gave little attention to its relationship to the outside world. Soon, George Howard Gibson and Ralph Albertson proposed publishing a magazine to "express to all men the truth that they apprehended." A minority doubted the wisdom of starting a journal when they lacked many of life's necessities. Albertson convinced them of its benefits and offered to assume all responsibility and indebtedness and give the paper to the colony when free of debt. Albertson prevailed, which then led to disagreements about the type of paper to publish, and like elsewhere in Commonwealth's life, there was no unanimity among a community of "theory specialists."[1]

The first issue, published on a fifty-dollar press using secondhand type, introduced the *Social Gospel* as "published in the faith that the wrongs of society can be righted and that the ideals of society can be realized. It is a journal of the practice of Christianity. It will be its purpose to inspire faith in the economic teachings of Jesus." It was the mouthpiece for the Christian altruism that Commonwealth's brotherhood life demonstrated. Members were proud that it reflected their daily lives and expression of love as an inspiration to all. Also, it followed events and activities in the outside world. Albertson described it as the community's "chief means of communication to spread brotherhood doctrine" and the Christian Socialist message. He asked readers to "use all available means to help us multiply copies and find readers for it."[2]

When the *Social Gospel* announced Commonwealth's adherence to Tolstoyan principles, it attracted global attention. Worldwide, there were similar communities organized along Tolstoyan lines or feeling an affinity for his ideas.[3] In New Zealand, Harold Williams, a left-wing journalist, became enthusiastic about those communities in America, especially Ruskin, the Christian Commonwealth, and Rugby. He was most impressed with Commonwealth's literature and circulated copies to New Zealand acquaintances. He planned to come to Georgia in 1899 to "see with my own eyes the working of the Christ spirit in Commonwealth." The colony impressed another New Zealander, A. W. Bickerton, a college professor. In the flyleaf of a book he sent to Gibson, he praised Commonwealth for its Christian spirit under difficult circumstances and the *Social Gospel* for exhibiting "more truly the science of life than any other work extant."[4]

Gibson and Albertson, aided by a group of associate editors, shared managing editor duties of the journal. Gibson also served as Commonwealth's corresponding secretary and handled communications and inquiries from prospective members and the curious. Through their efforts, he and Albertson became prominent in reform circles.[5]

The associate editors listed on the masthead included George Herron, Ernest Crosby, James Kelley, Samuel Comings, Thomas Will, John Chipman, and the Reverends William Thurston Brown, Benjamin Fay Mills, and W. D. P. Bliss. Scattered across the United States, most never visited Commonwealth nor participated in day-to-day editorial work, but they often wrote for the journal.[6]

Comings was a Michigan fruit grower who owned an extensive cranberry marsh and had considerable money invested in agriculture. He had met Albertson in Chicago in 1894, and his interest in Commonwealth dated back to its inception. He and his wife Hattie came to Commonwealth in February 1898. Like Damon and Albertson, Comings had broken from the church but continued to be influenced by its beliefs. Despite his limited formal education, he frequently wrote reform articles for the *Coming Nation* and the *Social Gospel*. A social theorist of strong sympathies, Comings was profoundly idealistic. He compared Christ's law of brotherhood to the law of gravity in that one could not set them aside. He saw the "tramp, the city slum, and the honest worker" desperate for work as analogous to Moses's "burning bush"—a voice calling for a "state of brotherhood and mutualism" that will end "the horrible sufferings of the present."[7]

Mills was a Presbyterian evangelist converted to socialism by George Herron. In 1895, he settled in Boston to preach and published "Twentieth Century Religion," a series of pamphlets explaining his ideas. His message was simple: faith, hope, and love—faith in the fatherhood of God, hope for the Kingdom of Heaven, and love as the path to the Kingdom of God. He believed only a conscience enlightened by love and revival of the brotherhood of men could abolish the poverty created by Gilded Age business practices. Mills believed the Christian Commonwealth contributed to that revival, but he perceived the wealthy differently than Commonwealth members. They embraced Herron's position that Christianity and wealth were contradictory. Mills argued that only the rich who reveled in luxury while others suffered would experience eternal torment. His larger concern, as it was for Commonwealth, was churches' indifference to poverty while accumulating wealth and yielding to their wealthy members. The church must "wake up" and care for its people's physical needs instead of merely preaching the Gospel. Mills's moderate stance on wealth had little effect. When he lectured on his economic views in Boston, his wealthy patrons withdrew their support.[8]

Optimism filled the *Social Gospel*, but Mills's faith in human spiritual and material progress exceeded everyone's. He believed the day was coming when a boy would ask his parents, "What is poverty? What is injustice? What is war?," and the parents would lack the language to answer. Gibson quoted Mills often in the *Social Gospel*, but by 1899 Mills had lost his faith in evangelism and become a Unitarian pastor in California.[9]

William Thurston Brown, a Yale Divinity School graduate, had been tried for heresy by a Connecticut Congregational Church for accepting Higher Criticism and promoting George Herron's social and economic views. He then received a call from the liberal Plymouth Congregational Church in Rochester, New York, before turning to Unitarianism in Boston. To Commonwealth, his decision represented an encouraging change in the pulpit's perspective on social questions.[10]

Brown wrote extensively on social Christianity, contributed to the *Social Gospel*, and donated to its General Expense Fund. He believed capitalism was the root of social problems. Under capitalism, "men weigh nothing at all in the balances of commercialism, which is the religion of this time. It must be apparent," he wrote in the *Kingdom*, "to most of us what was true of slavery is

now true in respect to the wage system and indeed the entire economic order.... One cannot conform to the existing system and preach a gospel which
is in any sense good tidings to the poor.... People are asking for bread, and
what are we giving them? Words, words, words!"[11]

He believed Christianity and socialism had the power to fix these problems. Brown saw Christ as an emancipator born to free men and women to
love and serve others, and he argued that Jesus and Marx were preaching the
same "gospel." However, the modern church and social class structure hindered that emancipation by promoting selfish materialism over moral con-
summation.[12]

Brown thought that his contemporaries had "lost the sense of simplicity
of the faith and vision and message of Jesus." The foundation of his message
was "the kingdom of God," which meant the absolute sovereignty of love in
human life. It was "self-sacrifice in the service of love" that manifested divinity in man, and a true Christian would experience suffering, sacrifice, sorrow,
and defeat. The modern world was a mass of conflict, hostility, selfishness,
and materialism, but in places like the Christian Commonwealth, the "law of
service, the law of love between man and man, holds the future."[13]

Brown's rhetoric was more radical than Commonwealth's. He agreed with
Tolstoy that the "wealthy members of society are literally riding on the backs
of men and women who toil" and with Herron's assertion that there was a
"moral contradiction in the present system." Brown then argued that "the
workers were justified in revolting against railroad kings, coal barons and
landlords" and, paraphrasing William Lloyd Garrison, "if the Constitution
of the United States bulwarks a system of industrial slavery, so much the
worse for that Constitution." Later, the *Social Gospel* chimed in with a Garrison quote stating that monopoly drove women into poverty, starved children, and turned laborers in cities to drunkenness. Tolstoy would never support the rhetoric threatening violence but agreed that the "ever-widening
chasm between rich and poor" was a "terrible danger."[14]

Brown predicted the emergence of a new religion to replace the mainstream church and its individualism, aristocracy, privilege, oppression, tyr-
anny, darkness, superstition, and faithfulness to capitalism. Its adherents
would manfully reject the modern church and achieve Herron's "authority
of love" by moving toward socialism.[15]

The *Social Gospel*'s popularity caused a problem meeting demand because of their limited and outdated printing equipment. In the summer of
1898, Walter Vrooman of St. Louis and his brother Hiram of Washington,

D.C., gave Commonwealth a two-thousand-dollar printing press with sixty fonts of type and time-saving accessories. A New York brother chipped in seventy-five dollars to pay the freight. Before the press arrived in September, the colony doubled the size of its print shop. Steam powered, the new press gave the print shop the ability to not only preach its ideology but also seek out job printing as a source of additional income.[16]

Even that press proved inadequate, and their equipment continued to hamper them. Within months, workers expressed a need for both a cylinder and jobber press, which would equip them for more printing business. In January 1899, they appealed again for another press after the older one stalled the January edition of the *Social Gospel*. It was in such poor condition that one of the pressmen said it was the only job press in the country that required three men to operate. They lamented the fact that there were good presses everywhere going unused—wrecked on "the sea of competition." Two Boston women gave them one hundred dollars to help meet their need for a press, and a Washington, D.C., brother sent twenty-five. They located a secondhand press that could buy for two hundred twenty-five plus fifty dollars for freight. Another hundred dollars would buy the type. It would put the journal "on its feet," and they pleaded for help to raise the balance. At the same time, they hinted that five hundred dollars could buy a cylinder press and type that would fulfill all their needs.[17]

Donations became unnecessary when, in March 1899, Paul Koetitz of Pennsylvania donated a large, high-quality power cylinder press to Commonwealth. It was a two-revolution job and book press with a capacity of fifteen hundred compressions per hour. Seven years old, the press had originally cost $2,225. Commonwealth used the $165 in contributions to pay to ship and install the press. In April, the press arrived by railroad, and Koetitz arrived a few days later after visiting Ruskin. Koetitz, Charles Cook, and a visiting printer set up the press and printed the *Social Gospel*'s May edition. The editors rejoiced over having a first-class press, which would "increase their usefulness." They could easily publish the journal and books of brotherhood literature and "do great educational work for social regeneration." To them, it was an indication of the community's progress.[18]

Despite obstacles, the *Social Gospel* continued to improve. They enlarged the print shop and added presses but still had to postpone filling subscriptions and were unable to provide back issues for lack of supply. They purchased new photographic equipment, and George Damon produced a set of group pictures and village landscapes that, with aid from T. Atworth of the

Brooklyn Daily Eagle, were published in the *Social Gospel* and sold to the public.[19]

When a lawsuit filed by a textbook monopoly forced the *Kingdom* to stop publication, the *Social Gospel* agreed to fill some of its subscriptions, which put more pressure on the print shop.[20] Nevertheless, it was a tremendous success. The journal circulated widely, and its circulation could have been larger except for their limited press capacity.

It was sent to every state in the union and seventeen countries, including New Zealand, Australia, Canada, England, Palestine, France, Belgium, England, Scotland, Switzerland, Germany, Hungary, Russia, Austria-Hungary, Japan, and several in Africa. The editors had to convince skeptics that the colony was a real, live, working colony. In a rosy portrayal, they assured the curious that none at Commonwealth were "ever hungry, or cold, or insufficiently clad, or out of work, or anxious for the morrow." Despite its size, it was a movement that planned to "everywhere meet the needs of humanity." It disappointed some radicals because it was a careful "appreciation of the good that is everywhere" rather than a journal of "the ranting kind of cocksure socialism."[21]

The *Social Gospel* received praise and support beyond anything the community expected. By August 1898, internal opposition had vanished and there was wholehearted support to make it the best reform publication in the country. Lack of equipment hindered their efforts, but they had learned from experience and practiced excellent workmanship regardless of their equipment. The *New York Sun* praised the journal's craftsmanship: "Considering the exceeding cramped facilities, the typographical neatness of the journal alone is remarkable. Published right out in the woods, in a little one-story building, it is a magazine that would do credit in general appearance to a good-sized publishing house."[22]

As a reform journal, it was well received across the nation. The *Commons*, a Chicago journal edited by Graham Taylor and presenting the "social settlement point of view," called it "the brightest, cleanest, most sweet-tempered publication. . . . There is never a harsh or hateful word in it from cover to cover, and never a flat or platitudinous line."[23]

Columbus newspapers called the *Social Gospel* a "neat and attractive" magazine filled with information about the colony and its "neighbor-love" movement. Even though published in a small building with inadequate equipment, the journal's "appearance typographically, compared well with the foremost magazines of the day." To them, it reflected credibly on Commonwealth's energy and ingenuity. The *Macon News* called it a "neatly printed" publication with "excellent" typographical work.[24]

The *Social Gospel* reported on Commonwealth's activities monthly. It described conditions honestly and cautioned readers that one could be miserable there. People who drew their pleasures from material goods, choice foods, expensive clothing, fancy furniture, and fine homes would find little to enjoy. One's happiness depended on one's spirit. If living unselfishly in the moral sphere was appealing, there was no better place than Commonwealth. Living freely and faithfully as brothers and laboring with love for all would bring joy to one's life.[25]

The journal warned potential members not to come to find ease or to think that Commonwealth had resolved everything and that all its people were angelic. They had withdrawn not to escape evil but to grapple with it to prove that good was stronger. Mutual respect was not universal, but members were moving toward perfection through revelations of their imperfections. They reminded readers that "in the ordinary family, imperfections are expected and mutual forbearance is exercised." So it was in the larger family called brotherhood.[26]

The *Social Gospel* reported members' accounts of their experiences. One of the most poignant was a letter from Ruth Damon to a northern friend "who is still out in anarchy." Ruth, sixteen years old, was an earnest and enthusiastic worker for Commonwealth's principles and, like most of the children, among the "best cooperators." Sweet tempered, loving, and affectionate, she did everything she could to make others happy.[27]

In December 1898, she wrote,

> There are about eighty of us in the colony now, and we are all of us happy and contented.... Everything here is classed as ours, not yours or mine. Nearly everything is held in common.... We are one big happy family, and this is the most unselfish way there is to live. We are nearly always happy. Every individual looks out for the other's needs and wants, and by that way none are left to suffer. I would not exchange this life for any sum of money.
>
> Our motto is "From each according to his ability; to each according to his need," I think it is the only way this wicked world can be awakened to righteousness and Christianity.
>
> If everyone lived as we are living here at Commonwealth, there would be no rich and poor.
>
> I most sincerely believe nothing could induce me to give up this grand,

noble work which, I am convinced, meets with God's most sincere approval. . . . I WILL become something more than a mere self-seeker who breathes, eats, sleeps and works a little and cares only for worldly pleasures.

Think of these hard headed business men who glory over their gains and live off of the poor, while the poor are dying from cold and starvation, and even the ground they are buried on, sometimes, is all but denied them. Some men are rich in money, but poor . . . in God's blessings. Think of John D. Rockefeller, what he is making off of the poor and needy! It's an awful sin, and the older I get the wiser I become on such things, and the less I love riches.

I would rather be as poor as a church mouse all my life, but one of God's chosen helpers, than to live in luxury and wealth, but be one of Satan's followers.[28]

Commonwealth received thousands of letters of interest and support. Community members came together weekly to hear letters read. They made listeners aware of the quality and strength of their influence, which boosted community morale. The accolades were endless. People from outside commended Commonwealth with admiration and love. "Rich men, businessmen, college professors, even two men prominent in politics added their words of praise." "You will show the world that Jesus' teachings are practicable." "As I read The Social Gospel, my heart burned with joy." "The Social Gospel goes to the heart of the social question." "You are inspired by the spirit of Christ." A well-known international scholar and thinker wrote, "I trust that The Social Gospel's mission as an illuminant will be accompanied with increasing proof of successful effectiveness."[29]

Letter writers frequently "expressed longing for the life at Commonwealth." A Missouri "Cooperator" wrote critiquing "the old machine—commercial, state, church, society" as decrepit, cumbersome, and wasteful. Taking Commonwealth as his model, he appealed for a new industrial machine—an Equitable Labor Co-partnership, an educated, self-governing, nonresisting, service-rendering, voluntary, federated Commonwealth.[30]

Gibson answered many of the queries in the Social Gospel. In August 1898, he printed two pages of "Questions and Answers." It is not clear if he fabricated and then answered them or if he extracted them from Commonwealth's correspondence. Regardless, they answered many questions about the community, including size, relations with outsiders, living and working conditions, family life, amusements, and religion.[31]

One St. Louis preacher, after he heard about a surplus of single men at Commonwealth, asked if the community had room "for cultivated, Christian single ladies, thirty-five to forty-two years of age." They were church members seeking a secure home and society. The editors responded that they would be welcome, quoting the Bible: "He setteth the solitary in families." Appealing to both sexes, they acknowledged that Commonwealth had single men and women, "delightful bachelors and 'picturesque schoolma'ams,'" and if someone wished for a wedding, ministers' services were free and a cottage provided.[32]

Reverend E. N. Potter, president of Hobart College, wrote an encouraging letter to Gibson:

> The Commonwealth may be circumscribed in means and members, yet . . . the last shall be first, the least greatest, is the law of Christ's kingdom. *The Social Gospel* and the "Social Incarnation" are . . . for Christians who, in increasing numbers, are asking, what shall we do to make life less worldly, selfishly self-seeking, and more Christ-like? An earnest and inquiring spirit is abroad, and there is growth and movement toward the consummation when the kingdoms and governments of this world shall become the kingdom of our God and of His Christ.[33]

Some letters offered well-meaning criticism. Others were highly critical and expressed disappointment. In July 1899, a "good man" who was interested in Commonwealth wrote that he and his wife were depressed over the deaths and disease at the community:

> We were not surprised at the trouble but believe insufficient food made not only ugly people but weak people. . . . You are so infatuated with your own ideas that you cannot or will not see that there is a limit beyond which it is wrong to pass in taking in penniless people . . . jeopardizing the whole colony by reducing rations to the danger line.
>
> How do you expect to get such men as I am, to work to earn money for other men to consume in tobacco eating?
>
> It is a shame that the kingdom of Heaven should be begging for something to eat all the time when there are Sons of God with plenty kept out by a horde of penniless tobacco-eaters and imbeciles.
>
> I am full of sympathy with any movement that will help society and promote the interests of Christ's kingdom. But whatever you people may be able to do living on horsefeed, I am certain we can never live that way and do anything.
>
> I was making all calculation to see you very soon. But now I am rattled.

Gibson responded that the sickness and deaths were not attributable to poor food but valued the letter because it furnished a basis for every reader to test himself.[34]

The *Social Gospel* promoted a correspondence exchange with British workers interested in social democracy and labor reform, which led to significant English support and interest. Keir Hardie, a Scottish socialist and the first Labour Party member of Parliament, supported the colony. After reading its journal, several members of Bruce Wallace's Brotherhood Church expressed an interest in working at Commonwealth. Two of them, Daniel Franks and his wife, came from London and joined the community. Both of them were "strong of heart, cheery, sweet-spirited and lovable," and the community offered a hearty welcome. Their commitment at a time when Commonwealth was struggling was appreciated. Daniel worked in the nursery and orchard and cared for the rabbits. A few weeks after his arrival, he conducted the morning service and gave an account of the Christian Socialist and brotherhood movements in London. He told them about Wallace's Brotherhood Church and the Brotherhood Trust as well as lesser-known groups of social reformers. Greatly appreciated as a teacher and song leader, he took over the children's group in Sunday school. Another Londoner praised Commonwealth for living as "economic Christians," seeking not to get but to give.[35]

Back home, a Pennsylvanian wrote, "We are in hearty sympathy with you in your work, and have many times talked of coming to you," but we are not clear on our part. A reader from New Jersey wrote, "Your reform work is destined to occupy a place of honor for actual results and influence for good," and the *Social Gospel* "is the most interesting, the most inspiring" paper. A Kentucky writer asked the Lord for help and permission to cast his lot with Commonwealth and "endure hardness." But an Ohio man desperately wrote, "I wish I and mine were with you. I am tired and sick of the struggle," but his wife's resistance and their finances kept him away.[36]

Agnes Leonard Hill, a Chicago evangelical pastor and esteemed lecturer on social questions, wrote that Commonwealth burned in her heart. It was like the Star in the East leading one to the Messiah. Demonstrating the Christ spirit of brotherly love was a splendid cause. The *Social Gospel* published her poetry, which reflected the colony's values. "Joy to labor doth belong.... Work is worship," she wrote as she appealed to the "pilgrims" to have courage. A Florida couple liked their way of living because it was the "Bible way."[37]

The editors welcomed letters of praise but admitted that the most gratifying letters were those that ordered subscriptions or offered donations.

There was no shame in their appeals for donations, and they were thankful for them. The donations were intended not to help members themselves but to spread the gospel of brotherhood "for the world." In June, they had overdue debts and needed a small engine to run the printing press, wood saw, cane mill, irrigation pump, and anticipated laundry machinery. In each case, they appealed to "friends" for help. Requests were not limited to cash or equipment. In mid-1898, they asked for twenty-five or more songbooks.[38]

In one response, a Wisconsin letter writer paraphrased the twenty-third Psalm, hoped the Right Relationship League would be Commonwealth's "right hand," sent a donation, and ordered a subscription to the *Social Gospel*. Joseph Baker of Iowa made a generous offer to help settle the debt. He put an eleven-room house in Des Moines up for sale to pay one-fourth of Commonwealth's debt outright and loan it the balance for five years at no interest.[39]

The *Social Gospel* tried to acknowledge all donations, even the smallest. The journal thanked two Augusta, Georgia, men, Berry Benson and Andrew Mulcay, for theirs. Mulcay was an organizer for the American Federation of Labor. Benson had been a Confederate sharpshooter during the Civil War who later supported textile worker strikes, helped feed poor black families in Augusta, and defended Leo Frank in his Atlanta trial for the alleged rape of a young girl.[40]

Many *Social Gospel* readers and writers were "leaders among the people" and prominent in social reform. George Herron, Edward Everett Hale, and Sam Jones sent testimonials. Boston reformers Vida Scudder and Reverend Charles Dole were subscribers and correspondents. In Britain, readers included Vladimir Chertkov and J. Bruce Wallace, who edited the journal *Brotherhood*, one of Commonwealth's most prized exchanges. The *Social Gospel* recommended it as a matter of pure love to extend the brotherhood movement's influence.[41]

Herron's writings frequently appeared, especially in the early issues. He asserted, in "Christ's Economic of Distribution," that none of Jesus's teachings were "practicable in any other than a communistic order of society." The first summer, he wrote that Jesus was "the most radical revolutionist that ever came to the earth." Tolstoy, Marx, and George were "dogged conservatives" compared to Jesus. Only he risked and lost his life in the cause of revolution.[42]

Later that year, the journal quoted a Herron graduation speech at Kansas State Agricultural College describing the difficulty businessmen faced when following Christian principles and competing with those who did not. But

Herron also deprecated Christian reformers who formed colonies. The *Social Gospel*'s editors asked that he clarify his position, and he responded with a long article. He warned that colonies had social separation as their goal and that one could not save the world by giving it up. He admitted that colonies had value educating people by illustrating socialist principles. He commended Commonwealth and Ruskin for their sacrifice and remained a defender and supporter of their efforts. Nevertheless, Gibson took exception to Herron's implication that colonies were escapist and that "we must all sin together until we are all willing to be saved together." Holding a more conservative perspective, Gibson believed that individuals who repented of their sin and turned away from a sinful world could bring social salvation and thought that Commonwealth's people demonstrated, as individuals, God's standard for the whole world.[43]

Despite the disagreement, when Iowa College trustees asked Herron to resign because of displeasure with his biblical interpretations and their impact on endowments, the *Social Gospel* jumped to his defense. It raised the issue of academic freedom and printed a letter in which Herron defended the "liberty of truth" against the "control and intimidation of money" and rejected any concern for his fate, stating that he was ready to give his life to "destroy the spirit of materialism." If he was unsuccessful in using biblical truth to destroy materialism, Herron asked, what would the world and the church do with the message of Jesus? George Gates, the college's president, defended Herron and diverted the attack, but most observers thought he would not return for another year.[44]

They were right. Herron resigned on October 13, 1899. The *Social Gospel* printed a supplement containing his magnanimous, four-page letter of resignation in which he defended his teaching but acknowledged that the trustees had the right to remove him for the college's welfare. The editors added a biting critique: "Institutional Christianity will not peacefully permit Christianity to be applied even to itself."[45]

The following month, the editors revisited the issue, publishing statements by Herron's colleagues and the college board of trustees. The faculty were complimentary. Praising Herron for the "manly way" in which he performed his duty, they assured everybody of the cordial and kindly relations between them. They thanked Herron's patron, Mrs. Rand, for continuing her endowment and reaffirmed support for the Department of Applied Christianity that Herron had chaired. Last, they assured Herron he would always be welcome and hoped to hear his voice among them.[46]

The trustees essentially repeated the faculty's opinion of Herron. They found him kind, considerate, and respectful of their position. Admitting that they did not agree with his views, they believed that they had been careful not to interfere with his freedom of speech. They supported the fundamental teaching of his department, that the religion and spirit of Jesus Christ should guide the conduct of men, and concluded that Herron was doing much good. Finally, they thanked Mrs. Rand for waiving the conditions attached to the endowment and allowing the trustees to manage it.[47]

The *Social Gospel* followed up by fabricating a "symposium" using letters received from prominent national leaders, including Reverend William Thurston Brown, of the journal's editorial staff, and Henry Demarest Lloyd, Bolton Hall, Franklin Wentworth, and George Shibley. Brown commended Herron for "breathing the spirit of manliness and love." Wentworth believed that Herron's resignation was inevitable because he challenged the special privilege that was perpetuated by American higher education and refused to let it muzzle him. James Canfield, the chancellor of the University of Nebraska, which had Herron speak at its 1894 commencement, to the chagrin of the plutocratic governor and conservatives, called Herron a prophet and dreamer who could never be a mere instructor in an educational institution. Shibley asserted that academic freedom regarding class did not exist in colleges and universities controlled by wealthy donors and their political allies.

Lloyd, on the other hand, was angry that Herron refused to withdraw the endowment from the college. He could have used it elsewhere to advance the "true spirit of the 'social gospel.'" Instead, they would use it to replace him with a conservative professor. Eltweed Pomeroy agreed with Lloyd. The endowment was for Herron's teaching, and he should not have left it at the college. The radical cause was impoverished and could use it. The publication of Lloyd's letter opened a rift with Gibson. Lloyd had intended for his letter to be private and was disturbed by its release because he reversed his opinion after corresponding with Herron. He cautioned that reformers would not have success until they "learn to pull together."[48]

The editors concluded that Herron's forced resignation demonstrated the church's commitment to the "present selfish order of society." Dependent on the wealthy elites, it would not allow professors or preachers to criticize its methods or apply Christianity to life's affairs.

Vida Scudder, inspired by Saint Francis and a visit to Assisi, was a *Social Gospel* reader and active supporter of the community. Realizing "that the difficulty is not to state the truth, but to make it operative," she admired Commonwealth's commitment to Christian simplicity, love, and brotherhood. She frequently wrote to the editors "because you out in Georgia are furnishing the example, which stimulates ... many of us are watching you wistfully and lovingly." A few months later, she explained why she could not join. Like Lloyd, Crosby, Bliss, and B. O. Flower, she belonged "to that inferior and outer circle ... of persons who ... still seem entangled in the present state of things by many threads of private duty."[49]

Gibson was impressed with Scudder's optimistic vision of social progress toward social democracy. She believed that diverse groups of people were striving for the regeneration of society under conditions of universal freedom, justice, and fellowship. Her view that democracy required sacrifice resonated in the community's ideology. The editors liked Scudder's work so much that they published excerpts that supported Commonwealth's ideals. In "The New Intuition," she argued that ideals and beliefs were rapidly changing in the nineteenth century, and reformers were reasserting with renewed resolution the words of Christ spoken nineteen hundred years ago. Believing that conscience and thought would inevitably lead to socialism, she praised the Christian's impulse to make it "his business to translate the great social petitions of the Lord's Prayer into action."[50]

Long before diversity became fashionable, the *Social Gospel* published articles one would not expect to see in a Christian journal. An article on social ethics used excerpts on Taoism from Laozi's *Tao Te Ching*. After criticizing Confucianism as shallow compared to Taoism, the article reinforced Commonwealth's values: have compassion, live economically, do not strive to come to the front, practice nonassertion, excel but do not rule, act but do not take credit.[51]

Ernest Howard Crosby compared Burmese Buddhism favorably to Christianity. He began ironically, noting that England sent missionaries to uplift the Burmese race by offering "counterfeit civilization and religion." The English made war everywhere, while Buddhism forbade killing. The English spent their lives accumulating property while a Buddhist was satisfied with a few simple wants. Buddhists believed government control was one of life's great evils. Crosby acknowledged the similar ideals of Buddhism and Christianity but thought Buddhists practiced them better. But he believed that the Christian Commonwealth could also realize those ideals.[52]

Despite its optimism regarding its fate, Commonwealth felt anxiety about global conditions. Some members feared revolution but hoped it would be peaceful and orderly. It would need to follow God's truth to avoid violence, and the conservative classes would have to allow such change. However, they were not optimistic about breaking conservatism's hold. It was full of sublime self-satisfaction, worship of the past, and contentment with the present order and feared change, even less extreme, in America.[53]

In response to the inequality and business panics that representative government showed no signs of addressing, the editors again anticipated progressivism by supporting "pure democracy" through "direct legislation," the initiative, referendum, and "imperative mandate." To achieve those goals, they proposed revising the constitution, which they thought was out of date. Voting reforms would challenge the professional politicians, secure the municipal ownership, and nationalize the "natural monopolies" and be a step toward the cooperative age. They supported Eltweed Pomeroy, a *Social Gospel* contributor and president of the National Direct Legislation League. They quoted the *Direct Legislation Record* on its progress, citing, as examples, South Dakota, as the first state to adopt it, thirty-one laws in Iowa providing for the initiative on subjects such as highways, textbooks, and liquor, and Switzerland's successful use of the direct vote. They insisted that legislation should be direct and should extend suffrage to women. They also modified their view of militaristic nationalist Theodore Roosevelt, commending him for his progressive attitude on the question and his independent conduct on making appointments.[54]

In addition to publicizing Commonwealth and its ideals, the *Social Gospel* reviewed current events in a desire to remain involved with the world and not escape it. Its monthly column "Progress" disseminated information on reforms and provided contact information for reform papers and organizations. The column often presented issues and publicized organizations that reflected the community's efforts.

Commonwealth paid close attention to municipal reform because of Albertson's and others' experience with urban life and their Chicago supporters. Cities and industries that did not show progress in reform received harsh criticism. Comparing Boston to New York, the *Social Gospel* noted that Boston held summer camps for poor boys, offered free baths, swimming lessons, and outdoor concerts, and built a huge bathhouse and gymnasiums. What had New York done? Built an eight-million-dollar "speedway" for horse racing. On the other hand, the journal praised the construction of the underground and elevated rapid-transit system, which would provide "needed relief to the thousands of salary-slaves of New York" who lived far from their workplace. Still, they wondered what New York would be like when the "mad rush ends." Would the living be better in "Jawgy"?[55]

The *Social Gospel* favored municipal ownership, an important progressive proposal. Many in Commonwealth supported it, and the journal reported positively on Huddersfield, England, which furnished transportation, gas, electricity, stoves, fuel, houses, and beef from abattoirs to its residents. On the other hand, it printed an article by W. H. Van Ornum, an anarchist, who argued that piecemeal government-sponsored reforms, such as municipal ownership or public washhouses, changed nothing. The old conditions would remain. "Jesus had said sell all and give it to the poor. All, not a part." In a statement that found support in Commonwealth, Van Ornum stated that only the communism of the early church could abolish poverty and raise the poor to equality. Ernest Howard Crosby followed that with an alternative to municipal ownership that accomplished the same thing without strengthening government power. He proposed "voluntary associations of citizens" who subscribed to stock in a trust that would render services at cost and without profit.[56]

When Jones ran for reelection, the *Social Gospel* viewed his supporters as a better measure of Toledo's Christianity than the city's church rolls. The editors celebrated his victory as an independent who received nearly double the votes cast for the Republican and Democratic candidates combined. An avowed Christian Socialist, Jones supported municipal ownership, a minimum wage, and labor unions and overcame charges that he would implement ruinous taxes, which would drive investment away from Toledo.[57]

The *Social Gospel* regularly reviewed and recommended pamphlets on cooperation and Christian Socialism. Imogen C. Fales, a Populist turned socialist, had a pamphlet that described worldwide attempts at cooperation, published by the National American Woman Suffrage Association. C. W. Woolridge, an English immigrant, medical doctor, and utopian writer, wrote *The Kingdom of Heaven Is at Hand*, which the Ruskin community published. The *Social Gospel* reviewer commended it highly.[58]

The journal regularly passed on information about other colonies and colonization schemes. It referred to Ruskin often and printed the proposal of Luther S. Kaufman, a member of the Christian Socialist Church of Philadelphia, to start a joint-stock colony on the Ruskin model. To finance it, he proposed to sell shares at one hundred dollars each and then incorporate it. There is no evidence that the colony ever functioned, but years later

Kaufman ran for political office several times on the Progressive ticket. The *Social Gospel* also publicized the Niksur Cooperative Association and its *Niksur Magazine* from Minneapolis, Minnesota, and the Ridgeville Cooperative Association in Illinois, both colonies based on the Ruskin plan.[59]

Commonwealth and the Ruskin Cooperative Association differed in significant ways. Still, the *Social Gospel* spoke reverently of John Ruskin's ideas and frequently printed brief quotes from Ruskin that had much in common with Commonwealth's ideology. His militant exposition of Christian economics and biting critique of the anti-Christian character of the existence of luxury side by side with miserable, unacceptable social conditions resonated in the minds of Commonwealth's members. When John Ruskin died in early 1900, the *Social Gospel* printed a testimonial by the artist John Ward Stimson, who praised Ruskin highly but warned reformers not to neglect the beautiful. "Religion must comprehend Love-for-the Beautiful and service-for-all."[60]

When Ruskin's weekly, the *Coming Nation*, solicited news from Commonwealth, Gibson responded pleasantly and spoke kindly of Ruskin, praising it as a prosperous colony whose ideal was brotherhood. With two hundred fifty members, there was no colony practicing industrial cooperation and political socialism that was better known. Despite the praise, Gibson was somewhat self-righteously critical. Ruskin's membership fee of five hundred dollars "shuts out of brotherhood association all who have less." Commonwealth had "open gates dividing everything we have with everyone who comes, tramps and all." Ruskin's "narrow, stock company" approach was a "selfish sort of salvation."[61]

In July 1899, the *Social Gospel* sadly reported Ruskin's breakup and the sale of its land. Some members reorganized as the Ruskin Commonwealth and purchased the *Coming Nation*. They merged with the Duke colony west of Waycross, Georgia, two hundred miles east of Commonwealth, where the local population warmly welcomed them. Commonwealth's August business meeting passed resolutions congratulating the Ruskin Commonwealth on their "wise plan of organization." They foresaw them becoming "a city set on a hill" as they "labor for the coming of the Kingdom of Heaven."[62]

They noted the success of Fairhope, the single tax colony attempting to prove that Henry George's theories were workable and recommended the *Fairhope Courier* for more information. The *Courier* reciprocated, publishing articles about Commonwealth that led to letters of inquiry about the community.[63]

Albert Owen, the founder of the Topolobampo, Mexico, community, received positive accolades for his writings. *A Dream of an Ideal City* was his notion of a perfect city and society. In another work, he proposed creating jobs for the unemployed by using scrip-paid labor for public improvements and utilities instead of incurring the debts and interest expense of bonds. The scrip would then be receivable for taxes.[64]

The *Social Gospel* reported on the Jewish agricultural colonies that became numerous in late nineteenth-century America. The Jewish National Farm School in Pennsylvania, whose purpose was to train Jewish boys as scientific farmers so that they could become managers in agricultural colonies, was preparing "the way for socialistic farming in the brotherhood life of the future."[65]

Outside of the United States, a New Zealand cooperative got their attention, which demonstrated Commonwealth's interest in the outside world and the world's interest in them. Founded by A. W. Bickerton, a professor of chemistry and physics, Wainoni was a "federative home" influenced by the Christian spirit of Commonwealth and Bickerton's reading of the *Social Gospel*.[66]

Contributors to the *Social Gospel* gave cooperative plans and societies positive attention. For most, cooperation was a form of service and sacrifice, which was the essential spirit of religion. Frederic O. MacCartney, a Unitarian minister and socialist politician, wrote about the Rochdale Plan, which applied the spirit of religion to the production and distribution of goods. He stated that a socialist administration with unity and community in commodities could supply the needs of everyone. MacCartney reinforced Commonwealth's faith in itself when he wrote, "A movement which is permeated by the spirit of service and sacrifice, which has brotherhood for its ideal, will produce an environment favorable to an awakening of the God-consciousness in the hearts of men."[67]

When Eltweed Pomeroy convened a National Social and Political Conference in Buffalo to consider "what is the next step to take" to reform American politics and economics, Albertson parroted Charles Sheldon by asking, "What would Jesus do?" He answered his question with the Commonwealth creed, "Demonstrate Love." Over a hundred fifty delegates attended the conference. Over four days, a brilliant body of reformers discussed everything from municipal ownership to temperance, industrial cooperation, and the formation of a new political party. They had a stormy debate over Bolton Hall's resolution demanding the immediate withdrawal of American troops from the Philippines and adopted a resolution by George Herron condemning militarism and plutocracy.[68]

Commonwealth's ambitions reflected that goal. Education was important, and the *Social Gospel* regularly reviewed "progress" in that field. They were especially interested in the Commonwealth University, a correspondence college presided over by E. N. Potter, former president of Hobart College. It was a free tuition institution devoted to academic instruction. It was open to both genders and offered no degrees, only certificates showing the courses taken. Commonwealth's editors viewed it favorably because it would enhance the "progress of the plain people." It enrolled over twelve thousand students in its first few months and claimed to have more students than were attending all of the colleges and universities in the country.[69] With free tuition, no admission requirements, and no degrees, it resembled, minus the electronics, some of the contemporary MOOCs. Similarly, some "legitimate" universities strongly attacked it.[70]

Political repression in higher education was endangering academic freedom, not because of its radicalism but for expressing views that displeased the colleges' wealthy donors. Gibson and Albertson became disturbed when the Kansas Republican governor, responding to protests, replaced two Populists on the Board of Regents of the State Agricultural College with Republicans and then had the board discharge the college's president, Thomas Will, and four professors for "violating" their contracts. The board accused the professors of rejecting the divinity of Jesus. The truth was that they had invited George Herron and William Jennings Bryan as commencement speakers and were in "opposition to the selfishness which dethrones Jesus, opposition to the rule of economic might, and insistence that the law of love and of equal right has some claim and is a higher wisdom." The fired faculty were on a "free, fearless, severe search for truth along economic and sociological lines, which search of course is dangerous to established error and injustice. But the party in power now proposes to change the course of study by cutting out much if not all study of sociology and political economy as branches not needed by the sons and daughters of farmers and mechanics."[71] In the *Social Gospel*, they urged Will and the professors Frank Parsons, Arnold Emch, Edward Bemis, and Duren Ward to join John R. Commons, who had just been fired from Syracuse University, to "gather together and open a school of Sociology for the people."

In July 1899, the Buffalo Conference, attempting to prevent the wealthy from controlling education, founded the College of Social Science to teach and study social and economic subjects without fear of repercussions. Modeled on the Chautauqua correspondence school, it offered seven courses on social and political issues, history, and economics. Its board of trustees raised fifteen thousand dollars for faculty contracts. Thomas Will became the first president, and recently fired faculty became the professors. The *Social Gospel* editors heartily endorsed the college, provided its contact information, and asked that responses to letters of inquiry and application mention the journal. The conference also proposed a New School of Economics, with the same faculty, a physical plant, and a journal.[72]

When Gibson learned of Will's ideological perspective, he invited him to become an associate editor, and Will began writing regularly for the journal. His first article was a history of education and how it had evolved from an institution dominated by theology into a field deeply influenced by modern science. Humans too had evolved from seeking salvation in the next life to accepting their duty to redeem humanity through the Kingdom of God on earth. Impressed by the material gains created by modern science and technology, Will asserted that the wealth produced must be distributed equally and justly.[73]

Will repeatedly criticized the harmful influence of wealth on politics and education. He wrote that in 1900 "wealth rules the world," passes self-serving laws, and strikes down or evades laws that it finds inconvenient. For Will, "We must educate or perish" and teach political and economic history and ethics in every college and university. That is why the Buffalo Conference organized a new educational institution, "independent of the paralyzing influences of monopoly and class privilege."[74]

A year later, Will wrote an article called "Tendencies towards Socialism." Modern capitalists, in pursuit of maximum profits, adopted the principle of concentration. He accused department stores like Marshall Field's of ruining small shopkeepers and trusts like Standard Oil of destroying small producers. Simultaneously, the government was concentrating courts, armies, schools, utilities, and transportation to benefit its citizens. "What shall we do with the trusts?," Will asked. "Nationalize them in the interests of the public!" was his answer. He noted that education at Kansas State Agricultural College had been free, and the school provided students with meals, goods, and services at cost. Was it socialism? Yes, but wasn't everything that came from most governments socialism? It was, so how could anyone argue that the tendency toward socialism was bad?[75]

An interesting column in the *Social Gospel* was that of the "Old Gentleman." He was a child during the Civil War, but his identity is not clear. He might have been a teacher in the school because he wrote about students handing in papers. He admitted to not being a scholar but believed that "the 'untutored mind' is competent for valid thinking about the greatest subjects." His observations were brief, sometimes biting, insights into the world's activities. He thought the war with Spain was "hideous" but did not rule out the possibility that the United States had a "destiny" to create "a better order of life in the world." The courage and heroism American soldiers and sailors displayed impressed the Old Gentleman. Still, he was concerned for the "soldier boys" who were subjected to "all manner of moral and physical infection, neglected, cheated, starved, stormed at with shot and shell, herded for transportation like cattle, landed on their native shore in the last stages of exhaustion and dejection." Fortunately, the suffering would end, but the global, industrial, and commercial war would be "stretched out to the crack of doom" by the wealthy and conservative classes.[76]

There was little that escaped the Old Gentleman's observation and curmudgeonly tone. He thought sarcasm was not necessarily a bad thing. Commenting ironically on the "degradation of literary style" and "bad workmanship" in publishing, he blamed it on the pursuit of profit and the "coming of cooperation," which gave the "blunderers" roles in the production of literary works. Another target was Theodore Roosevelt, who "rode roughshod over the English language" the same way he rode over the hills of Cuba.[77]

During the Christmas season, the Old Gentleman's sarcasm was in full force. He was "going to start a subscription paper to raise a handsome little purse for the minister, who is struggling along on a salary of four thousand dollars." Convinced that charity begins at home, he was going to get him a family Bible with "Morocco binding, hand-made paper, full gilt, and illuminated title page." The cost would support an Armenian orphan for months, so he would send a dollar to the Armenian relief fund. "A little would go so far!" Finally, he would "meditate on the bubonic plague, Russian famine, the war in Luzon, and the little disagreement in South Africa." It would calm his spirit to reflect that he was not afflicted like other men.[78]

Like Albertson, the Old Gentleman touted the "vigorous virtues" and "aggressive traits" of strong men. He was sure that "the gentleness of a strong man is gentler than the gentleness of a clam," and "abuse of gentleness is not only enfeebling and emasculating but calamitous and cruel." He also agreed with Albertson on settlement works' slow pace. He referred to the "Settlement Conference" issue of *Commons* as "pathetic" for its naïveté about the use of "sweetness and light" to ease people's burdens. "The economic problem which must be solved before right relations, good morals and good manners can be thoroughly achieved."[79]

"A black felt hat on a black wooly head under the blazing Georgia sun" seemed ridiculous to the Old Gentleman. His deeper concern was the vulgar Gilded Age society women who wasted more money on fashion than it would take to house a family for a year. The adoption of reasonable attire would make it possible for everyone to be properly dressed.[80]

Reaction to external affairs sometimes demonstrated the ambiguity of Commonwealth's ideology. Pronouncements of love, brotherhood, and non-resistance within the community were one thing, but members often took conflicting positions on the Spanish-American and Filipino wars and imperialism. Albertson, an inconsistent pacifist, opposed both wars. Others, torn between pacifistic love and patriotism, opposed imperialism but thought the wars helped unite a nation still divided by the Civil War.[81]

Initially they were mildly critical of the war. They pointed out the hypocrisy of celebrating a high mass with a choir singing Easter hymns on a naval ship in the Brooklyn Navy Yard while alongside the *Mayflower* was loading powder into her magazine and hammers and drills gave their chorus to Odin, the god of war. The church and state had entombed the teaching of Jesus. "Christ is not risen. He is crucified by their fighting."[82]

Ultimately, they accepted "that there must be war" but prayed for peace, mourned the deaths of soldiers on both sides, and asked that the vindictive, heathenish war cry "Remember the *Maine*" be replaced by "Cuba Libre." War for the "country's honor" was unacceptable. Only a war for peace that stopped the "needless shedding of Cuban and Filipino blood" was justifiable, and the United States must extricate itself quickly from both territories.[83]

Commonwealth's equivocation on war and imperialism disturbed Ernest Howard Crosby. He refused to believe the alleged humanitarian motives. As a member of the American Peace Society and head of the Anti-Imperialist League, he wrote that "there should be no 'but' and 'ifs' for Christians in this matter of war. War means hate; Christianity means love, and there can be no truce between them.... No argument whatever is admissible in its behalf, and only on the plea of some kind of insanity can the lips that defend it be recognized as other but savage and pagan." The war in Cuba "is a mad orgy of slaughter, it is a grand national 'drunk.'" It is a mockery of the "Prince of Peace."[84]

By July 1898, the editors noted a decline in the "war spirit." The Fourth of July festivities demonstrated that there was no decline in the love of the country, but the people preferred peace to war. The volunteer soldiers complained about conditions, which suggested that they had lost their enthusiasm. A few months later, the editors read George Kennan's testimony that the American wounded had endured suffering without complaint, but they countered that the rejoicing at war's end was dampened by mismanagement in the treatment of the sick and wounded, which resulted in unnecessary suffering and death.[85]

In the aftermath, the *Social Gospel*'s equivocation continued. They were glad that the war was short, the killing had ended, and the casualty count was low, and they celebrated the citizen-soldiers' manhood, fighting ability, and heroism. They were thankful that the Catholics had demonstrated loyal Americanism while fighting Spain. They were not yet aware of any aggrandizement or enrichment by the American government or any catastrophic result for the Spanish. Still, they did note the "melancholy spectacle of seemingly needless misery, starvation, and death which the nation had witnessed since the close of the war."[86]

Henry Demarest Lloyd, who had inspired Gibson and Albertson, was less equivocal than the *Social Gospel*. In the aftermath of the war, he wrote a biting article for the *New York Journal* in which he referred to capitalism as the "religion of Self-Interest" that brought America, "in peace and war," slums and camps, workless men and working children and soldiers dying of typhoid because capitalists and politicians would not provide shelter, food, and medicine.[87]

From the children's song on the accomplishments of Commodore Dewey to Walter Vrooman's pronouncement of the "beautiful possibilities of Cuba," some members viewed American imperialism as progressive. But a few months later, Commonwealth abandoned its ambiguity with a more critical posture. It represented the community's diverse views, but many articles were unsigned, so individual attitudes were unclear. In January 1899, the *Social Gospel* published a blistering evaluation of America's postwar behavior. "Our greed has put [the Spaniards'] greed in a mild light. We have grabbed all we could and kept it fast. We are hungry for more, we need it. We are well known by millions of people as Yankee pigs. We have lied to all the world about territorial expansion.... In remembering the Maine, we have forgotten Christ."[88]

James Kelley offered a more nuanced perspective. Acknowledging that, in the beginning, the United States had denied any desire to control Spanish possessions, Kelley chose not to see it as a "lie." He believed that pragmatism, military necessity, and events had created a need for a responsibility that we could not evade. He even delved into the constitutionality of acquiring territory in a way that resonated with the modern debate over the original document. The founders had acted "according to their own lights and the logic of events." Now, "we shall make our constitution as we go along."[89]

After Rudyard Kipling's poem "The White Man's Burden" came out, the *Social Gospel* printed a lengthy article analyzing its message. Many believed that the United States would govern the captured colonies better than Spain and saw taking up the "white man's burden" as a "duty" to "weaker and semi-civilized peoples," not a benefit. However, they feared that the rationale of moral obligation would furnish "a cloak for the ambition and greed of those who are in power." In referring to "strong races" and "weak child-peoples," it also reflected the racial and ethnic temper of the times. The Dutch in Indonesia, the British in India, and the Americans elsewhere had mixed motives, but they were bringing peace, infrastructure, and medical care to these territories despite the exploitation. "War to prevent war," building railroads, and stamping out yellow fever were fulfilling a moral obligation.[90]

After the war, the editors were encouraged that Congress convened a committee to investigate the corporate greed that had been widespread during the war and had aroused an avalanche of popular anger. The *Social Gospel* reported several examples. The government was paying fifteen hundred dollars per day for each privately owned ship sitting in Manila harbor waiting to be unloaded. Some had been waiting for as long as forty days. The same thing was happening in Santiago, Cuba. In Tampa, Florida, railroads were charging the U.S. Army higher local freight rates for the long-distance traffic passing over their lines. The editors hoped the committee's findings would arouse popular support for government ownership.[91]

The *Social Gospel* became increasingly impatient with affairs in Cuba and the Philippines. They conceded that brigandage was down and the United States was controlling yellow fever better. Still, starvation and industrial prostration continued while the American governor-general spent a hundred thousand dollars to renovate a palace for his headquarters and received an allowance of seventy-five hundred dollars a year to maintain his trappings of royalty. They insisted it was time for Cuban home rule, quoting the congressional pledge: "The United States hereby disclaims any disposition or intention to exercise sovereignty jurisdiction or control over said island, except for pacification thereof, and asserts its determination ... to leave the government and control of the island to the people."[92]

Drawing on its ideals, the *Social Gospel* stated the "truth is that we belong to the Filipinos, as to the Cubans, and must render them any and every possible service in their political and industrial and moral life." It suggested that we learn from Father William Duncan's efforts with Alaska Natives at Metlakatla. He encountered a "degraded set, many of the tribes being cannibals." He formed a cooperative community of one thousand educated Natives who lived peaceably and comfortably in a communistic way. Nevertheless, Commonwealth remained skeptical of a positive outcome in the Philippines. It condemned the press censorship and presidential silence when the slaughter of the Filipino insurgents and the "orgy of looting and wanton destruction" became known. Was McKinley merely the "high-handed instrument of American mammonistic ambition" or the executive of great democratic duties? The editors could not decide. Commenting on the soldiers' suffering and the deaths of "deluded" Filipinos, they feared subjugation was necessary to "convince the Filipinos that we are their friends." Despite their fault finding, they continued to laud Admiral George Dewey for his courage, discipline, good sense, and success. The manhood of a warrior who demonstrates the "supreme beauty and worth of the higher life" should not be invalidated by his achievement on a lower plane.[93]

The *Social Gospel* thought Emilio Aguinaldo displayed encouraging abilities and powers despite representing a "low order of civilization." They believed a Filipino government would be as effective as a McKinley government, but a native government would not promote the interests of American capital and commerce, a priority after the war. Responding to a *Munsey's* article arguing that "development, exploitation, and investment" would increase the demand for products of the American worker, they stated that only capitalists would benefit. To confirm their views, they quoted Senator Beveridge: "We value them by the standard of their commercial usefulness, and by no other."

They feared that the Filipinos would be ill fitted for serfdom or citizenship because of their deep hatred of those who had "whipped them." Neither the Tagalog Christianity of Aguinaldo nor the Methodist Christianity of McKinley would mitigate their bitterness.[94]

Other recent American acquisitions also got the *Social Gospel*'s attention. The Americanization of Puerto Rico had occurred peacefully, but the editors were concerned the Puerto Ricans "have been denied citizenship" and a tariff prevented free trade. They thought the presidential power to appoint the Puerto Rican Senate and give it unlimited control over granting franchises was "nothing short of high-handed piracy." Similarly, they considered the requirement that men owning a thousand dollars' worth of real estate sit in the Hawaiian Senate was a "serious political menace, the making of a plutocracy."[95]

Commonwealth's ambiguity reappeared once more in reporting on the revived interest in a Central American canal stimulated by America's new acquisitions. The *Social Gospel* seemed positive, concluding that the canal would allow us to protect Hawaii, Puerto Rico, Cuba, and the Philippines. It would shorten trade routes to Australia and South America's Pacific Coast, and best of all, the government, not private capitalists, would own any canal.[96]

The *Social Gospel* criticized churches' overseas missions, which favored personal evangelism and charity over improving social conditions:

> The churches will spend thousands of dollars in an effort to teach Christian Cuba the falsity of certain Roman dogmas. The government may spend more money to relieve famine and distress. But ... the Cubans need free land and seeds and tools and education, a fair opportunity as men to provide for themselves. Charity will do them but little good and may even do harm. Industrial democracy will be their salvation, and neither the superstitions of Romanism nor the wage-slavery of Protestantism could stand before it.[97]

When they heard that over thirteen hundred Student Missionary Volunteers had sailed for foreign lands, they thought it "a pity they have gone to organize their converts for commercial warfare and pit them against each other for all the work and in all the interests of this life."[98]

The militarism generated by the war frightened Commonwealth. They feared that the "poverty-spreading, wealth-concentrating, enormously powerful monopolies of America" would use the military to serve their interests. They attacked Brooks Adams's "stupendous program of militarism, for the support of a policy of fierce industrial militancy" and noted, with fear, the situation in Italy where the military served the economic powers by imprisoning thousands of oppressed workers who were protesting their conditions. Without citing Frederick Jackson Turner specifically, they suggested that free land in America had relieved that type of pressure here but feared that now, without free soil, that pressure would reappear. They concluded that only the elimination of property selfishness could prevent the rise of revolution in America.[99]

The *Social Gospel* received unsolicited books regularly and published reviews of books on religion, reform, and the "social question." Reviewers recommended, without reservation, Anne L. Vrooman's *Silver Text Bible Lessons: A Sociological Interpretation of the Bible from Genesis to Joshua,* and it became one of the works that the community sold by mail. Anne, Walter Vrooman's wife, believed that God had intended to make the earth like heaven, but sinners from Adam and Eve to corrupt Hebrew leaders had undermined his plan. Believers in unselfish brotherhood would return humanity to the plan. Commonwealth's reviewer, reflecting the community's perspective, rejected Vrooman's reliance on "legalism," which had already failed to establish brotherhood, in favor of "entirely free individuals" bringing brotherhood into being.[100]

Sue Fay Hinckley was one of the few colony women who contributed to the *Social Gospel.* In the fall of 1899, she redesigned the front cover and wrote several book reviews, including a positive account of Charlotte Perkins Gilman's *Women and Economics.* Subtitled *A Study of the Economic Relations between Men and Women as a Factor in Social Evolution,* the book outlined the effect on humanity of the unequal economic conditions between men and women throughout history. As the female leader of the community, Hinckley remained convinced of the book's truth and the need to become earnest advocates on behalf of women.[101]

Hinckley's review of Paul Sabatier's *Life of St. Francis of Assisi* celebrated the saint's life and excerpted many passages that were underpinnings of Commonwealth's philosophy. Francis believed that the Church had failed its mission, and a return to gospel poverty was the path to reform. Seeing property as a cage with gilded wires, he took a vow of poverty, which became a vow of liberty and a victory of love over materialism. Francis's rejection of material goods resonated within the community, where they viewed the pursuit of luxury as cruel.[102]

Charles Sheldon, author of the best seller *In His Steps: What Would Jesus Do?,* supported and contributed to Commonwealth, but his book received a mixed review in the *Social Gospel.* The reviewer, "K," who may have been James Kelley, criticized the text's style and errors in expression. Nevertheless, the reviewer thought its primary message, "to imitate Christ was an absolutely valid solution to the problems of life." Sheldon thought, and the reviewer agreed, that no rigid scheme would save society and bring the

Kingdom of God. When the book became popular, the *Social Gospel* thought that its appeal was to "sound Christian sentiment." Later, when Sheldon proposed to start a daily newspaper run according to what "Jesus would do," the editors defended him against critics who accused him of seeking financial gain.[103]

CHAPTER 7

✦ ✦ ✦

The Outside World

In the world, while not of it.

—*Social Gospel*

THE CHRISTIAN COMMONWEALTH did not seek to isolate itself. Members admitted to separating from the selfish world of America's Gilded Age but had unlimited love for it. Throughout its existence, the community maintained intimate human relationships with outsiders and carefully observed and commented on their activities. When they felt the world's pulse, they believed that it was progressing to a new order of God's kingdom, and by upholding their standard of brotherhood, they could contribute to that progress.[1]

After settling, to facilitate trade and communication, the leaders asked the Central of Georgia Railway to establish a station at the colony and petitioned the federal government to create a post office. Both would be named Commonwealth. The Post Office opened in February 1897. It was a money order post office with two daily mail deliveries. George Damon was the first postmaster, and Irene Albertson became his assistant. In early 1899, when Damon left to photograph in Cuba, Irene succeeded him, and they both put their federal pay into the common fund.[2]

Commonwealth's relations with its neighbors, urban and rural, started from curiosity, which decreased with more familiarity. The local people viewed the colony as a "novelty" but were interested in its "Arcadian existence" and often visited, and most held a favorable opinion of the community. Commonwealth received respect and friendship, and in contrast to many communitarian experiments, there is little evidence of hostility. An adjacent landowner, Captain Oattis, a former Confederate officer and school principal, saw "good in his new neighbors," and Columbus businessmen presented the community with a plantation bell as a gift. The colonists believed that their neighbors took their "truths" seriously and enjoyed the camaraderie with the new arrivals.[3]

Many African Americans lived near the colony, but there are few details about their relationship. At the turn of the century, most progressives did not prioritize the plight of African Americans. It was not a primary issue at Commonwealth, but the community created a bond with the impoverished blacks. Members got to know them well, cooperated with them, and maintained positive relations. Sometimes it was a sharecropper relationship, but their treatment toward the blacks was unlikely as harsh as that of other white landowners. Usually it was more equitable and charitable. One Sunday, a party of Commonwealth adults rode in a wagon to the lower end of the colony's property to visit two black families who lived rent free on colony land. Uncle Asa was an eighty-six-year-old sharecropper whose work ethic and attitude inspired Commonwealth. Born a slave, he cultivated thirty acres of cotton and ten acres of corn by himself. A victim of the sharecropping system, he spent his earnings before he harvested his crop.

Nevertheless, he worked from dawn to dark and was always cheerful. "He believes in God ... and God will not disappoint him ... he works like a horse and prays like a saint and sings like a lark, and he's all right." When Asa's only mule died at the same time as one at Commonwealth, the colony, its team broken up, gave the remaining mule to the "old darkey."[4]

Most of the colonists were new to the South and exposed to southern racial attitudes for the first time. Their ignorance took away any sense of superiority, and they viewed blacks as comrades more than as servile lackeys. Albertson compared their abilities favorably to community members who had book learning but knew nothing of gardening, raising crops, cotton, or fruit, or caring for animals. Nonetheless, there was a paternalistic tone to the relationship. Albertson wrote that "divine law is making us our colored brother's keeper" as Commonwealth's members showed the African Americans "how to do things and gave them training in new arts. Their homes showed the effect immediately; their gardens improved, and their children went faithfully to school." When the colony learned that there was a slave burial ground with one hundred unmarked graves near their water tank, they beautified it as a botanical garden.[5]

Some Commonwealth sympathizers expressed the prevailing attitude on race in America. Listening to the debate over territorial expansion and imperialism after the Spanish-American War, a *Social Gospel* writer concluded, "An inferior race in our own land is problem enough. How, then, can we rightly govern a far-away dependency of eleven millions of ignorant, superstitious, half-civilized and degraded (by the Spanish) people?" In another context, while discussing the Boer War in South Africa, the editors considered the Filipino a savage compared with the Boer. Another example of racial views was a reference to slaves in a review of John Woolman's *Journal*. The writer defended the slaves' rights, condemned cruelty, and advocated kindness. Nevertheless, he referred to slaves as "lower animals" and "dumb creatures." As he often did, the Old Gentleman took a contrary view. He commended the black soldiers as stalwart men who were writing with their blood a new chapter in military history that would win even more glorious victories in peace. In any case, the conflicting attitudes and behaviors reflected diversity within the community.[6]

When it came to more intimate relations, both Commonwealth members and African Americans acted with tact and common sense in the context of southern race relations. Despite their socialism, the local whites perceived Commonwealth to be traditional in their politics and wishing to be "identified with the southern people as citizens of repute and standing." There were community zealots who were anxious to demonstrate their commitment to brotherhood by accepting African Americans into membership. Little evidence exists that any blacks sought to join, but members induced one, who had been inspired by Albert Pease's religious fervor, to put in a formal application. Albertson sympathized but counseled delay, believing that the colony had enough obstacles to overcome without provoking an adverse reaction from local whites. It would "endanger the safety of the movement.... It would not matter if we employed negroes, but if we allowed them to work on an equality with us we should have to leave the country." Abstaining from voting, he was willing to wait, as was the African American who sought membership.[7]

Commonwealth's relations with the black sharecroppers remained decent. In early 1900, the community had a surplus of fruit trees in the nursery and offered them to their neighbors. At the post office, Albertson encountered a black sharecropper whom he had never met and proposed that he plant some trees on Commonwealth's terms, which meant "without price and no strings tied on." The seventy-six-year-old sharecropper appreciated

Ralph's generosity but rejected the offer. Exposing the conditions that existed, he told Albertson that if he had fruit trees, his landowner would force him to pay more rent or move off the land. Other black neighbors did "risk it" and took a few hundred of the trees despite the "prohibitive tax" that prevailed in the South.[8]

After they cleared pine trees and burned brush on land in the northeast corner of the colony, they offered it to another black neighbor. Following local custom, he got it rent free because he was making the first crop on a newly cleared piece of land, but no evidence exists of the subsequent relationship. In the spring of 1900, they formed a typical sharecropper relationship with a disabled black widower and his three daughters. Commonwealth furnished land, a mule, and all provisions with the expectation that he would return the cost in cotton that fall. Rachel, the oldest girl at fourteen, ran the plow, cooked, and chopped wood. The other girls were also good workers and helped their father "make a crop." In appreciation, they brought beautiful bouquets of wildflowers to Commonwealth.[9]

Albertson was impressed by the honesty, industry, and integrity of the black families near Commonwealth. He felt that his experience gave him a more positive view of African Americans and their possibilities than that held by most of his friends and American society in general. The community gained intimate knowledge of African Americans' need for better economic conditions but also expressed its hope for higher ideals and moral betterment.[10]

While not oblivious to the African American condition, Commonwealth more often saw them as part of a larger worldwide population of exploited poor people. In 1899, the *Social Gospel* editorialized that "the manner in which southern farmer negroes are living this winter would put to shame many a foreign missionary's story of barbarian conditions I have read labeled famine." The editors spoke out against lynching, associating it with imperialist actions. When an American consul called for intervention against piracy on China's Red River because their government was unable to suppress it, the *Social Gospel* asked if it would be appropriate for another country to intervene in the United States to suppress lynching since our government refused to stop it. Their outrage at lynching was not limited to African American victims. When a mob of thirty in Covington, Georgia, martyred three Mormon elders, the editors expressed their dismay. In another article, James Kelley attacked the widespread Malthusian and Social Darwinist perspective that saw the dying out of the "less favored classes" as a solution to the labor problem. He cited African American death rates in Philadelphia and Baltimore, which were twice as high as those for whites, and he noted that wealthy white Christians spent money on luxurious pleasures rather than aiding the dispossessed.[11]

Albertson did not have as high an opinion of Commonwealth's white rural neighbors who he thought were of a "lower order." Many were from Georgia families whose lives had peaked before the Civil War and whose "intellect, self-respect, industry, ability, integrity and hope were gone." They still lived off of black labor while "their properties were rundown in a shameless and unnecessary manner. They talked much about their pride, but showed no evidence of it." They maintained white superiority and refused to eat with blacks while having their children nursed at the breast of black women. Untidy in their persons, they were attached to whiskey and snuff and had intellects not nearly as keen as their black neighbors. These whites did not cause the community any problems, and some were neighborly, although in a condescending way.[12]

Despite these negative attitudes that remained private, Commonwealth established mutually beneficial relationships with its neighbors. It loaned its logging trucks to them to haul logs to the sawmill, where colony men milled them into lumber for a one-half share. The cane mill also worked on shares, which provided the community with a source of sugar. They gave waste paper from the printing office to neighbors who used it to fill in chinks in their cabins.[13]

Commonwealth had closer relations with the whites in Columbus, with whom they conducted business and found to be pleasant. Albertson, viewed by many as the "most prominent" colonist, visited Columbus regularly and discussed conditions at the colony.[14]

In July 1898, Commonwealth reached out to the local community through a seven-day religious revival at Wildwood Park in Columbus. The Commonwealth ministers, aided by Harry C. Vrooman, pastor of Fountain Park Congregational Church in St. Louis, did the preaching. Colony members disseminated a handbill that promoted the revival and expressed their religious ideas by challenging the local population with a series of questions. Are you and your country saved? Do you, your politics, and your business belong to Christ? Do you "worship the Almighty Dollar in place of Almighty God"? Do you know the meaning of the Social Gospel? In conclusion, they invited everyone to listen to Commonwealth's men and women preach about giving themselves and their property to God.

Colony members and Columbus residents jointly conducted other well-attended revival activities. Recitations, phrenological examinations, music, and singing by "the leading voices of the city" accompanied the sermons. They used the songbook of Sam P. Jones, a southern evangelist who rivaled Dwight Moody in popularity. The programs included such topics as "Georgia, a Holy Land Like Palestine" and "Modern Atheism and the Heathen of Muscogee County." One guest speaker, who had organized the New York Society for Parks and Playgrounds, told stories about the "little tots who live in the 'hell of poverty' in that wicked metropolis." Others preached the coming of the Kingdom of God and the application of the truths of Christianity to the Gilded Age's "heathenish, cannibalistic, corrupt monopolists and usurers of America's business and industrial systems."

Over five hundred people attended the opening meeting. Walter Vrooman, a Bellamyite socialist from St. Louis, was the opening speaker. He appealed to his audience's Christian conscience to accept the gospel of neighbor love and commended Commonwealth's members for living according to that law. He addressed the Spanish-American War and contrasted the "beautiful possibilities of Cuba" with the destruction and suffering that human greed had produced there. Later in the week, before another sizable audience, Vrooman criticized monopolies and other undesirable features of Gilded Age capitalism and spoke on the unity of the interests of the rich and poor and how the prosperity of one depended on the success of the other. Afterward, the children and young ladies of Columbus, whom Vrooman had encouraged to attend so they could be educated and "grow into the work of socialism," put on an exciting program.[15]

Other Commonwealth members talked about socialism and related biblical religion to life in the present rather than to eternal life. The subject of the final meeting was "Thy Kingdom Come; How, When and Where?," in which community members explained what they were attempting to achieve. Vrooman spoke on the "Kingdom of God on Earth," and Albertson offered an interpretation of the Lord's Prayer and told how it applied to contemporary life and business.[16]

Overall, the local press complimented the revival highly but found the religious meetings "peculiar" because of their focus on "real life" issues. It took issue with a reference to "camp meetings," noting that this revival was significantly different from the traditional Methodist camp meetings. In particular, the press criticized Vrooman's unorthodox interpretation of scripture. They also noted his tendency to criticize the modern church.[17]

Two Columbus residents, Armel Alexis Marchand and his wife, were important supporters of the community. Armel had been a founder of the Icarian Community in 1848. Later, he became president of the New Icarian Community in Iowa, and he and Marie remained until its dissolution in 1895. Devoted to Etienne Cabet's communism, they were not as enthusiastically Christian as Commonwealth's members. Nevertheless, the Marchands embraced its values of brotherhood and equality and were frequent visitors and helpers in the community. Armel was close to many Commonwealth members, and when he died in 1898, Albertson conducted the funeral service in Columbus "in a very impressive manner." Mrs. Marchand's commitment to peaceful communism was rooted in her childhood recollection of the revolution of 1848. "Deeply embedded in her soul are the truths that separate her girlhood from the force methods of her co-patriot French communists." When she died at her daughter's home around Christmas 1900, Gibson and Calvin Reasoner conducted her funeral service, which was attended by several Commonwealth members. Their daughter, Marie, had edited *La Revue Icarienne*, Icaria's journal, and, after arriving in Columbus, married William A. Ross, a local schoolteacher. Ross was a frequent donor to Commonwealth and often visited his colony friends on Sundays.[18]

The Columbus newspapers published excerpts from the *Social Gospel* describing community activities and repeatedly complimented their new neighbors: "They have shown themselves to be an honest, hard-working, and intelligent people, and good citizens." Criticism of the community was rare and often implicit. After revenue officers found a stash of moonshine on a farm that abutted Commonwealth property, a local newspaper noted that it was "near, very near" to the community. Such an implication seemed farfetched, as many of Commonwealth's members had their roots in the temperance movement.[19]

Throughout the United States, people regarded Commonwealth with interest and curiosity. Mrs. J. W. Spencer, a visitor from Pensacola and future resident, wrote, "I have shown the colony photographs to many people here, and they are all surprised that the colonists look and dress just like other people. But their ideas change somewhat after my little story about our colony and our people." A Macon newspaper called it "one of the most unique towns in the country," and noted its commitment to economic equality, cooperation, and "loving thy neighbor." Twenty miles south of Jackson,

Georgia, on the Southern Railway, Commonwealth inspired a cooperative colony that engaged in textile production, although it, like Ruskin, had a five-hundred-dollar entry fee.[20]

A young man from Salem, Massachusetts, Fred Tay, came to Commonwealth to study and work before entering Amherst College. He stayed with James Kelley in the newly erected Growlery under the pine and persimmon trees east of the Albertson cottage. Tay planned to stay for a year to gain a greater understanding of the community. His arrival provoked a thoughtful response from one member. Feeling that outside interest validated the "greatness of our mission," he believed that outsiders who did not experience the trials of self-denial and pioneer work could not appreciate the hardships necessary to realize Commonwealth's ideals.[21]

Looking beyond its relations with the local community, the *Social Gospel* served as a means of communicating and exchanging ideas with the larger world. Through its subscriptions and exchanges with other reform journals, the community kept close tabs on what was happening. To spread their values beyond the colony's borders, Commonwealth also planned to hold semi-annual assemblies on the ideals of brotherhood and Christian civilization.[22]

The community paid close attention to other communal and cooperative activities, always supportive but also offering suggestions or insights regarding those efforts. Members believed that any socialism concerned with individual and social improvement would have to be Christian. It would evolve toward perfection and would revolutionize not only the factory but the kitchen, parlor, and ballroom. It would fulfill God's purpose of creating strong, happy individuals. They believed that cooperation and socialism had millions of supporters but took issue with so-called scientific socialists who criticized communal efforts. In all ages, they suggested it was the children, the poets, and the lovers who had been right, and the wise men, the philosophers, and scientists who too often had been wrong.[23]

In return, Commonwealth got support from advocates of cooperation. One, Edward Keyes, founder of the Right Relationship League, published the "Commonwealth Story," a pamphlet written by Gibson. Subsequently, several papers republished it, and thousands of copies were printed and sold.[24]

Commonwealth's supporters were not always well received in the outside world. When Reverend Carl Thompson of the Prospect Street Congregational Church in Elgin, Illinois, began preaching the *Social Gospel* message, it divided his church. The majority stood by the pastor, but a wealthy minority stopped contributing, which had a significant economic impact on the church. To the journal's editors, it was another example of the conflict between Christ and commercialism. Later that year, the editors saw it as a sign of progress that the church gave Thompson "perfect freedom to preach 'The Social Gospel, cooperation, economics and socialism' in his pulpit." However, the following year, Thompson left his church to become a devout Christian Socialist.[25]

He also began writing for the *Social Gospel* in support of Gibson's proposed Order of Brothers. He called brotherhood the "real Christianity" and spelled out its essential features that would be true to the ideals of Jesus: universality, democracy, cooperation, and regulative control of production and distribution. Thompson's ideals did not deviate from Gibson's, but to implement them he turned to the state. To him, it was the only hope to cope with the gigantic trusts. Influenced by Christian Socialism, he turned toward progressivism and orthodox socialism. Later he became a socialist congressman from Milwaukee and active in the international peace movement.[26]

While it was never prominent, Commonwealth received national attention from the mainstream press. When the *New York Sun* published a description of the colony, it attracted requests for further information from readers who considered joining. In early 1899, the *Chattanooga News* described the colony as "flourishing" and "composed of many talented men and women." It noted that the community had good schools and published an excellent magazine. An Illinois newspaper called it "peculiar" and Arcadian but praised its extraordinary members who had overcome poverty and harsh conditions to create a community that lived according to Christ's principles and demonstrated the potential of "practical socialism."[27]

Commonwealth became well known within the national communitarian movement. In September 1899, Reverend A. B. Ellis of the Brotherhood of Burley in Washington detoured from a Boston trip for a three-day visit. Ellis, a Harvard graduate and the son of a Universalist preacher, spoke to the membership about Burley on Saturday and preached "acceptably" on Sunday, telling the community that he had gone to work with brotherhood cooperators because he believed that practicing love was a priority.[28]

Ruskin's newspaper, the *Coming Nation*, praised Commonwealth and the *Social Gospel*, referring to it as an "attractive monthly." By spreading the news of its plan and brotherhood spirit, it was multiplying Christian joy and religious socialism and "leading the thought of the world on neighbor love and brotherhood questions." Commonwealth reciprocated the praise and viewed the *Coming Nation* as a leader in the industry and a phenomenal success for a reform paper.[29]

The community shipped copies of the *Social Gospel* worldwide, arousing interest and enthusiasm. Some readers became correspondents, while others contributed funds and real property. Edward Everett Hale offered the group three hundred dollars to build a cottage for invalids and sent copies of his books to the community. Luther Burbank sent flowers and fruits from his home in Santa Rosa, California. John Wood, general secretary of the Brotherhood of St. Andrew in New York, anxious to know more about the colony, sent a letter of inquiry. His organization's sole purpose was "the spread of Christ's Kingdom among young men." Bolton Hall, a leader of the Brotherhood of the Kingdom, was another supporter.[30]

Most correspondents supported Commonwealth, but some praised their motives but suggested modifications to their plan. Others warned them that they were bound to fail. Herbert W. Gleason, editor of the *Kingdom*, which had been the medium for the founding of the community, spoke kindly of the colony as "fairly successful" and "heroic." Later, he concluded that its members were "unrepresentative of humanity" and leading a brotherhood life that "does not furnish any actual solution to the social problem." By separating itself from the world, the community was selfish, and by selling towels in the world, it was engaging in selfish competition. Finally, Gleason asserted that "the colony was never Jesus' method."[31]

Gleason's critique inspired letters to the *Kingdom*. John Moore of Atlanta accused Commonwealth of being "limited to one class and one condition" in its suicidal pursuit of pure altruism. He quoted Romans 15 to imply that Commonwealth was strong but self-serving and unwilling to bear the infirmities of the weak. The *Social Gospel* editors took umbrage with Moore, stating that anyone who knew even a little about Commonwealth knew that the weak were there "in force." Commonwealth was open to all, blue-blooded aristocrats, poor folks, ex-presidents and millionaires, even tramps, "but the head of a trust, or the 'standard-bearer' of a political party, would no doubt need to give a pretty thorough account of himself." It would take in all men if it could do so without defeating the end for which it existed.[32]

W. D. P. Bliss, the evangelist, supported Gleason's position. Ironically, Bliss's Christian Socialism had helped inspire the community, and he served briefly as an associate editor of the *Social Gospel*. However, in an article titled "Self-Serving Colonies Condemned," published in both the *Kingdom* and the *Social Gospel*, Bliss wrote that Christ never lived apart from the world but entered ordinary life and made it divine. Admitting the divinity of cooperative life in the countryside, Bliss asked, "What about our present ordinary city life?" To abandon the city was "running away" and undermining the "'solidarity' of mankind." Bliss admitted that colonies set an example but thought they accomplished so little for so few people that reformers should concentrate their efforts on urban reforms.

Nevertheless, Bliss concluded that all colonies were not harmful, and the Christian Commonwealth was serving the interests of a unique group of people. On the other hand, people in ordinary life had opportunities to bring about reform and progress. Gibson disagreed with Bliss and referred readers to Albertson's chapter on "Selfish Socialism" in *The Social Incarnation*, where he insisted that the dominant role of their community was social sacrifice and not saving themselves.[33]

Gibson always defended Commonwealth and pointed out the errors of the critiques. He insisted that Commonwealth was reestablishing the universal brotherhood that the Church of Christ had ceased to be:

> By giving up private property and its pursuit, and making ourselves brothers to all men we have for all time joined ourselves to the world, instead of having separated ourselves from it.... We have solved the problem of getting men to live together as brothers.... We have brought into brotherhood relation here professional men and common laborers, the highly cultivated and the unrefined.... We have made real brothers of men who belong to orthodox churches and to no church. In politics we have blended Republicans, Democrats, Populists, Prohibitionists, and Tolstoyan nonresistants. We have welcomed people who come to Commonwealth in Pullman coaches, in box cars, and on foot. Not a tramp has been turned away from our doors. We have all lived for months and months on less than three cents each per meal, in order to divide with the world's destitute ones.

Gibson noted that their towel making and other industries were doubly virtuous. By making and selling products with free hearts and loving hands, they were providing the world with "the greatest possible service"—providing material goods at an affordable price. Their advertisements read, "We can undersell the each-for-himself world if we will." Instead of separating themselves, they were "making connections with and commending all forms and degrees of unselfish cooperation." Finally, they were emulating Jesus, the apostles, and the early church by having "a common purse" and "all things common."[34]

Other critics of Commonwealth tried to use the extremism of George Herron's lectures to condemn it. Although skeptical of its success, Herron had inspired and supported the community, but he also believed that those who separated themselves from suffering humanity were neglecting the need for human solidarity to create brotherhood. Gibson denied that Herron was talking about Commonwealth, which was expanding brotherhood life one man at a time.[35]

Despite its size, its relatively short life, and the limited circulation of the *Social Gospel*, the Christian Commonwealth received significant international attention. Leo Tolstoy was its most prominent foreign supporter. He followed its progress closely with keen but cautious interest. Even before the *Social Gospel* began circulating internationally, Ernest Howard Crosby wrote Tolstoy about Commonwealth's practice of his ideas, especially non-resistance, and that he planned to visit the colony in Georgia. Tolstoy asked Crosby to send him his observations from the visit. A year later, Tolstoy made the same appeal to Aylmer Maude.[36]

After publishing the first issue of the *Social Gospel*, Gibson sent Tolstoy a copy and told him that he was "entirely committed to Christ's non-resistant teachings" and that the journal's other editors and writers were becoming more interested in the "truth of love." He asked for Tolstoy's help to create brotherhood and separate from the selfish commercial struggle. Tolstoy responded that the magazine and Gibson's letter afforded him "great pleasure," and the articles were "very good."[37]

Tolstoy ordered extra copies of the *Social Gospel* to circulate to friends and supporters and recommended it to his correspondents as a model of Christian anarchism. Its appeal, which peaked in the 1890s and 1900s, created a worldwide following that was interested in the activities at Commonwealth and other communitarian experiments. The *New Order*, a British publication, publicized the community regularly. Tolstoyans in the Netherlands were also in touch with the colony. Tolstoy's letter to the colonists at Commonwealth, written in March 1898, appeared in translation in *Vrede*, a Dutch Christian Socialist and peace newspaper a few months later.[38]

Despite spreading the word about Commonwealth, Tolstoy had grave reservations about communal experiments. He wrote to Gibson,

The contradictions between his surroundings and his convictions are very painful for a man who is sincere in his Christian faith, and therefore the organization of communities seems to such a man the only means of delivering himself from those contradictions. But this is an illusion. Every community is a small island in the midst of an ocean of unchristian conditions of life, so that the Christian relations exist only between members of the colony but outside that must remain unchristian, otherwise the colony would not exist for the moment. And therefore, to live in a community cannot save a Christian from the contradiction between his conscience and his life. I do not mean to say that I do not approve of communities such as your commonwealth, or that I do not think them to be a good thing. On the contrary, I approve of them with all my heart and am very interested in your commonwealth and wish it the greatest success.

I think that every man who can free himself from the conditions of worldly life without breaking the ties of love—love the main principle in the name of which he seeks new forms of life—I think such a man not only must, but naturally join people who have the same beliefs and try to live up to them. If I were free I would immediately even at my age join such a colony. I only wished to say that the mere forming of communities is not a solution for the Christian problem, but is only one of the means of its solution.... The ideal will be attained only when every man in the whole world will say: Why should I sell my services and buy yours? If mine are greater than yours I owe them to you, because if there is in the whole world one man who does not think and act by this principle, and who, will take and keep by violence, what he can take from others, no man can live a true Christian life, as well in a community as outside it. We cannot be saved separately; we must be saved together.... We must all work together—men living in the world as well as men living in communities.[39]

Gibson explained his position and that of his cofounders to Tolstoy:

If two or more families do not begin to live the life of love, it cannot spread and reorganize society and make it Christian. The individual cannot remain in the midst of the selfish struggle without being involved in it.... It seems to me, wherever modern machinery and capital having taken the power of independent Christian action away from the individual and compelled him to gather his living through the selfish machinery processes, prices, relations, he is called of God to come out of such evil combination.... If he be too poor and helpless to support life apart from himself and family, they must be redeemed by those who have the means.

In addition to the charitable motive that Gibson mentions, the founders discussed separation as creating a beacon for the rest of society. Despite Tolstoy's criticism, Gibson encouraged him to "be very free to advise us always."[40]

In 1899 in the Netherlands, the Vrede group established the Blaricum colony, which reflected Commonwealth's values. The group acknowledged Tolstoy's reservations but reiterated Gibson's position that community was a means to an end, not an end in itself. Van Mierop, the leader, maintained that there was no better way to live than in the spirit of Jesus and love.[41]

In January 1899, the *Social Gospel* printed a letter that Gibson received from T. Altaresky in Palestine: "The fame of '*The Social Gospel*' and of 'The Christian Commonwealth' has reached even these shores.... Is it really a fact that you and your comrades are about to solve the social problem? Is it possible that the glorious promises of God to mankind, to establish His kingdom on earth, are on the eve of fulfillment? What a glorious mission you are entrusted with." Altaresky asked for copies of the journal and other Commonwealth publications and expressed his desire to join such a community. He sent a gift of "flowers plucked from the holy fields around Jerusalem"—rose of Sharon, hyssop, lily of the field, and others—which were mounted on cards and became a collection of rare and beautiful blooms at Commonwealth.[42]

Altaresky may never have fulfilled his desire to join a community, but there was a colony in Jerusalem that was "filled with the same Spirit of Love" as existed at Commonwealth. The *Social Gospel* reprinted an article about it from the *Christian Guardian*, a Toronto-based journal. Started by Horatio Spafford during a pilgrimage to the Holy Land, the community was committed to the self-sacrifice and service that was expressed in the question "What would Jesus do?" Spafford gathered around himself members of every imaginable religious denomination—Protestants, Catholics, Armenians, Abyssinians, Copts, and Syrians—as well as Muslims and Jews. Muslims referred to the community as the House of the Peace of God because it reduced violence and conflict among the various Christian sects and between Christians and non-Christians.[43]

In March 1898, Tolstoy asked Gibson about the possibility of the Doukhobors settling in the United States. They were nonresistant conscientious objectors who refused military service in Russia. After years of government persecution, the czar granted the sect permission to emigrate. They hoped to migrate to England or America, but the Russian government confiscated their wealth and property. Tolstoy estimated that around ten thousand would emigrate and told Gibson he planned to publish an international appeal for aid. "He then asked Gibson and his friends, Herron and Crosby for suggestions about the matter."[44]

Gibson responded that Commonwealth would "help them to the utmost" and thought they could find land to buy in the United States. He agreed to contact Crosby and Herron about raising funds but also encouraged overseas supporters to raise money to finance the migration. Gibson recommended Georgia as a destination. It had a healthy climate, moderate temperatures, and timber for both fuel and construction. The land was affordable, and with fertilizer, the soil could produce two or three crops a year.[45]

Tolstoy considered Commonwealth as a destination, but it was impractical. The *Social Gospel* sent out one hundred letters asking about "the advisability of attempting to move them to America" and seeking land or aid for them. Many responses were positive, and the paper reported, "The question of getting land for them will not be an over-serious one."[46]

Tolstoy passed along the *Social Gospel* to Vladimir Chertkov, an advocate for the Doukhobors who had written a book on their martyrdom in Russia. He subscribed to the journal, thanked Commonwealth for its assistance, and kept up with the community's progress. The *Social Gospel* published a lengthy article by Chertkov, which described the Doukhobors' plight and appealed for help for their emigration. He asked for recommendations of locations with cold winters and a dry climate, requested vessels for transportation, sought financial aid, and solicited the dissemination of information through leaflets, letters to editors, and book sales. In an appeal to Commonwealth sympathizers, Chertkov stressed that anyone contributing would "become sharers together in a movement which directly tends to the coming and establishment of the kingdom of God amongst men."[47]

C. F. Willard of Commonwealth suggested that the Doukhobors settle in Texas. Tolstoy forwarded the suggestion to Chertkov and the English Committee for Emigration and asked Crosby to find out about land availability, price, and transportation. He also requested that they start a subscription in America to raise funds.[48]

The *Social Gospel* followed the Doukhobors' situation closely. It commended the Society of Friends for their sympathy for and financial aid to the sect. Contrasting them to churches that had no problem advocating war, Commonwealth celebrated the Society of Friends as martyrs to the cause of peace and brotherhood. A temporary Doukhobor settlement on Cyprus was not working out, and Commonwealth received a letter from Eliza Pickard, an

English supporter of the Russians, appealing for assistance and publicity in arranging to send two thousand Doukhobors to Canada.[49]

Crosby and the *Social Gospel* repeatedly called attention to the Doukhobors' plight by publicizing the Tolstoy Doukhobortsi Fund organized in New York. In late 1898, Crosby pointed out that Canada was opening its doors to the exiles and appealed for financial aid to cover their transportation and settlement. To help secure financial support, he started a subscription fund in the *Social Gospel* but was disappointed by its results. He raised only "$600 or $700" and complained to Tolstoy that no one sympathized with pacifism.[50]

When Aylmer Maude, Tolstoy's biographer, came to North America as a spokesman for the Doukhobors, the *Social Gospel* reported his activities and lecture in New York. Before returning to England, Maude publicized Tolstoy's views and arranged for seventy-five hundred Doukhobors to migrate to Canada. He compared the Doukhobors to the Huguenots and Puritans who had migrated to America earlier and drew an analogy between the nonresistance of Tolstoy and of William Lloyd Garrison. In January 1899, a Philadelphia Quaker informed the *Social Gospel* that several thousand Doukhobors from Cyprus had landed in Nova Scotia and would migrate to land near Winnipeg. By March, they had settled and were preparing to start their spring planting. The Canadians held them in high regard as "a superior class of people"—intelligent, diligent, clean, courteous, kind, and respectful. Commonwealth saw them as a bright spot in the moral complexion of the western hemisphere as they, like Commonwealth, demonstrated that love and Christianity were practical.[51]

Despite his sympathy for Commonwealth, Crosby never joined the community but served as an associate editor and regular contributor to the *Social Gospel*. He advocated the application of Christian teachings to socioeconomic problems and later wrote an account of Saint Francis's "subversive" principles of political economy. He agreed with Gibson that to compete with the Gilded Age trusts that "pull the wires," one must learn their secret and improve on it. For Crosby, that secret was "voluntary cooperation—of mutual attraction," which is what the Christian Commonwealth was doing.[52]

At the *Social Gospel*'s inception, Crosby encouraged Gibson to write Tolstoy and John Coleman Kenworthy, the British founder of several Brotherhood Churches and Tolstoyan communities. He thought they would write for the paper when they learned its philosophy. On Tolstoy's seventieth birthday, Crosby wrote a lengthy article that spelled out the Russian writer's life and thought. Tolstoy's belief in the "actual brotherhood of man and the evil of distinctions of rank and wealth," his complete nonresistance and condemnation of all governments, his advocacy of self-sacrifice and the simple life, and his faith in the Gospel of Saint Matthew and the Sermon on the Mount could have been a description of the Christian Commonwealth's ideals.[53]

Ironically, a few months later the *Social Gospel* severely criticized a New York banquet in honor of Tolstoy. Quoting a British writer, they noted that the elite literary figures at the dinner, dressed in their elegant clothes and indulging in a gourmet feast, totally contradicted Tolstoy's values. Instead of reflecting "high culture," it was time for them to adopt the simplicity, humility, and plain living of Tolstoy's thought.[54]

Crosby introduced the socialist artist William Morris to the pages of the *Social Gospel*. Acknowledging that religion was not part of Morris's perspective, he drew parallels between Morris's belief in the value of work that was worthwhile and pleasant and Commonwealth's commitment to labor as a form of service and worship.

He often wrote on the conflict between war and Christianity. He viciously attacked the "Christian war" in Cuba, which must have made some Commonwealth friends uneasy because they believed the conflict promised uplift and "Christianity" for the Cubans. He thought the Filipino war was "sickening" and that it was unlikely that Americans would understand or sympathize with Filipino culture. His greater fear was that America would bring the "blessings" of civilization to the Filipinos. We would awaken "new physical wants" and "our greed for 'things'" to "an uncivilized people." The West had imposed its civilization on Egypt and Japan, which led to the exploitation of men, women, and children. Was it fair, he asked, "to ram down the throats of the Filipinos all the miseries of our slums"?[55]

In prose and poetry, Crosby asserted that America was losing its freedom and global leadership by using armies and navies to spread its values and frontiers. In *War Echoes*, a pamphlet of spiritual poems published at Commonwealth, Crosby pictured the horrors and madness of war. Rather than world conquest, it was time to "establish first the kingdom of heaven there, and all things should be added unto you." His book of poetry, *Plain Talk in Psalm and Parable*, received a rave review from Gibson for "its faithfulness to the Spirit of Love" and was sold through the pages of the *Social Gospel*.[56]

Like Crosby, Tolstoy criticized American jingoism and patriotism in a private letter, which the *Social Gospel* published after the Spanish-American

War was over. He was disappointed in Commonwealth's equivocation regarding the war. He was sorry that he had not been able to convince his brothers that patriotism "must lead to lies, violence, murder, and the loss not only of material well-being but to the greatest moral deprivation." The *Social Gospel*'s editors took exception to Tolstoy's criticism. Initially, they blamed it on the language difference but conceded that evil could arise from patriotism. Moreover, they admitted that universal brotherhood and the love of all countries, while appearing unpatriotic, were superior to the love of one's country. The spirit of brotherhood "does away with all artificial barriers and gives one natural connection with all one's kind" regardless of tribe, nation, caste, class, sect, or religion. Tolstoy thought their defense of patriotism was "sad" and that too much intellectual cleverness plagued Commonwealth.[57]

Tolstoy put Jenö Henrik Schmitt, a Hungarian philosopher/anarchist, in touch with both Albertson and Gibson and introduced Commonwealth to other Christian anarchists in Europe. In London, the *Brotherhood*, a journal of peace and reform, said that the *Social Gospel* was spreading its message "far more clearly and forcibly" than it had done in its eleven-year existence.[58]

The *Social Gospel* and other periodicals attracted many visitors to Commonwealth. The colony had no hotel but provided accommodations and a welcome for everyone. Visitors from all over the United States and the world had their names and origins published monthly in the *Social Gospel*. The most prominent Americans were Jane Addams and Ernest Howard Crosby. Addams came in March 1899 accompanied by her niece, Mary Smith. She knew Albertson from his Chicago visits and knew of the colony from its beginning. She had a keen interest in its work, as she did in all efforts to better the conditions of human life.[59]

Addams had just visited Tolstoy, who deeply influenced her. She thought that Commonwealth

> portrayed for us most vividly both the weakness, and the strange august dignity of the Tolstoy position. The colonists at Commonwealth held but a short creed. They claimed in fact that the difficulty is not to state truth but to make moral conviction operative upon natural life, and they announced their intention to "obey the teachings of Jesus in all matters of labor and the use of property." They would thus transfer the vindication of creed from the church to the open field—from dogma to experience.
>
> ... We inquired if the policy of extending food and shelter to all who applied, without test of creed or ability, might not result in the migration of all the neighboring poorhouse population into the colony. We were

told that this actually had happened during the winter until the colony fare of corn meal and cow peas had proved so unattractive that most of the paupers had gone back, for even the poorest of the Southern poor-houses occasionally supplied bacon with the pone to prevent scurvy— from which the colonists themselves had suffered. The difficulty of the poorhouse people had thus settled itself by the sheer poverty of the situation, a poverty so biting that the only ones willing to face it were those sustained by a conviction of its righteousness of the experiment.[60]

She suggested a member had "a fanatic's joy in seeing his own formula translated into action." Albertson dismissed her observation. Commonwealth's message was one "of courage and cheer to those who are capable of an earnest and faithful and cool-headed obedience to a high social ideal." He denied that the community saw its poverty as a sign of its righteousness. "We believe," he wrote, "in a gospel of material prosperity . . . someday there will be houses and lands and food and raiment and useful labor for everybody." The colonists embraced neither asceticism nor poverty, but their situation perpetuated them. They believed a brotherhood could not function if it prospered. It would become exclusive and attract only the selfish.[61]

While Gibson and Albertson were fund-raising in Chicago, Samuel Comings left for a visit to the North and stopped off at the Ruskin colony in Tennessee. He was interested in their work and pleased with their progress. In turn, they were intrigued by Commonwealth's comprehensive plan for cooperative industrial education, which Chicago socialist Walter Thomas Mills designed at the instigation of Comings. They spent the week discussing education and colonies and received great support for a "college of the new economy." Comings believed that Ruskin would be the seat of a model school before long. Other Commonwealth members also visited Ruskin, a celebrated oasis of social justice.[62]

Gibson would travel anywhere for the cause. In the summer of 1899, he received an invitation to the Conference of the Brotherhood of the Kingdom in Marlborough, New York. The attendees included the most important figures of the Social Gospel and Christian Socialist movements, including Walter Rauschenbusch. Gibson presented an address on "Communal Cooperation," and Ernest Crosby spoke against imperialism. Commonwealth supporters, "Golden Rule" Jones and N. O. Nelson, gave addresses on "Municipal Cooperation" and "Industrial Cooperation," respectively. However, the following year Jones, possibly influenced by Gibson's disillusionment, repudiated "the colony idea." Albertson thought his aspirations to be governor of

Ohio and president of the United States may have influenced him. Nevertheless, Albertson repeated his support for Jones's political ideas.[63]

Gibson's wife and son accompanied him on his trip to Marlborough. After the conference, they visited friends and relatives in New York and Maine. Jacob Troth, who was well known among Quaker societies and peace organizations in the East, arranged to attend the annual meeting of the Universal Peace Union in Mystic, Connecticut. On his trip, he was going to canvass for more *Social Gospel* subscriptions and join Gibson, who was going to address the Mystic meeting, but Albertson's illness forced Gibson to return to Commonwealth, where problems were increasing.[64]

PART
THREE

APOCALYPSE

CHAPTER 8

✦ ✦ ✦

Nonresistance Abandoned

To live we had to fight.

—Ralph Albertson,
"The Christian Commonwealth in Georgia"

B Y THE END OF 1898, there had been much progress at Commonwealth. The population had hovered around one hundred throughout the year, and construction and food production had increased.[1] Those positive developments reversed themselves in early 1899. In February, the temperature dropped below zero, and three inches of snow covered the ground. The first crops froze, and the late frost destroyed much of the fruit. That spring, dissension, in the form of malingering, crippled efforts to repair the damage. It led to a food shortage that lasted into the following winter. It was so bad that in November, the *Social Gospel* asked its northern friends who had a surplus of fruit to ship it, regardless of quality, to Commonwealth.[2]

Given the conditions, minor disputes were part of Commonwealth's day-to-day experience despite its commitment to love and brotherhood, but serious dissent was rare. In June 1898, Gibson, in a Sunday talk, pointed to the existence of three classes—those who want more than their share, those who want precisely their share, and those who think only of giving. Only those in the last group were truly Christian, and they needed to be the most influential. Moreover, instant equality was impossible.[3]

The problems evolved into the first major dissent in community history, and its appearance was a serious blow. As the number of newcomers increased, they felt excluded from power, despite the democratic structure. Most new members were good citizens, lived harmoniously, and worked faithfully. But there were, among the "Whosoever will, may come" contingent, several "tramps" and even more "cranks" who were incompatible with the leaders. As they examined the community's ideals, some questioned certain actions of the leadership and the original members.[4]

When Commonwealth's management refused to provide more funds for the towel-making business after its initial failure, their decision angered Felix Loiselle, who had come specifically to start the enterprise. He became a spokesman for the newcomers who complained that leadership was unresponsive to their input and needs.[5]

Dissenters charged colony leaders, especially Albertson, with hypocrisy in their unfaithfulness to the ideals of the "Kingdom of God on Earth." Their accusations were not without merit. Gibson's mother had not given all her wealth to the community. The founders were among the first to have newly built private cottages. Irene Albertson kept her piano at her cottage (although she gave lessons and played for community events) and had eggs when others did without. Damon's wife wore fancier clothes than the other women (although she made them herself). Each example created the impression of privilege, not equality.[6]

Frustration over poverty, poor living conditions, and inadequate diet led some critics to blame poor management. Damon and Albertson admitted there was poverty and occasional food shortages but stated that majority rule determined the diet and living conditions, and they believed sacrifice was necessary to achieve the Kingdom of God. James Kelley defended their "sacrifice" as "altruistic, wholesome and noble self-expression." Brewer countered that the colony had, on one occasion, expressed a desire for better food, but could not get Albertson, the head of the commissary, to comply with their wishes.[7]

The founding members were a majority, so there was no way for disaffected newcomers to alter their decisions. Many protested by malingering to express their sense of powerlessness and loss of morale. Others became more vocal in criticizing the leaders and their policies.[8] After working hard for a year or more, some newcomers forgot the hardships from which they had come and realized that they had personally accumulated little in the interim. Some missed the lure of civilization but found it hard to conceive of leaving Commonwealth empty handed. They expressed a wish to gain ownership of a share of Commonwealth's property.[9]

In May 1899, several dissenters, led by Brewer, Albert Hall, and S. W. Martin, accused the leaders of trying to force them out and "colluding to convert the property to their own use." They also said that, in an attempt to "starve" them out, they received less weekly rations.[10] The protesters said, "Feed us better and we will not kick."

The *Social Gospel* downplayed the founders' defensiveness in the face of the dissenters' complaints. After devoting their assets, time, and labor to the colony, the original members were protective of their investment. The leaders defended the power structure and its actions by asserting that it expressed the democratic will. But as the disaffected element became more vocal and more outsiders answered the invitation to "come out of individualism and into mutualism," Gibson admitted that the founders drew closer together and "developed a narrowness and a clannishness." Still, he labeled the critics as dishonest and uncharitable egotists who wanted to overthrow the leadership.[11]

The dissenters' motives appeared mixed. Some wished to break up the community and acquire its assets instead of participating more fully, but Brewer's was more personal. He had had an erratic tenure at Commonwealth, and the community expelled him in January 1899. Brewer had been there for over a year, wrote for the *Social Gospel*, was a good worker, and seemed to be honorable. Experienced as a preacher, he expressed his ideas forcefully, often in opposition to the leadership. In Albertson's opinion, he was a dogmatic "crank" with a considerable amount of intellectual conceit who was annoyed by Albertson's pragmatism, flexibility, and influence.

When Commonwealth expelled Brewer, he vowed that he would "destroy" the community. Weeks later, he returned and started a commotion near the print shop. He told members that he was going to publish his manuscript and file a lawsuit against the colony. He also informed them that he had notified the Right Relationship League that Commonwealth had violated its ideals. In an ironic response, some of the colony's most committed nonresistants became a mob that threatened to tar and feather Brewer. Albertson defused the situation by threatening to abandon his leadership role if the crowd used violence. The next morning, he went to Columbus to ask the sheriff to come out and remove Brewer.[12]

Brewer had an ally, Tannager, a tough, physically imposing man. Heavily scarred, he had been a cowboy, and Commonwealth suspected him of having "a record of gun-play in Texas." He was not a deep thinker and had a great deal of personal venom. He had contributed heavy physical labor to Com-

monwealth but regularly supported Brewer and was the only voter opposing his expulsion. He also spread rumors that undermined the reputation of
some young women in the community. He and Brewer threatened to kill Albertson, which led Damon and Justin Cook to keep an armed guard at Albertson's house. After the sheriff removed Brewer, he returned to remove
Tannager. The incident gravely harmed the community as members bewailed
the loss of their ideals of nonresistance and love by resorting to the "force"
of civil authorities. It was a precursor of things to come.[13]

Brewer returned a few months later to stir up dissent again. He attended
a prayer meeting where anyone could speak and began to read a speech that
bitterly criticized Albertson, Damon, and Gibson. He accused them of pre-
venting free expression and Albertson of trying to establish an "intellectual
autocracy." In response, the leaders adjourned the meeting, but a few members remained to hear Brewer. Albertson, Gibson, and Cook returned, blew
out the lights, and put an end to Brewer's speech. Afterward, they had the
Columbus sheriff arrest Brewer.[14]

Affairs became more intense with the arrest of S. W. Martin. He had been
a resident for eighteen months but was never a member. Everyone who
worked at Commonwealth signed a contract, which explicitly stated that
"board is and shall be accepted by me as payment in full for the labor I perform and I hereby relinquish all claims whatsoever to any wages." Nevertheless, when the membership gave Martin notice to leave, he demanded payment for his labor. Without it, Martin refused to go, and Albertson called out
the sheriff again to remove him.[15]

Since September 1898, Commonwealth had given Martin four notices
asking him to leave. In response, he wrote a letter to William Damon, which
a Columbus newspaper published. In his letter, Martin falsely claimed to be
the only southerner left in the colony, which had expelled the others. He referred to the community leaders as "broken down Yankee preachers" and
compared them to the "Northern pulpit" that had long been responsible for
spreading stories of southern "deviltry." He went so far as to compare them
to "'Ku Klux Klans,' and 'white-cappers' by conducting star chamber courts,
using the sacred name of Christ as a trademark." They hold secret meetings,
decide who is "persona non grata," and "give them notice to quit." Martin was
protesting in public because he feared others would construe his silence as
evidence of his guilt.

Damon and Albertson responded to Martin's accusations. They stated
that his effort to inject sectional prejudice into the conflict was unwarranted.

Martin, they claimed, was not a southerner, but there were many southern members in residence. Moreover, Commonwealth was grateful for the kindness they had received from their southern neighbors.

Similar to events at the Amana and Burley colonies, a dispute over the control of assets led to legal problems that would hasten the demise of the Christian Commonwealth. In May 1899, the dissenters, led by Brewer, Martin, and Loiselle, asked Colonel C. J. Thornton, a Columbus attorney, to file a petition in the Muscogee County Superior Court for a bankruptcy order to appoint a receiver, disband the colony, force the sale of its property, and distribute the proceeds to its members.[16]

The litigants did not reject the idea of a "brotherhood" colony nor consider it a failure but were alleging mismanagement. They produced a letter from a former member that emphatically expressed the belief that Commonwealth conducted on the right principles would be successful. They told a *Sunday Herald* reporter that if they won their suit, they would start a new colony with ideal theories and conditions.[17]

They argued that Commonwealth could not expel a member without civil action in the courts because the charter was invalid and members held individual property rights. They charged a "ring of leaders" with trying to "freeze out" members who did not support them. The dissenters told a reporter that twenty-seven disaffected people had recently left the colony. In addition to the dissent leaders, fifteen other colony members signed the petition. Except for S. W. Martin, all were members of the community.[18]

The dissenters directed their petition at the Christian Commonwealth and William Damon, Sue Fay Hinckley, Jule Talmadge, Jacob Troth, Ralph Albertson, and other officers and members. It accused them of conspiring to convert Commonwealth's property to their benefit. To that end, they had secured the support of a majority of members and were continually making "frivolous charges" without proof against dissenters. Then they expelled the accused. The petitioners claimed that it was common knowledge that the leaders denied members their "equal right of participation," which the charter guaranteed, and intended to discharge every member who disagreed with them. They stated that they were powerless to protect themselves without the court's support and asked for two thousand dollars in damages. The petition also asked the court to require the defendants to account for all property and money that they acquired during the community's existence. Finally, the petitioners wanted the defendants enjoined from expelling any members without just cause.

The petitioners had some knowledge of the community's liabilities and assets, and their list exposed its economic condition. They were aware of a debt of over six hundred dollars to several individuals and believed there were other debts of which they did not know. The community's assets included around five hundred dollars' worth of livestock and movable equipment worth over twelve hundred dollars.

The lawsuit created an uproar in Commonwealth, producing trauma, turmoil, and conflict among the members. Tolstoy had advised the colonists that if they quarreled, "it is better to give up everything than to act against love," and believers in nonresistance opposed contesting the lawsuit even though it might destroy the community. They believed a legal defense would mean the end of their ideal. Albertson, on the other hand, refused to allow the colony's members to be "put out on the sandy highway of Georgia empty-handed." He believed that if "they had taken away our horses or money or any property we should not have prosecuted them," but "it was a situation that could not be met by anything in our philosophy. If we were to live we had to fight. It was the end of our dream of strictly obeying the Sermon on the Mount." After an intense debate at the colony's general meeting, Albertson and those who wanted to contest the petition won the day and abandoned nonresistance to preserve the community.[19]

Years later, in *Thy Cloak Also*, a fictionalized account of his life, Albertson recalled his dismay:

> Hugh [Albertson] . . . knew. . . . It would have to go through the court. . . . The wickedness of it! The falseness of it! Failure! Utter, irrevocable failure! Ignominious failure! The triumph of lies! The loss of his ideal! The wreckage of his dream!
>
> He had wanted to follow Jesus. He had wanted this colony to follow Jesus, . . . "Resist not evil!" Resist not their evil. . . . Let the whole conception of an orderly peaceful city of love become a byword and a snare!
>
> Jesus? Yes, they had crucified him. They had lied about him. They had proven him wrong. They had killed him. . . . They had certainly rejected the good words of Jesus. Then there was a new rejection and a new crucifixion. Nothing had been resurrected. It could not come back. Love was crucified. . . . Herron had said that only crucifixion could await any man who undertook to do as Jesus did in his life. No man could live and love his neighbor as himself. He could talk about it—cheap, hollow talk!
>
> To follow Jesus was to have no property. . . . There is no social gospel. There is no hope for common property if you follow Jesus. The poor will

take it all, and when the poor are fed, the selfish will take the rest. There is
no social salvation.... There is only ... the triumph of selfishness.

So this was the crucifixion. the land would be sold. the libels would
stand. The gospel would be disbelieved. Overfed preachers would stand
in their pulpits and read pompously: "Go, sell all thou hast and give to the
poor—" Smug capitalists would continue to expound Christianity. They
would even talk about Jesus as a good businessman....

To follow Jesus now means to let the Christian Commune be sold out
and wiped out.

Well, should he die—without a struggle? Without going on any further? Strange he had not realized before that Jesus was still on the cross!
Why shouldn't the world fight, and be cruel?

Hugh Cotton resolved to fight. He knew Jesus wouldn't. So, he would
stop trying to follow Jesus.[20]

Despite his despair, disillusionment, and cynicism, Albertson took charge of
the community's defense and hired two Columbus attorneys to represent
the community in court.[21]

When the dispute became public, Tolstoy expressed concern for the
Christian Commonwealth, but he remained positive about its future. In a
letter to Ernest Crosby, he wrote, "I feel especially concerned about all that
goes on in The Christian Commonwealth. I read all their journal with deep
interest and never cease to rejoice at the firmness of their views and beautiful expression of their thoughts. I should like to get as many details concerning their life as possible."[22] The *Coming Nation* chastised Commonwealth in
the wake of the lawsuit. The relationship between the communities was cordial, but there was an undertone of rivalry. Commonwealth had never failed
to promote its open admission policy, in contrast to Ruskin's high entry fee.
Writing about the lawsuit, the newspaper stated that Commonwealth, with
no admission fee, should have expected hardship, hard labor, and scanty
fare because of its lack of capital. The result was disgruntled members who
lacked patience with pioneer conditions and charity for the shortcomings of
others.[23]

Damon and Albertson were confident that the petition would be rejected
but spent time in Columbus talking to people about the issues. It was the
most severe crisis in the community's history, but they denied that it proved
the colony was a failure. It had prospered far beyond their expectations and
was still improving. He challenged anyone to "find a happier or more con-
tented community" than the majority at Commonwealth.

Albertson blamed the trouble on the indiscriminate membership policy, which allowed "virtual tramps" to become members. Conditions caused the departure of about half of the newcomers, who did not have the character, work ethic, or moral standards of the colony or found it uncongenial. There were fifty-three voting members in the community, but only fourteen names on the petition, and two of those persons said that their signatures were not authorized. The majority of members and nonmember residents approved of its management, and none of the colony's original members, "those who have made it what it is," were part of the conspiracy.

He believed that the troublemakers were mainly people who had come since early 1899. Unless he was making a distinction between members and nonmember residents, he was speaking incorrectly. Of eight known petitioners, five were mentioned in the *Social Gospel* as early as October 1898 and one arrived in January 1899, but it is not clear when the others came.[24]

Gibson acknowledged that they "had to take each other on trust," which led to members who stirred up trouble. Egotistical and thirsty for power, they organized to discredit the leadership and break up the community. Dissenters stopped attending religious meetings, mocked prayer, and displayed materialistic tendencies that contradicted Commonwealth's values and the pledges they made when they joined.[25]

Some petitioners took exception to Albertson's condemnation, and the entire affair played out in the newspaper. Asked who the tramps were, Brewer replied that Albertson and Damon were "dead broke" when they came to Commonwealth, and Albertson was living off of a Michigan socialist.[26]

Albertson and Damon responded to the charges for an *Enquirer-Sun* reporter. It was absurd that the leadership was benefitting financially, and they noted that the revenues of the community were not that remunerative. They stated that the benefits the petitioners had received were equal to or exceeded the value of labor, money, and goods that they had contributed and that many members were "tramps" who had brought nothing to the colony.

Asked if the leaders "fared any better" than the rank and file, they replied that all fared the same, despite incidental evidence to the contrary, including Albertson's comments in his manuscript history. Also, they noted that prominent members had made personal sacrifices to benefit the entire community.

The trouble at Commonwealth aired some "spicy charges" and created quite a sensation in Columbus. People were aware that problems had been brewing and the newspapers covered them thoroughly, sometimes on the front page. It is not clear where the local people stood on the issues, but the colonists did have many personal friends in town. Nevertheless, others were critical of the leaders. Mrs. Washington, a local slum worker, visited and saw several unpleasant things. She thought the leaders were "heathens" in their unorthodoxy and lived better than most colonists.[27]

Legal proceedings began on June 1 but did not include the case against Commonwealth. The community was pressing trespass charges against Martin because he remained in Commonwealth after being given notice to leave. Albertson and Damon testified that Martin was not a member, was not entitled to any property or benefits, and had no right to remain. Martin testified on his own behalf. He admitted to not being a member but denied trespassing because, having worked on the property for eighteen months, he believed he was entitled to share in the material holdings and have every privilege except voting. The jury found Martin guilty and fined him twenty-five dollars or six months in jail.[28]

Illness forced the postponement of the main trial. In the interim, Martin paid his fine and was released from jail. Then he, Brewer, and Hall sat for an interview with an *Enquirer-Sun* reporter. Hall stated that his family had been at Commonwealth for eighteen months. They had arrived well clothed and contributed eighty dollars and a set of tools to the community, where he worked as a blacksmith. Now, he said, their condition was "pitiable." They had been insufficiently fed and had received only some shoes and minor articles of clothing.

The three men denied they were tramps. Albertson's charge was unfair, and they presented countercharges against the leaders, stating that one "religious leader" of the community had spent time in state prison. Another member of the majority, Justin Cook, had been on his way to Commonwealth, was arrested as a tramp, and spent thirty days on a chain gang. A third prominent official had "tramped" for forty miles to reach Commonwealth. Given the diversity and nature of the community, these charges could have been accurate. Unfortunately, there is little evidence supporting or disproving the claims, but they aroused tension and interest.

The petitioners also accused the leadership of amending the constitution to serve their interests. The original constitution stated that a member should contribute "all he had" to Commonwealth to be used for the public good. According to the men, one leader's wife inherited a "neat little fortune," and her husband used his influence to have the constitution revised, allowing her to keep the money. Again, the record is vague as far as constitutional amendments are concerned.

The constitution stated that there should be no private property or wealth except for personal items. The dissenters claimed that nearly everyone in the colony who could scrape up cash kept it. Moreover, Irene Albertson kept her piano, and Jule Talmadge kept his Civil War pension and his tobacco.[29]

On June 6, the Superior Court took up the Commonwealth case. It was a lively event. The majority of the audience, including many colony "ladies," sympathized with the leaders as they listened with amusement to the petitioners' recitals of the alleged abuses. However, the petitioners also had significant support.

Both sides restated their positions depicted above. Albertson and Gibson reiterated that the petitioners had received more than they had brought to the colony. In a legal maneuver, Commonwealth's attorneys forced the petitioners' attorneys to present affidavits that they had initially decided not to offer. The trial records have not been found, so it is impossible to know if something beneficial to Commonwealth was revealed.[30]

The next day, the colony's attorneys finished reading their affidavits, which challenged those of the petitioners. Each side finished with brief arguments, and the case went to the judge, who denied the petitioners' application for a receiver.[31]

The dissatisfied element held a mass meeting at the Red Men's Hall in Columbus. Colonel Thornton, the petitioners' attorney, stated that he would appeal the case to the Supreme Court. About thirty people heard Brewer, John Steffes, and William McHenry criticize Commonwealth's leadership and plead for money to cover the cost of an appeal. In response, George Damon, William's son, invited anyone who wanted to know the truth about Commonwealth to come for a visit.[32]

Commonwealth had proved itself competently managed and prosperous. Furthermore, everyone had equal rights and benefits. The judge upheld the community's charter and approved the expulsion of members who violated its bylaws. With one exception, Commonwealth did not have to expel or abridge the membership privileges of any dissenters. They all left of their own accord—fifteen departures in June.[33]

The following day, the grand jury charged Brewer with trespass and disturbing a public meeting. He was arrested, posted bond, and claimed it was the colony leaders, not him, who had disrupted public worship. Brewer wrote a letter to the *Enquirer-Sun*, repeating his charges against the leaders. Albertson and Damon were broke. Damon did not want to come but was facing "starvation or the workhouse." Gibson and Cook were "stranded paupers" in Nebraska; Gibson was brought by David Brown, whom he ran out of the colony, while Cook "tramped" through Tennessee before arriving in Columbus on a freight train.

At his trial, Brewer denied the trespass charge and stated that members of the minority faction still lived at Commonwealth and invited him back after his expulsion. The state argued that the colony, through its leadership, had the privilege of determining who could reside at the community. Despite Brewer's impassioned defense, the jury found him guilty. He was sentenced to pay a twenty-five-dollar fine or serve three months on a chain gang.[34]

Despite Commonwealth's court victory, the proceedings caused much reflection. Gibson felt compelled to share their newfound wisdom for the benefit of those who would follow. He acknowledged that the community organized based on trust. With no test for membership, some early members had harmful faults, especially selfishness, and withdrew quickly. Still, with their need for manpower, the colony was vulnerable to smooth talkers whose goals differed from theirs. The whole episode caused pain and sadness within the Commonwealth, but Gibson believed that good would come of it. They were determined to keep their doors open but would "more carefully guard the inner circle of membership" and wait until they saw the "Christ spirit" in newcomers before making them voting members.[35]

The court victory was marked by moral defeat. The lawsuit produced an ideological split among the members that poisoned the atmosphere, undermined solidarity and morale, provoked further disagreements, and cost them support from the outside world. Believers in nonresistance thought that by using the courts, the community had turned from its fundamental principle and abandoned its hope for the Kingdom of God. They were no longer different from the rest of the world. Critics noted that expelling people violated their ideal to "open their doors to everybody." No longer did their love and industry include even the least of God's children. They had turned to force and expelled some. They had drawn a line around themselves and called on the state for protection. They had wanted to deed their land to Jesus Christ, but now they had "driven off some of those for whom Jesus Christ had died. The ideal was gone."

Nevertheless, Albertson believed that the community was beginning to find itself. He thought that Commonwealth had been uncertain as to its character. It was now clear, and they could concentrate on building something permanent and useful. The majority had supported the fight and understood that the choice was to see the community destroyed or make a pragmatic choice to modify its principles and survive.[36]

He saw Commonwealth and communities like it doing two things. They would "rescue some souls from the seething mass of overcrowded city life and greatly bless them in the pure air and healthful occupations of the country" and "lift up a standard and show to the world a pattern of right social life." Commonwealth had come through its troubles "sweet and with a strong hold on life" and would continue its joy of loving sacrifice.[37]

The lawsuit forced Commonwealth to clarify its charter. The corporation, not the membership, held title to the property. There was no individual ownership, and members owned no stock. This prevented future legal challenges to the community's existence. Albertson wanted to take it one step further and deed the property "to a board of trustees of national reputation" to create a relationship similar to that of universities. With no property to covet, they could avoid the fate of Ruskin or another lawsuit from selfish members.[38]

They had completed the hard work of starting a community and continued to grow spiritually after the trial. Poverty and imperfect brethren continued to test their faith. They knew that they had much to learn, but they also knew that it was right and safe to love and had neither the right nor the desire to turn from the brotherhood life to the old life of self-seeking. Nor were they willing to resort to a "sifting process" to perfect the membership. They remained committed to the belief that undying love "shall work miracles in the moral status of imbeciles and reprobates."[39]

They were convinced that devotion would lead to victory over economic hardship. Nothing could shake their confidence that the brotherhood life was right and God would fulfill his promises and supply their needs. Such serenity could not have existed in the "sinfully selfish system of competition." They had first "sought the Kingdom of God and His righteousness of brotherhood and were convinced that the promise of God was being wonderfully and graciously fulfilled."[40]

But their optimism was misplaced. In addition to ideological conflict, the lawsuit dealt Commonwealth a severe economic blow. Legal expenses diverted money from food, supplies, and equipment. Members could not afford beans, rice, sugar, and syrup. They were compelled to live off of cornmeal, shorts, and vegetables from their gardens. Nevertheless, a member concluded that the legal victory was worth the cost of a bread-and-water diet.[41]

Not everyone viewed the court victory positively. When the community violated its ideal of nonresistance, contributions dried up. Edward Keyes was disappointed that the colony was no longer living according to its ideals, and the Right Relationship League refused to make further payments on the two-thousand-dollar mortgage, which put Commonwealth under severe financial strain.[42]

Other sympathizers wrote letters criticizing Commonwealth. Buoyed by the legal success, Albertson rejected the criticism and sarcastically caricatured the critics' position:

> It was too bad, they said, that so glorious an ideal should have been given up so easily. Would it not have been possible with a little more love, with a little more tact, to keep the "kickers" from rebellion? . . . Is not such love possible? You were going to show us, we hoped, that it was. Well, we are hurt, our faith is hurt. We are almost but not quite broken hearted (as we sit here in our office in a northern city and dictate this letter to our stenographer). Naturally we shall take less interest in what you are doing.[43]

CHAPTER 9

✦ ✦ ✦

A Loss of Courage

Every man for himself.

—William Damon,
"The Christian Commonwealth"

THE DEATHBLOW TO THE Christian Commonwealth came from within. Just as its most promising enterprise—its extensive orchards—was primed to bear fruit, twin catastrophes struck. The lawsuit and, more importantly, the community response to it played the most significant role in the community's decline and disintegration. While tensions were still high, a typhoid fever epidemic killed several members and sickened many more. The twin calamities resulted in members losing faith, and one by one families drifted away. Nonresistance proved powerless against slander, climate, and disease, and abandoning the principle to fight the lawsuit broke the spirit of many in the colony.[1]

Of the original members, the Gibsons, Albertsons, Damons, and Hinckleys remained. Albertson was optimistic that the community had solved the problems caused by open membership and that it could thrive. However, the loss of workers weakened their ability to produce the necessary resources. A winter snowstorm and the dissenters' malingering added to the colony's food shortages.

In April 1899, the community picnicked on beautiful grounds outside the village. They used water from a nearby brook to make lemonade and coffee. Three weeks later, four members became feverish. They soon developed typhoid symptoms, and they feared the cause was contaminated water from the picnic. Slow to respond, the community used quarantine and disinfectants to halt the spread of the disease, but a month later there were five more cases.[2]

Two members died in the initial outbreak. Eora Henry, the doctor, was one of the first. Members buried her at Commonwealth with Albertson and Damon officiating. She left three sons, the oldest four years, and the youngest, born at Commonwealth, only four months old. A week later, her husband Leroy, also a doctor, was stricken but recovered. After his recovery, he and his children left for Terre Haute, Indiana, from where he kept up with Commonwealth and continued his reform activities. He called Gibson's essay "A Society of Brothers" the "best and most practical thing yet," and asked for fifty copies that he could distribute at Reverend J. Stitt Wilson's meetings.[3]

The loss of both doctors was a severe blow at an inopportune time, and the community hoped that Henry would reconsider and return. Nevertheless, with Columbus doctors, food, and careful nursing, members thought they were free of the disease by August as all of the patients were recuperating. A generous shipment of fruit and food from Dr. and Mrs. Dorcas Green of Pennsylvania helped them get back on their feet. The disease and the losses exhausted and strained the community, but they remained confident that God would intervene on their behalf.[4]

The typhoid epidemic disrupted Commonwealth's social gatherings, such as the Shakespeare Club, throughout the summer and fall. John Chipman tried to rally the community from afar. The "warfare upon us" has "tried our courage," but he urged colonists to take the sum of their "joy of personal comradeship—the joy of battle with wrong—the joy of love and of hope and of faith—the joy of God near to us." His encouragement helped. As the disease declined, community socials became regular occurrences, and the Shakespeare Club restarted. There was rejoicing as people "who have looked Death in the face" reappeared in their old places within the community.[5]

When the Shakespeare Club restarted, it met in the general parlor, a large, comfortable room with a sizable old-fashioned fireplace. The Commonwealth women brought in their "fancy work," and John Karmen sketched the place and its participants. They read *King Lear*, then dropped Shakespeare temporarily to read and discuss Bolton Hall's *Things as They Are*. Readers enjoyed the work and saw Hall's advocacy of urban homesteading as parallel to their efforts.[6]

Commonwealth also resumed periodic talks and lectures. Calvin Reasoner's daughter Elsie visited during a lecture tour of the South. She had been a correspondent for *McClure's Magazine* when the Spanish-American War broke out. In Jamaica, she met Clara Barton, who took Elsie on a Red Cross ship to Cuba, where she became America's first woman war correspondent.[7]

Meanwhile, the public's opinion of Commonwealth was declining because of the revelations in the legal case, the lack of financial success, and the disease epidemic. There were some intimations, confirmed by Albertson, of laziness on the part of colony members. One staunch friend of the colony rejected the accusation as a total injustice. A frequent visitor, he argued that Commonwealth's members worked hard but had one of the worst pieces of land in the county—land ruined by profit-seeking, slave-based plantation agriculture. Nevertheless, their efforts had improved the property significantly.

In September, Albertson, after a summer of the burden and strain of caring for others, became ill with typhoid. He and eight-year-old Fannie Croyle were the last to come down with the disease. Fannie quickly recovered, and Albertson, with a good physician and the best of care, improved but then relapsed. His condition filled the community with anxiety and prayer. Critically ill and near death, he barely survived and was not able to leave his bed until late October. At one point, he was a "sack of bones weighing only eighty-nine pounds." He credited Lucy Fay with saving his life, but no details about his care exist. He may have had some unusual ideas about medicine, for in a book review in the *Social Gospel*, he commended a doctor's support for avoiding medicines and using the bath method for curing disease.[8]

When Albertson's illness prevented him from serving as an editor of the *Social Gospel*, Gibson, the managing editor, brought in new contributors and maintained its high standards. He gave Justin Cook, of the Farm Department, permanent work in the printing office. He was "quick and bright" and knowledgeable about machinery, which made him useful in both the composing and printing rooms. Sue Fay and Daniel Hinckley, Calvin Reasoner, and Derrill Hope got opportunities to write more, and when Gibson left, they helped keep the *Social Gospel* going. In January 1900, Gibson invited all members to contribute to "Colony Notes" for the February edition. Almost everyone was willing, and nineteen members wrote something for publication.[9]

Hope reviewed popular fiction and wrote an analysis of the language of the Lord's Prayer, concluding that the contemporary world had strayed from its teachings. In her view, love, compassion, and courtesy had disappeared in the pursuit of pleasure, convenience, and wealth. Parents had abdicated their authority as the worship of Mammon had devalued discipline and corrupted the domestic atmosphere.[10]

Sue Fay reviewed art books and historical romances and wrote an insightful critique of W. Walker Stephens's *Higher Life for Working People*. Applauding him for his understanding of the problems faced by the working class—dangerous working conditions, unemployment, poor housing, unequal distribution of wealth, and lack of security in old age—she faulted him for preferring evolutionary schemes of reform and rejecting socialism. Her husband Daniel gave Bolton Hall's *Things as They Are* a favorable review while the Shakespeare Club was reading it. An optimistic book of fables, it criticized the "logical absurdities" of many reform methods, such as charity, while advocating education as the path to the Kingdom of Heaven.[11]

Despite signs of improvement, Gibson was discouraged. He first showed despair in a letter to Tolstoy in mid-1899, after the first typhoid deaths. He wrote, "I open my heart to you, for advice and conference concerning the things of the Kingdom of Love." Defending Commonwealth as evidence of the ability to overcome individual and family selfishness, he admitted to its imperfection in taking people out of society. He asked Tolstoy about starting a "religious Order of Economic Brothers" that would establish a spiritual bond "across space." It would adhere to Commonwealth's principles of universal love and service but would allow people to stay "just where they are." Gibson first embraced this idea in August 1898, when he suggested that "it may be necessary for some individuals to hold what they possess, directing its use unselfishly that greatest service may be rendered to the most needy ones."[12]

There was evidence in the *Social Gospel* that some members, while holding to their general principles, were on the verge of giving up on the colony. In late June, Ruth Damon, the sixteen-year-old daughter of Commonwealth's president, died after a battle with typhoid fever. Ruth had a "happy, loving spirit" and led the young people. In Commonwealth's early days, she had copied a list for them of "rules of life" that helped explain her beautiful character:

1. Learn to govern yourselves, to be gentle and patient.
2. Guard your tempers, especially in seasons of ill health, irritation, and trouble, and soften them by prayer and a sense of your own shortcomings and errors.

3. Never speak or act in anger until you have prayed over your words or acts.
4. Remember that valuable as is the gift of speech, silence is often more valuable.
5. Do not expect too much from others, but forbear and forgive, as you desire forbearance and forgiveness yourself.
6. Never retort a sharp or angry word. It is the second word that makes the quarrel.
7. Beware of the first disagreement.
8. Learn to speak in a gentle tone of voice.
9. Learn to say kind and pleasant things whenever opportunity offers.
10. Study the character of each friend and sympathize with all their troubles, however small.
11. Do not neglect little things if they can affect the comfort of others in the least degree.
12. Avoid moods and pets, and fits of sulkiness.
13. Learn to deny yourself and prefer others.
14. Beware of meddlers and talebearers.
15. Never charge a bad motive when a good one is conceivable.

Ruth's death hit the colony hard, and her father, whose son was also ill, hung on until the fall but finally gave up on Commonwealth. Out of despair, he cried, "Every man for himself."[13]

That fall, Damon and his wife, with Jacob Troth, left for Virginia to investigate a site that Troth had inherited from his Quaker ancestors. It adjoined Mount Vernon, and Troth thought a colony might work there. The Damons agreed and decided to start a new brotherhood colony with Troth and several other interested parties. They started the community in Gunston, Virginia, on the land of professor Edward Daniels, but the Damons stayed only a few months, having had enough of communism. The colony ended as well, and Troth ultimately died on his family estate.[14]

The community deeply felt the loss of the Damons. They had been among the first to come to Commonwealth and had been instrumental in its development, but their involvement in a new colony somewhat eased Commonwealth's disappointment.[15]

Despite the losses, members remained encouraged by their agricultural progress. The farm was not hopelessly inadequate but merely "run down," and workers were learning how to get good results from the soil and the climate. With care, they expected both farm and garden to improve yearly. They solved their hay shortage by planting several acres of millet. They began preparing a fall garden with collards, cabbage, lettuce, radishes, and beets. Only a shortage of labor and fertilizer limited their ability to raise more vegetables. Loving friends encouraged them by providing emotional and material support during their time of affliction. Two offered generous loans without interest to help the community "set its house in order." They tried to reassure everyone that they had quite a stock of happiness at Commonwealth, gathered in by their brotherhood spirit and relations.[16]

Gibson and the Hinckleys tried to hold the colony together, but when Gibson announced that he planned to leave, their effectiveness was weakened. In his letter to Tolstoy, Gibson had pleaded for a story "that we may print" to attract readers and asked permission to put him on the masthead as an associate editor. Anything "would serve our cause much." Feeling hopeless, Gibson lost faith in establishing a physical location for the Kingdom of God. Still devoted to the ideal but disillusioned by the disappointments at Commonwealth, he no longer believed that communal experiments were the best path. Looking for a new opportunity, he proposed, in the September 1899 *Social Gospel*, the organization of "An Order of Brothers," inspired by Commonwealth's ideals, but larger and broader and composed of people everywhere. Under the rule of love, a religious Order of Business Brothers could "economize labor, facilitate service, and perfect fellowship."[17]

Gibson asserted that Commonwealth had demonstrated the value of living in a brotherhood but had failed to demonstrate how men could follow that standard where they were in their current economic relations. His model was the disciples of Christ who, though personally separated and compelled to conform to economic custom, were able to remain united in spirit and have all things common. A spiritual brotherhood should take precedence because it allowed members to remain where God had placed them. He advised that no one should come to Commonwealth unless they were certain they could serve the world better there. Accepting incremental reform, he suggested that men should temporarily use the industrial system while cooperating to "increase their power of service." They should establish city colonies, social settlements that had economic features, and cooperative stores, factories, and farms. In those circumstances, even a few men could extend brotherhood by serving and sharing as brothers. Once organized, these small groups could share their earnings, fulfill others' needs, and accumulate surpluses as brotherhood capital to found or extend brotherhood industries. In conclusion, Gibson followed his proposal with additional articles and solicitations for support and asked for letters from readers who had questions or suggestions.[18]

His solicitations generated support and opposition. He received enough positive response that he believed he had a plan that would lead him to a larger field of usefulness than Commonwealth had been. He wrote Tolstoy that he proposed a "love movement in mutual service" that would "emancipate individuals from the entanglements of the selfish system of life." But, he then said that he would "make whatever use can be made of the church and government in their very imperfect state." Not believing in bullets or ballots, he nevertheless said that with "some mixing in politics," he would get the attention of people who otherwise would not hear him.[19]

Tolstoy responded favorably but urged caution. He had always sympathized with and challenged Commonwealth. He agreed with the community's simple ideology that "reason and love" were the only rules of God's organization. Now that the colony was in decline, he reasserted his belief that all human organizations were false and needed elimination because they prevent men from seeing God's truth. He warned that too many rules and definitions would hinder the activity of Gibson's Order of Brothers. Finally, Tolstoy confirmed that he would send the *Social Gospel* a story for publication.[20]

Ernest Howard Crosby agreed with Tolstoy. He sympathized with Gibson's proposal for a broad-based brotherhood, drawing from Swedenborg the idea that "people who think alike are ipso facto together." He also appealed for a second level of membership for weak brothers like himself, who were not able to extricate themselves from mainstream society. Crosby dismissed the need for geographical unity and believed that Commonwealth undermined its own goals because not everyone was ready to accept colony life, even if they agreed with the community's ideals. Moreover, communitarians could not be effective because they were too isolated. Finally, he feared an organization could become an end in itself and turn into an empty form that mistakes the instrument for the spirit.[21]

N. O. Nelson responded positively but also urged caution. He agreed that Christianity needed a new start but thought that Gibson had ignored the example of Saint Francis. To prevent the evils of materialism, the order had to declare itself against large possessions or many wants.[22]

Thomas Will offered support, and a socialist minister from Kansas, G. E. Etherton, expressed his fullest sympathy and was ready to join with Gibson

to develop the plan's details. Etherton agreed with Commonwealth's founders that charity and incremental reform were merely tampering with a dis-
eased social organism. On the other hand, the colony method narrowed the
field of influence, could not be evangelistic, and was never Jesus's way. Remaining in place, but uniting, was a practical solution given modern tech-
nologies in transportation and communication. The printing press, the railroads, and the telegraph would allow the order to be scattered everywhere
but still "touch the present system at all points." Etherton closed by telling
Gibson that he waited eagerly for details on the order. A month later, Etherton offered his ideas about how to actualize God's kingdom on earth. He saw
it as a simple and natural process of evolution. Form local circles of believers
in universal love. Have them communize their interests and provide mutual
help to one another. Such a community would "grow by the Christian law of
natural-spiritual selection" rather than coercion, and it would "convict the
world of its sin, shame it out of its selfishness and draw all men unto Christ
and His way."[23]

After Gibson published his pamphlet, Etherton called it "clear, compact,
comprehensive, consummate" but expressed frustration that many were not
able to understand or see the same vision. He explained that vision in a long
Social Gospel article a few months later. Comparing the Order of Brothers to
the early disciples of Christ, he assured everyone that abandoning individual ownership and the single-handed struggle for one's livelihood would not
result in poverty, as communism's critics argued. Etherton stated there was
no evidence that Christ and his disciples suffered in poverty, and the Brothers would also be cared for by those to whom they ministered. Gibson recommended a work that supported Etherton. It was *Christ-Like Christianity*
by Edward Eels, a Presbyterian preacher in West Virginia. Eels argued that
Christianity was organized as a brotherhood and not as a church assembly.
He devoted an entire chapter to the Greek word *koinonia*, which he translated as communion, fellowship, and "putting money together," and which,
in 1942, became the name of another Georgia intentional community sixty
miles southeast of Commonwealth.[24]

In response, critics reprised their earlier doubts about the Commonwealth plan. A New York minister stated that a brotherhood "cannot be a success—as long as human nature is as it is." The *Social Gospel*'s editors agreed
that it might not be the best way, but it would suffice until the "churches required their members to be industrial and economic brothers," as taught in
Christ's gospel.[25]

Gibson took the letters seriously and wrote a column listing vital questions that he would address in the future. He was aware of the concerns but was optimistic that if each person found "at least one who wants to be your brother," it would start a movement that would be a "way of escape." He also proposed a conference to "discuss the brotherhood ideal and obligations."

At Commonwealth, the Order of Brothers became a topic of conversation at Sunday services, with Calvin Reasoner supporting Gibson. The order would unite people "in spirit whereby property shall become subordinate to cooperation of soul." Not being ecclesiastical, denominational, or hierarchical, it would be Christian to the core.

Commonwealth's Executive Board also discussed the order during its meetings. Whether they thought it was a threat to Commonwealth is not clear, but they realized that Commonwealth's people would "be ready to act along new lines as rapidly as light breaks upon them and providence makes possible an open way."[26]

In December, Gibson wrote a pamphlet, "A Society of Brothers," for people who were interested in brotherhood life but were bound by love, duty, and economic necessity to remain where they were. The *Social Gospel* advertised and circulated the pamphlet widely. Gibson wrote that God wants us to form a Society of Brothers that can exist anywhere. To promote it even more, he started a new department in the *Social Gospel*, "The Brother-Love Evangel." Its goal was to throw light on the problem of forming brotherhood societies anywhere and everywhere.[27]

The department received much correspondence. Mary Stuckenberg, a leader of the Woman's Christian Temperance Union, called the *Social Gospel* beautiful and Commonwealth's example and the Order of Brotherhood "great work." A Wellesley College professor, probably Vida Scudder, differed on some details but loved the *Social Gospel* and would join Gibson's Brotherhood if it "matured." She would have to remain in the "inferior but outer circle" suggested by Crosby because of entanglements in "many threads of private duty." In a poignant letter, a Princeton-educated minister asked how a preacher, bound to his church, could enter, except sympathetically, the Order of Brothers. He tearfully longed for love and brotherhood but saw little in the church. Gibson read his letter with "intense, painful interest." He responded that the minister should free himself by faithful preaching. He may be "cast out" for doing so, but he would also attract a harmonious society of brothers who would love him as he had never been loved. Letters and requests kept coming. A Massachusetts correspondent questioned whether men or our social system were capable of following Jesus's teachings. Then he described encounters with his pastor and a union leader, both of whom were readers of the *Social Gospel*. They said they were with him on brotherhood, although all three were doing more thinking than acting. Gibson assured him that God was calling him and he could not refuse. It was education, particularly of children, that would prepare them for a future society rooted in love and brotherhood.[28]

Gibson continued to promote the order in his monthly column. Organizing societies of brothers who Christianized capital would conquer the selfish, commercial world by including no profits in its prices and by using its surpluses to extend its business and provide employment for an ever-increasing number of workers. He believed even a single person could call a Society of Brothers into existence and encouraged people to "talk the matter over by letter" after reading his pamphlet.[29]

Albertson reiterated his support, repeating Commonwealth's message of practical Christian Socialism:

"Have faith in men.
Unite.
Surrender your self-interests.
Don't be afraid of the devil.
The love of God is the best policy.
Keep a level head.
The kingdom of Heaven is at hand."

"We hope to portray this truth and show that the truth is workable and livable and rational and feasible and possible of realization to common men and women." He admitted that "Commonwealth has made mistakes ... and never attained her ideal," yet it "stands as a rock for the vital principles of Christianity" and raises high the beacon of a right social order. "We are not expecting crucifixion."[30]

While the discussion of the Order of Brothers proceeded, members, discouraged by the conditions, began to depart. Nevertheless, a Columbus visitor assured everyone that there was no truth to the rumor that the colony was disbanding. He stated that newcomers were replacing those leaving, keeping the membership numbers stable. In the short term, he was right. New arrivals had come from New Hampshire, Alabama, New York, and Pennsylvania, along with a family of seven from South Dakota.[31]

While Albertson was ill, the community elected him president for the first time. He had resisted the post to demonstrate his humility, his devotion to the Kingdom of God more than its temporal manifestations, and his anarchistic leanings. The other leaders had departed or lost faith and courage, but Albertson still hoped for Commonwealth's success. When his condition got better, he needed to find a solution to the threat of typhoid and feared the community lacked the resources to do so. Not fully recovered, Albertson called an election in which Charles Cook replaced him as president. In October, to recuperate, Albertson took his ghost-like form north to visit his relatives on Long Island. Accompanied by his daughter Phyllis, he planned to return to Commonwealth in January 1900. After leaving his parents' home, Albertson visited friends of the colony in Boston, New York, Connecticut, and Ohio. In western Pennsylvania, he visited Ernest Hammond, a major Commonwealth benefactor. Albertson also met Hammond's daughter Hazel, who made such an impression that she would later become his second wife. Immediately after Christmas, he went to Chicago to discuss his plans with Chicago reformers.[32]

Dozens of members left while Albertson was ill, and he came to realize that the end might be near. Samuel Comings joined the Fairhope single-tax colony in Alabama, where he became a prominent member until his death in 1907. Sadie Pease, whose husband Albert had joined Vrooman the year before, followed Comings to Fairhope after the Vrooman colony failed. In early November, James Brower and his wife left for Ohio. Prominent members, they received the community's love and good wishes. Daniel Franks and his wife returned to England, which pained Commonwealth's membership, but they tried to see the bright side. The Franks could do more significant work promoting the Commonwealth ideal in London than in Georgia. With love and prayers, the members sent them off to spread brotherhood life.[33]

Meanwhile, the *Social Gospel* made one last effort to alleviate the labor shortage. Its appeals in late 1899 told a sad story: "We need a doctor." "We need a blacksmith and more carpenters and farmers." "We need textile workers." "If the carpenters could also farm, it would be an advantage." They needed almost everything and looked for people who would be content living in the South. The appeals continued into the new year. They required three carpenters with tools, a sawyer, and an all-around mill man and still needed a blacksmith. They promised a home among brothers and no fear of losing their positions.[34]

With Damon gone, the need for a good nurseryman became essential. They had peach and plum trees and grapes that, with a good man in charge, could make the nursery and orchards quickly profitable. They pleaded for someone from the fruit or nursery business to join them.

Despite the problems, the community welcomed the love of distant friends and supporters, found pleasure in their environs, and continued to persevere. The fall weather was delightful. The mockingbirds were singing, and autumn brought the full glory of omnipresent blooming weeds and trees presenting the splendor of their dying leaves. The goldenrod, growing as high as a man's head, was luxurious with large and perfect flowers. The children and adult flower lovers, led by Sam Byerly, gathered bunches and arranged them with other October blooms to adorn Commonwealth.[35]

There were good reasons to push ahead. In less than four years, they had built a sawmill, a central kitchen and dining room, a print shop, a blacksmith shop, a flour mill, a cotton mill for the production of towels, additional barns and farm buildings, a school, a bachelor's dormitory, and fourteen family cottages. They always appeared on the verge of continuous and permanent success. After three years of love, equality, and common property, most could not conceive of abandoning brotherhood relations and returning to the individualistic, commercial world.[36]

In December, John Croyle took over as superintendent of the farmers, and the warm weather allowed them to plant a field of oats. A team plowed part of the orchard and began clearing additional rich bottomland for spring planting. In January, Croyle left for the Apalachicola colony. The community shipped his trunk by riverboat and expressed hope that he would return. Nevertheless, the farm work went on. In late January, workers set out one thousand young peach trees and followed with more fruit trees. They had another ten thousand young fruit trees in the orchard, mainly peaches and Japanese plums, and gave many to neighbors.[37]

On the industrial side, Commonwealth purchased belts to operate the sawmill, shingle mill, and gristmill using the large steam engine. The same engine would run the cotton mill when it restarted, and the mechanics began fitting the mill with steam heating connections, matching floors and ceilings, and more windows. Restarting the mill was a cause for optimism. The building was ready for the new machinery, but the loom factories were behind in their orders, which delayed the restart. Still, Commonwealth continued to send an agent to the Columbus mills to gather needed information.

They were met with courtesy and kindness and as much assistance as they desired. The *Social Gospel* also advertised for a loom fixer and predicted the need for all kinds of cotton mill workers as the enterprise grew.[38]

Circulation of the *Social Gospel* increased by one-third in the last two months of 1899, and the job shop turned out club calendars for two Ohio women's clubs and followed with four more custom jobs. They did more job work that winter than ever before, much for the local neighborhood. The demand for work had the force working every day and some evenings throughout the Christmas holidays. The work was lucrative, and the printers received commendation from their patrons. Cold weather, frost, and a New Year's Eve snowstorm made it difficult to run the big press, and the *Social Gospel* went out a week late in January. The heavy demands for printing required improvements in working conditions and mechanical upgrades, so they purchased new type and finished installing steam pipes to bring the heat to the press room.[39]

The *Social Gospel*'s staff remained optimistic. Their goal was to expand circulation to twenty thousand in 1900. They asked friends and readers to send addresses of potential subscribers and include, if possible, ten cents to cover the cost of a trial issue. If everyone did that, they could double their subscription list monthly.[40]

Albertson and Phyllis returned in January 1900 to a warm welcome. After months away and more than a thousand miles of travel, Albertson found Commonwealth and brotherhood life to have even sweeter beauty. His feelings confirmed his belief in brotherhood. The community had paid his doctor's bill and taken care of his family of five. They were not homeless, hungry, or in rags. He had not lost his honor or respect by relying on charity. He owed a debt, but it was "a debt of service and a slavery of love" toward his nurses and comrades. He felt like a brother among his brethren and recommitted himself to work needed in the community.[41]

When Albertson returned, Gibson left Commonwealth for vacation and to attend to business matters in Maine. He also planned to discuss his Order of Brothers with friends in New York and Chicago. Expected back in March, Gibson became critically ill in February in Chicago and went to the Battle Creek Sanitarium for treatment. He was impressed by the facility, which had started as a small stock company and then converted into a cooperative medical missionary society. The unselfish devotion of the doctors and nurses reinforced Gibson's belief that competitive industries could become places of brotherhood cooperation. By April, he had completed his planning for the Organization of Brothers and headed back to Commonwealth.[42]

After a brief stay, Gibson left for Edwardsville, Illinois, the location of Leclaire, N. O. Nelson's cooperative community for his industrial workers. James and Lou Brower, who had left Commonwealth earlier, followed the Gibsons to Leclaire. They joined forces with Nelson and Reverend Carl Thompson, the minister whose difficulties because of his Christian Socialism had been publicized by the *Social Gospel*. Thompson had expressed a profound interest in the Brotherhood. Under the aegis of Nelson, they coedited a monthly magazine titled *Social Ideals* and set up an Order of Brothers, but it lasted only three months.[43]

At Leclaire, Gibson saw that some families had already entered into brotherhood relations. He believed such acts would multiply Societies of Brothers and create brotherhood industries through education, study, and classes. By October, Gibson was at Thompson's headquarters in Elgin, Illinois. He continued to contribute to the *Social Gospel*, sending poetry and an article on the exploitation of local factory workers. He called again for enrollment in the Order of Brothers by assuring everyone that they were free to practice brotherhood in the light of their conscience. Ultimately, Gibson ended up in Chicago, where he continued to write about the "manhood destroying struggle" of an individualist society and called for a "national industrial corporation of citizen stockholders."[44]

Gibson's departure, while expected, was a serious loss. Still, most Commonwealth members chose to see it positively. The Executive Board passed a motion appointing him as a "missionary agent of the Christian Commonwealth to expand our principles of economic brotherhood as outlined in his pamphlet "A Society of Brothers." The board expressed its love and confidence and hoped that the bond with Gibson would never break. Albertson sounded less enthusiastic. He felt that "neither the imagined nor real superiority of scheme could justify the break." For him, "unity in effort and life" was more important than the method. Nevertheless, he admitted that "our work is all one."[45]

Gibson and Damon took important people and assets when they departed, and Albertson feared that they might have conspired with Keyes and left him out. Nevertheless, he remained committed to Commonwealth. The mortgage remained a problem even though Ernest Hammond had offered help, and Albertson admitted that Commonwealth's form of life was not for everybody. Supporting Gibson, he urged those who could not or would not come to the colony to remain in their old surroundings and form Societies of Brothers that put spiritual power above material interests.[46]

With the other leaders gone, Albertson made one last effort to keep the community functioning. It was time for spring work on the farm. Forest land needed clearing. They needed men at the mill. There were a hundred people to feed, and they needed a larger print shop. The Executive Board decided to build one near the dining room so the same steam plant would provide power and heat to both.[47]

After talking to *Social Gospel* readers, Albertson thought that the editors had done a disservice by portraying conditions at Commonwealth so badly. Many of those conditions were temporary, and there had been a great improvement. Crop yield was excellent, and the community diet was better than in previous winters. Food was more varied, healthful, and of a higher standard. Common breakfasts included oatmeal with both sugar and milk or cornmeal batter cakes with syrup. For dinner, they had collards, mustard greens, or sweet potatoes and soup made from beans, barley rice, macaroni, and onions with either soup stock or a piece of salt pork for seasoning. Suppers included apples, canned, dried, and raw, dried peaches and prunes, or wild grapes that they had canned themselves. Cornmeal mush with sugar and milk, coffee, and, on Sundays, peanut butter made regular appearances at the table.[48]

Disease was gone, general health was good, and members were gaining weight. The fear of typhoid fever remained, and they tried to improve the water supply, the suspected cause, but had no definitive solution. There were eight wells in Commonwealth varying in depth from ten to forty feet. It was unlikely that they caused typhoid, but members considered digging an artesian well, which would be safer.[49]

New equipment arrived. New members replaced those who departed. The print shop could handle more work. Subscriptions to the *Social Gospel* grew. For those who remained, brighter prospects and improved material conditions contributed to a sense of cheerfulness and a feeling of union and harmony—"not the gush kind" but one that could stand wear and tear. The good, moral atmosphere was increasing the spiritual force of their lives.[50]

Winter evenings were often "a jolly time" in the dining room, shelling peanuts and making peanut butter, ten pounds per session. The community planned to purchase a machine to do this work, but they enjoyed the manual labor as a time of fellowship. One evening, Albertson told stories of his trip—

most important, new contacts he had made with friends of the community. Finally, they had a hearty laugh reading selections from *David Harum*, a novel of cheerfulness and sympathetic treatment of love.[51]

By the first Sunday of 1900, the weather had warmed, which benefited the fruit trees, but caused worry that they might bud too early and be damaged if there was a freeze. The balmy weather coaxed the blueberries, violets, and blue gentian into bloom. The alders were rich with tassels, and the members hoped more warm days would bring out the wild plums. Everyone enjoyed the beautiful day. Derrill Hope taught Sunday school, and most attended the Sunday meeting to hear Albertson preach. In the afternoon, a large party strolled into the fields and woods. A wagon went along, and from it, members made excursions into the swamps to collect ferns and mosses and ornamental berries. The day concluded with Sue Hinckley leading the evening prayer meeting.

Better weather brought a surge of activity. Much of the work was being done by single men, who had become a majority of the males. They stayed busy in the print shop and moving logs to the sawmill, which was producing lumber for construction projects. Others pruned and transplanted fruit trees. But the labor shortage continued, and Commonwealth pleaded again for help, especially single men who would find pioneer life tolerable. After the sale and delivery of 2,750 young trees in the winter, new nursery stock was brought out and packed for shipment. Three men drove a team to Columbus to ship the stock and purchase feed. A few days later, George McDermott and Derrill Hope went in again, returning with another load of feed. In late January, there were rainstorms and warm weather, which brought out the wild violets and birds. The variety of birds was a natural wonder. Blackbirds, redbirds, butcher birds, blue jays, sparrows, robins, mockingbirds, woodcocks, meadowlarks, yellowhammers, quail, snipes, owls, hawks, crows, and buzzards all inhabited the local environs.[52]

A cold wave hit at the end of the month, bringing the coldest days of the winter. It lasted a few days and did not harm the fruit, but it interfered with other outdoor projects. One team finally finished plowing the orchard and another large field. Despite the weather, they thought the prospects for an abundant crop looked good.

Mid-February brought days of heavy rain, which shut in most of the workforce. The storm flooded the fields, washed down the hillsides, and floated away bridges. It was followed by cold, bracing, pleasant weather that allowed the men to return to work. The labor force was down to twenty-five men, six in the print shop, four chopping wood, three in the nursery, two each at the mill, the kitchen, and mending the washed-out paths, one doing carpentry, another taking a team to Columbus, and four unable to work. A few days later, temperatures in the teens and high winds prevented the men from doing anything but staying warm and fed.[53]

Daily life continued as usual in other ways. Using wagons or the train, members went into Columbus to tend to business, shop, or visit with friends. They brought back groceries and hardware for the community. Calvin Reasoner continued his Sunday morning addresses on themes drawn from the Sermon on the Mount. Sydney Fripp and J. B. Collette addressed the evening meetings, and occasionally Fripp taught Sunday school for Derrill Hope. They were among the richest pleasures of Commonwealth life.

On the other hand, the best log truck broke down. The mill shut down for a week, which left the colony without wheat flour. They ran out of sugar but were satisfied with unsweetened oatmeal and corn mush. The calves ate the collards in the garden. The steam engine in the print shop broke down, and they sent it to Columbus for repairs. Fortunately, it was back in a few days, and they were able to finish printing the *Social Gospel*. They were out of kerosene for a week until Brother Goodrich secured a barrel along with other supplies.[54]

Despite the problems, the community celebrated seemingly mundane events. After years of dining on a variety of dishes brought by members, they opened a cask of new dishes, which "marked an epoch in their history." No longer would they eat soup off of shallow dinner plates or deal with the poor condition of their tableware.[55]

New arrivals continued during these months. Some became members, others came just to see Commonwealth. Two of the most delightful were W. D. Honens and his wife, who came from Iowa in December with plans to leave in May. Brother Honens often spoke at the evening meetings, and both helped out elsewhere. Their sweetness, patience, and helpfulness inspired everyone. They were not formal members, but their presence reminded the community that membership was as much spiritual as anything.[56]

A sixty-nine-year-old brother showed up after spending three years and five hundred dollars in another colony. The *Social Gospel* did not name the colony, but it resembled the Ruskin Cooperative Association, which required new members to purchase a five-hundred-dollar share and had disbanded a few months earlier. Another young man, who had been with the Shakers, arrived from New York. They, like Derrill Hope, were examples of seekers of brotherhood life who made pilgrimages from one intentional community to another despite disappointments and failures. The ex-Shaker was disappointed that things were not as prim and proper as in the Society of Believers. Paul W. Koetitz, who had sent Commonwealth the printing press in 1899, came back from Ohio with his family. A printer and general mechanic, Koetitz, a valuable addition to the colony, got the sawmill running again. Another brother arrived from Iowa and went to work sawing wood. A poignant arrival in early January was a young woman with a baby who got off the noon train. Her husband had deserted her, and someone "had compassion on her" and bought her a ticket to Commonwealth. She knew nothing about the community or its religious and economic beliefs, but members welcomed her with food, clothing, and a room. They found work for her and taught her to read and write. Commonwealth expected the arrival of another Illinois family whose goods had preceded them. Community members set them up in a two-room house. Household goods belonging to a Pennsylvania brother arrived by freight and were so extensive they had to be put in the wagon shed. On February 2, a family of seven arrived on the night train for a two-month visit. Commonwealth had advised them to bring bed quilts because the community could not provide them. They had packed everything they needed, but the railroad lost their baggage, and members had to gather up quilts for the emergency. Despite their wait for accommodations, the family understood the difficult situation and managed it well.[57]

Not everyone who came stayed, and the departures indicated future problems. A Chicago brother left after only a few weeks. He had not brought his wife but concluded that life was too primitive for her. Another brother from Chicago arrived in his place. Fortunately, he had bedding because the community was running short. An Iowa brother left for Florida after two weeks. He had expected to find a community believing in a fundamentalist interpretation of Old Testament prophecies. Instead, he found no two biblical interpretations alike. A Dakota farmer complained that the red clay made his eyes hurt and thought that the thin, sandy soil would not make for successful farming, ignoring the fact that Commonwealth had been making progress for almost four years. He was sorry to notice the waste of fertilizing material, every ounce of which should have been conserved and utilized. On the other hand, the rapid growth of pine trees on the barren hillsides impressed him, but he regretted the clear-cutting of some hills as economic waste. He thought that the intensive growth of forests was a path to success.[58]

Outside support continued to come in. William A. Ross came from Columbus to encourage the colonists. He also bought land adjoining the community and set out fruits and berries for which Commonwealth men did
most of the work. In January, Dr. Dorcas Green sent canned fruit for everyone. An unexpected gift was a barrel of provisions for a prospective resident who never appeared. It was turned into the general supply and introduced variety to the community diet. Mixed Stocks Publishing, Keyes's
Chicago company, sent a box of "many useful presents." The contents were
unpacked and distributed to members. Another member received a "box of
goodies" from Michigan, and even more goods came by freight from Philadelphia. A Pennsylvania benefactor offered a carload of machinery, horses,
and farm tools worth two thousand dollars if the community would pay the
two-hundred-dollar freight cost. They needed those goods badly and sought
out someone to work with the donor to get the goods shipped.[59]

Two early contributors to the cotton mill fund, Leon and Delphine de
Brabant, had planned to come from Illinois the previous December. They finally arrived in March with five children and a small herd of hungry goats in
tow. Fortunately, the colony had a surplus of feed that the cattle and horses
refused to eat. An experienced fruit grower, Leon fulfilled a desperate need
at Commonwealth created by William Damon's departure, and his five children raised school enrollment to fifteen.[60]

The prospects for fruit, supervised by de Brabant, looked good. They
planted peach pits for a new nursery and set out four thousand new trees
in March for a total of six thousand for the season. When they had several
days of frost in March, they built fires in the orchards to create smoke, raise
the temperature, and mitigate the danger. Only slight damage occurred to
the small number of blossoms that had already opened. That was fortunate
because the trees were young and small. If their buds had borne fruit, the
branches would have broken under the load. The weather continued to be
unseasonably cold through most of March. Members plowed the land but
were unable to start gardens until the end of the month. Still, they expected
better weather and the rapid growth of vegetables.[61]

When the Ruskin Cooperative Association experienced a schism in mid-
1899, they admitted that they were not like the Christian Commonwealth
and went to great efforts to dissuade such a perception. They stated that they
could not adopt Commonwealth's practices because their members were
"very human" and had only a slight understanding of cooperation.[62]

One group formed the Ruskin Commonwealth and moved to Duke, Georgia. The Christian Commonwealth greeted them as "comrades" and neighbors. Ralph Albertson offered a resolution at the business meeting, congratulating them on their organizing plan. He commended their courage to carry on after their "unjust loss of property," and referred to their new home as "a city set upon a hill, whose light shall be stronger and brighter than that of old Ruskin." He saw a fraternal bond between the communities as they labored for the coming of the Kingdom.[63]

Later that winter, John Merrell of Ohio and Edward Keyes visited Commonwealth and the new Ruskin colony in Georgia. Keyes still led the Right Relationship League, which had saved Commonwealth from foreclosure. After their visit, they suggested that the two colonies form a federation on an equitable basis. In February, the *Coming Nation* raised the possibility of a union between Ruskin, Commonwealth, and Equality in Washington. Merrell and Keyes discussed the subject with Commonwealth's members, who voted unanimously to support a federation with Ruskin based on their fundamental belief in common ownership. Keyes encouraged the colonies to have an open discussion about the details of a merger. The *Coming Nation* responded that Ruskin people also supported the merger. Commonwealth passed a resolution proposing general terms and mailed it to Ruskin. The *Social Gospel* editors believed that there were no insurmountable problems in uniting and thought some good might come of it.[64]

The *Social Gospel* asked its readers to share their opinions on the proposed merger. When the editors received only three responses, they waited another month for additional comments. They questioned the value of formal and spiritual combinations of organizations, but expressed a willingness to modify their organization and work as long as it did not alter their devotion to Christian altruism.[65]

Albertson wanted to "see Commonwealth and Ruskin united in deed and in management as well as in spirit and in truth." He was aware of problems at Ruskin but thought that its natural advantages were superior and that both places could be maintained successfully. Asserting Commonwealth's commitment to its ultimate ideal, he admitted that it could impose a membership fee, drop the word "Christian," or even give up the colony effort and not violate it. He called for the discussion to continue with the "freedom of intelligent manhood" in hopes of a rational, pragmatic solution.[66]

Derrill Hope took over the correspondence with Ruskin, and discussions

between the two communities continued when Ruskin received a letter out-
lining Commonwealth's proposal for the union. Ruskin gave the proposal
careful thought and hoped for a union, but no positive steps ever occurred.[67]

Meanwhile, Herbert Casson, editor of *Appeal to Reason*, launched a hostile
attack on communal experiments. He had left Ruskin, embittered and disillusioned, after six months. Focusing on Ruskin, Commonwealth, and Equality in Washington, he believed that every socialist colony had been a failure.
He had never been to Commonwealth but knew the observations of "reliable
men." He thought that "Mr. Gibson's half-starved disciples" needed less religion and more food and asserted that garment workers on New York's Lower
East Side had better food, lodging, and pleasures of life. Colonies, dependent
on manual labor and lacking expertise, produced inferior goods that could
not compete with modern producers. Moreover, they relied on a small cadre
of socialist sympathizers as their primary market. He concluded that thousands had invested money to join colonies, but no one ever left a colony with
more than when they entered it.[68]

The April 1900 *Social Gospel* continued to be optimistic about the future.
Two months from a complete breakup, there was no sense of dissolution,
but a close reading exposed issues that were becoming critical. There was an
open discussion of the significance and value of community life. It was not
unusual because they took their Commonwealth life seriously. But Gibson's
plan, Herbert Casson's attack on colonies, and the problems that they faced
called forth some new concerns. The evangelical zeal of Christian Socialism
had not waned. They knew they were attempting work that was worth doing,
but they were not satisfied. They were concerned about those who were "of
them" but not "with them." They were thinking more of "community" than a
colony and of general altruism rather than promulgation of a scheme.

March had been an "ordinary month" marked by good health, peace, and
some progress, although the colony still faced shortages of resources. Departures, elections, new appointments, and some reorganization indicated
that significant change was occurring. W. L. Carman and Henry S. Croyle
both left, which left gaping vacancies in the workforce, but did not erase the
community's love and respect for them. Charles Cook added the presidency
to his duties as business manager, labor director, and foreman of the printing office. Daniel Hinckley took over the orchards, George McDermott managed the farm, and Justin Cook supervised the garden and the laundry. Sam
Byerly was in charge of the machinery and general mechanical work, while

Paul Koetitz ran the cotton mill. Finally, Derrill Hope had general supervision of the women's work.

The print shop acquired new type and equipment, which improved their ability to do more and better work. They had two publications in progress: *The Bible Plan for the Abolition of Poverty* by Reverend Jesse Jones of Massachusetts and *The Builder* by P. S. Sailer of Pennsylvania. Jones was the first Christian Socialist clergyman in Boston and had predicted that America would become the new Kingdom of God.[69]

The community started a small millinery business. A Brooklyn brother sent two cases of hats and trimmings, and the colony women began trimming and selling hats. They did not expect a large market, but the women were also treated to the first choice of hats for themselves.[70]

Even the departures did not cause alarm. The "spring exodus," mostly of drifters, was a regular occurrence and left them shorthanded. They had always been overcrowded in the fall and winter when there were not enough beds. Now there were too few workers for every department, and everyone had to increase their workload. Members left for Fairhope and others went elsewhere for a variety of reasons—to make a living "lecturing on phrenology" or because there was "excessive levity." One left after twelve hours because there was "absolutely no harmony in the colony."

April was a month of delights and little foreboding about the future. The profusion of birds and flowers provoked excursions into the woods and swamps to experience their beauty. The *Social Gospel* went to print and maintained a positive tone despite the mid-April exodus. Commonwealth had filled many positions, and the remaining members looked forward to continued progress. The editors were either naïve or unwilling to publicize the crisis that they were facing.[71]

Sue Fay Hinckley remained optimistic and in her diary raved about the beauty of the site:

April 13th, 1900. Oh, this South! Its blossoms are something to live always in one's memory. Lou just rode past with her arms as full as they could be of great pink azaleas, Wonderful just to see. Such a mass of soft pinks! A great handful came to me and is on our little stand. Just behind it is a branch, ceiling high, of dogwood with its great snowy blooms. On my dresser is a vine of fragrant yellow jasmine.... And in a vase is such a cluster of honeysuckle as it would seem wicked to pick it from a vine in the North.... A wonderful South![72]

Departures made things difficult, but Commonwealth took them in stride.
No one blamed people who sought better prospects or conditions than
the colony could provide. A few were viewed as uneducated, "egotistical,
narrow-minded cranks," but they "needed love most and must be loved just
the same."[73]

Departures also opened up opportunities. Irene Albertson and Lucy Fay
learned to set type and helped print the May issue of the *Social Gospel*. It remained successful despite the instability and shortage of printers. Charles
and Minna Cook had been reliable, but others had come and gone quickly
and often on short notice, delaying publication. Having permanent and reliable members ensured more stability.[74]

Despite the disruptions, other community routines continued. Calvin
Reasoner and Sydney Fripp and his son moved into the Gibson cottage and
did their housekeeping. In May, a married couple arrived from Norcross,
Georgia. The fourth wedding in Commonwealth history occurred in June
when Marie Hassler of Pratt City, Alabama, married William H. Dorchester
of Commonwealth and made their home in the colony. Young and talented,
they could contribute to the colony's success.[75]

The labor shortage brought construction to a halt. Everyone was planting
crops, so there was no one to haul and mill lumber. The large dining room,
which they had started a year earlier, remained unfinished, and they had to
postpone completion until the winter. They also had to pass up an opportunity to sell thirty-five thousand shingles because of the shortage of workers.[76]

The number of people remaining is unclear, but only twenty-two were
eating in the dining room. The kitchen staff had shrunk, and its hierar-
chy changed. Clarence Hough, who had been an assistant cook, took over,
aided by Marie Hassler and William Dorchester, who had previously run the
kitchen. Circumstances kept the diet plain, but the members commended
the cooks for making "good meals out of corn-meal, cotton-seed oil, onions,
and salt." There was meat occasionally, but a desire for it had diminished
during earlier periods of its absence.[77]

At the end of May, the *Columbus Enquirer*, which usually printed excerpts
from the *Social Gospel*, told a more ominous story. A visiting reporter stated
that only thirty persons remained at the colony, and they seemed to have
lost heart. Except for a pea patch, they had not cultivated much ground and
had to buy feed for their stock. The orchards were overrun with weeds and

the school population had dwindled to where closing the school seemed likely.

Another Columbus resident noted that on a midmorning visit no one was working, except in the print shop. He chastised them for not planting crops to cut their feed bill and noted that the farm had been profitable for its previous owners. Commonwealth's supporters called the accusations of laziness unfair. Colonists had worked hard, the defenders said, on one of the poorest pieces of land in the county that had been profitable only using slave labor. If the colonists had accomplished anything, they had improved the place. Nevertheless, it appeared on the surface to be a failure, but as a reform effort, the Commonwealth people had gained experience and new ideas, which they used in future endeavors.[78]

The people who remained had not given up and rejected the observations of the visitors. In the final *Social Gospel* published at Commonwealth, they repeated the hope and optimism of earlier issues. There was no sense of impending doom. They had more equipment than ever and could make their living from the land and the machinery. There was a large supply of cotton in the neighborhood and money in the treasury, and the mill was partially fitted and needed only workers, which, given the national economy, they expected soon. They announced a "great opportunity and need for good workers with loving hearts and willing hands." Rains had been frequent, so they had a good harvest of fruit ready for consumption—blackberries were ripe, wild plums plentiful, and there were more ripe peaches than they could consume along with ample plantings of garden vegetables. They planted thirty acres of peanuts and started sweet potatoes and melons, and the sugar cane was already growing well.[79]

Other contributors to the June *Social Gospel* offered a different picture. Albertson began to refer to his love for Commonwealth in the past tense and admitted that they could do nothing to save it. The experiment in communism had failed, and he announced his forthcoming departure to New York. They had not been starved out or lost their determination, but he claimed the *Social Gospel* had ceased to be a source of income, and it had not received adequate support from the colony. He wanted to continue the journal at any cost and thought leaving was the best way to do that. The same inspiration and purpose that had brought him to Commonwealth were now taking him away. The community sold some property to raise money to aid the members who were going to new homes or communities. School closed at the end of May, and Sue Fay Hinckley resigned as a teacher to follow Albert-son to New York.[80]

Albertson concluded that brotherhood was not confined to one place but could be everywhere and that "Commonwealth has been a nursery of this life." As he made plans to take a group to New York, he noted that Damon and a few others had gone to Virginia, Gibson and his followers had left for Illinois, and Chipman had wound up in Augusta.[81]

Some were determined to continue to build brotherhood life. Seventeen Commonwealth members departed for northern Florida, where they joined a colony founded by Reverend Hiram Vrooman. He had acquired over one thousand acres on Florida's west coast, east of Apalachicola, and aspired to the same social Christian goals as Commonwealth, although tinged with Swedenborgianism. The colony was called the Southern Cooperative Associ-ation of Apalachicola, which was a precursor to the Cooperative Association of America. It survived until he departed in 1904.[82]

In June, Commonwealth shut down the print shop. The large press be-longed to Paul Koetitz, who had been a printer on the Social Gospel. The Ex-ecutive Board released the press to him, and he took it to Tippecanoe City, Ohio. A considerable amount of equipment had been a gift from the Vrooman brothers, but it remained at the colony.[83]

The members voted to sell Albertson the remaining printing equipment and the publishing rights to the Social Gospel. He moved it to his boyhood home in South Jamesport, New York, from where he had agreed to fulfill over a thousand unexpired subscriptions. Albertson's parting word to Com-monwealth was a word of love. A group of about twenty other members who wished to stay together and continue living as brothers accompanied him. Besides his family, the group included the Hinckleys, the McDermotts, the Cooks, Lucy Fay, and Clarence Hough. Albertson thought effective work for social and religious reform might be more successful in the Northeast.[84]

Albertson hoped that the loyal souls left behind would maintain the Christian Commonwealth. Its assets exceeded its debts, and with some ad-ditional economic good fortune, it could be a happy home and continue to shine the light of brotherhood on the world.[85]

James Kelley loaned Albertson a thousand dollars to finance the move and set up a print shop. They formed a partnership, the Social Gospel Company, and enlarged the paper to fifty pages, raised the subscription price, and pub-lished it as coeditors. They agreed to give Commonwealth and the work of Gibson and the Order of Brothers a prominent place. Other than that, they had no real plan. Reflecting his anarchist leanings, Albertson dismissed programs as unnecessary, constitutions as crutches, and schemes as fetishes. Reform was "not in the letter of a WAY but in the spirit of a life." By August, they had the *Social Gospel*, with a less radical subtitle, "A Magazine of Christian Altruism," back in print. They published for about a year with Gibson, Derrill Hope, and both Hinckleys continuing to write for the journal. They acknowledged their role in the Christian Commonwealth but decided that the new journal would be a general monthly magazine and keep the publishers' personal and collective concerns in the background.[86]

On Long Island, the children, who had spent four years in Commonwealth's school learning cooperation, brotherhood, and communist philosophy, had difficulty adapting. When a hotel proprietor offered work to the Commonwealth women, the children were shocked. Why would he need to hire someone "when he has a dozen ladies sitting around all day on the front porch doing nothing"? Another couple tried to rent an apartment. "Rent, what's that?" their daughter asked. "Do you mean that we must pay … for using his rooms when he has a whole house that he never uses?"[87]

Derrill Hope remained at Commonwealth, became its corresponding secretary, and offered to furnish the constitution and bylaws freely to interested parties. She assured them that they had "changed a waste place into a valuable estate" that could "become a garden of homes for the children of God" if they came in the spirit of sacrificial love. Hope also promised Albertson a letter from Commonwealth for every issue of his new *Social Gospel*.[88]

By midsummer 1900, most of Commonwealth's members had left. One exception was the de Brabants and their children. Originally from Lyons, France, they had arrived that spring from Illinois. By the time they reached the community, they had had enough travel. Fortunately, they had retained their personal property when they joined. When the colony broke up, they bought some land nearby and still lived there twenty-five years later.[89]

On June 20, 1900, de Brabant petitioned the Muscogee County Superior Court for a receiver to liquidate Commonwealth's property. The petition stated that the colony's liabilities totaled thirty-eight hundred dollars. They owed two thousand dollars plus interest on their mortgage. Other major debts included six hundred dollars to James Kelley, two hundred fifty to William A. Ross, and two hundred to Andrew Allen. The primary assets were orchards, nurseries, physical improvements, and cash. The petition explained that they had had a near-total crop failure in 1899, and the membership had become discouraged and dwindled from over fifty to fewer than a dozen.

With such a small force, it was impossible to perform the necessary work, and they had voted to disband.[90]

Judge Butt appointed W. A. Ross as the receiver and directed him to sell the real estate "at public outcry." Ross compiled a report on Commonwealth's assets and liabilities, which the court reviewed in November. After the review, the court ordered two receiver's sales for December 1900.[91]

The first sale, on December 4, included 931.75 acres of land with its improvements, except for the right-of-way of the Muscogee Railroad Company. The improvements included the plantation house, nine cottages, stables, barns, cabins, and other structures. There were also sixteen thousand fruit trees with one-half of them beginning to bear fruit. Advertisements in the local paper raved about the large fruit-bearing orchards and the commodious residence.[92]

William T. and William Henry Harvey purchased the property for thirty-eight hundred dollars. William T. invested a good deal of money and turned its orchards and cotton land into profitable enterprises, "easily recouping his investment." By 1903, he had built a flour mill, cotton gin, and sawmill to meet the needs of the local farmers. Although corn and cotton continued to be erratic crops, Harvey's overall success undermined the argument that Commonwealth's land was no good, but, at the same time, his investment demonstrated that lack of capital might have been the greatest hindrance to the community.[93]

The second sale consisted of the movable property. It included a sawmill with a twenty-five horsepower steam engine, another twenty-five horsepower engine, a wood saw, six thousand feet of lumber, the shingle machine, four cotton looms, a machine lathe, a steam heater, a flour mill, a buggy, a blacksmith outfit, a washing machine, a hotel cooking range, cooking and heating stoves, household furniture, seven stands of bees, four cows, a two-horse wagon, a log wagon, two harrows, large and small plows, miscellaneous farming and household implements, and one lot of ladies straw hats.

Ross obtained considerably more for the colony's assets than had been expected. One week after the sale, he posted a "Notice to Creditors" that they had thirty days to present claims against the Christian Commonwealth, and by late January he was winding up the colony's affairs.[94]

No one thought that anything would be left for the colonists because most believed Commonwealth was insolvent. The constitution stated that a member who left had no claim to the colony's assets, so Ross had to resolve the question of who was entitled to the proceeds. De Brabant had made a list that included all who had left Commonwealth in the final six months. In his petition, he presented that list to the court and stated that they deserved a share of any proceeds once Ross paid the debts, even though that violated the community's constitution. Fortunately for Ross, the remaining sum was small and there were no disagreements over its distribution.[95]

In June 1901, the Superior Court issued its final decree. Ross paid the Right Relationship League the remaining two thousand dollars on the mortgage and paid all of Commonwealth's debts in full. He gave destitute members railway fares and money for basic needs. After Ross settled the debts, a balance of $669.30 remained. Out of that, the receiver and the attorneys, McNeil and Levy, each received $100. After court costs, Ross divided the remainder between the twenty-six colonists who were community members on the day de Brabant filed the petition.[96]

The members were Ralph and Irene Albertson, E. T. R. Tripp, Justin Cook, Charles A. and Minna Cook, Leon and Delphine de Brabant, Henry and Minnie Staiff, Lucy Fay, M. A. McDermott, Eunice D. Cushing, Samuel M. Byerly, Daniel T. and Sue F. Hinckley, Martha Bethune Jones, George H. Cushing, Clarence Hough, William H. and Marie D. H. Dorchester, Sadie Pease, Grace Pease, Leroy Henry, and John Chipman. In the final accounting, each of them received about fifteen dollars per share. Ross filed his final report, and the judge dismissed him as receiver in January 1902.[97]

For many, Commonwealth's demise was no surprise. One journal referred to it as "A Dream Which Proved Baseless." It failed as a socialist community despite starting with above-average intelligence and considerable capital. "For a time, the colony prospered, then dissensions arose, and now the usual fate of such projects has come."[98]

Other than the original plantation house, little physical trace of the Commonwealth settlement remains. The Harveys salvaged the cottages for their lumber. The Central of Georgia Railway discontinued its stations on either side of Commonwealth but maintained the flag stop at the community. By the early 1900s, it became known as Ordway.[99]

In a perverse irony, today most of the site of this Tolstoyan nonresistant community lies within the Fort Benning Military Reservation, where the notorious School of the Americas trained anticommunist Latin American death squads.[100]

CHAPTER 10

✦ ✦ ✦

In Retrospect
Failure and Success

I have fought His battles.

—Graham Taylor, *Commons*

THE CHRISTIAN COMMONWEALTH existed for three and a half years. Not part of a larger cooperative movement, it was unique in American communitarian history. It emerged out of a diverse set of ideas and influences: the Kingdom of God, Christian love and brotherhood, socialism, anarchism, nonresistance, Jesus, Saint Francis, George Herron, Karl Marx, and Leo Tolstoy.[1]

It did not succeed in creating the Kingdom of God, but it did create a "kingdom" of economic, social, political, and gender equality. Some members had advantages based on their education, experience, and personality, but none had an advantage regarding clothes, food, education, or health care.

During its existence, Commonwealth had over two hundred members and over three hundred fifty residents. Its members desired to serve humanity and sacrificed personal ease and comfort to achieve that end. Founded on a common vision of love and nonresistance, the community initially functioned informally. When its "open-door" policy welcomed members who did not share the founders' vision and affairs became complex, it became necessary to formalize the organization. That did not solve the community's emerging problems. The original members remained a majority in a direct democracy. The dissenters, a powerless minority, turned to defamation and intimidation to discredit the leadership. Unsuccessful, they finally resorted to the courts. There, the dissenters lost and Commonwealth won, but the case shattered their core vision.[2]

Although its agricultural efforts were modestly successful on exhausted land in an unpredictable climate, they did not lead to prosperity. Nor were other enterprises, such as its towel-weaving business, remunerative. Only the *Social Gospel* and the print shop generated significant revenue. Shortages of capital, labor, and resources, plus lack of skills and experience, poor business sense, and poor money management, limited Commonwealth's options and played roles in its failure. Unlike more successful communities, it also lacked a charismatic leader. Given its devotion to sacrifice, the Christian Commonwealth may have overcome these deficiencies. Still, the loss of its core vision because of a court challenge to its existence undermined the members' morale and courage and led to its disintegration.[3]

George Howard Gibson blamed Commonwealth's failure on economic collapse despite evidence to the contrary. Despite working hard, the community found itself in an "economic situation in which they could not produce enough to be self-supporting." He believed that "production, as a science and art, should be left in the hands of those who can most economically organize and direct labor." Ever the Tolstoyan, Gibson also believed that they trusted too much in scheme and organization and not enough in spirit. His departure from Commonwealth and creation of the Order of Brothers reflected his commitment to a looser organization of individuals functioning within the larger society and not limited by locale.[4]

To Albertson, the end of Commonwealth felt like a bad dream and "the end of a life." He thought the community could have lasted longer if it had not been for its debt and placed blame on Edward Keyes and the Right Relationship League for calling in its mortgage. His experience left him disillusioned with communitarianism, but his faith in reform and its religious underpinnings did not diminish. He had searched for brotherhood for years and thought Commonwealth was the most genuine expression of the brotherhood spirit he had experienced. Compared to mainstream churches, "the degree of altruism marking the whole undertaking would rank it as a brilliant success." It had produced more "spiritual growth in individuals" than any "regular channels of religious work." That alone justified it as a form of service. At the same time, he acknowledged the difficulty of "imparting the open-door spirit to whomsoever should come and the maintaining of it in whomsoever should stay." He resigned himself to the idea that observers would define the Christian Commonwealth as a failed socialist experiment, but he doubted that it furnished a definitive test of socialism's practicality. Nor did its failure provide evidence that socialism would not work. He believed that "wiser men, fair industrial equipment, or a different location, might have insured success."[5]

Albertson continued promoting his belief in Christian altruism in South Jamesport, New York. There, he published the *Social Gospel* and wrote a pamphlet called *Relecopol: A Christian Socialist Weekly Newsletter*. It was a brief, inexpensive publication "for progressive and busy people" and "not calculated to tickle the self-satisfied greed of the high-priced pews." Simultaneously, he fulfilled requests for sermons and talks on Christian altruism throughout Long Island.[6]

As American communitarianism declined, interest in cooperation grew, and Albertson embraced it. He shut down the *Social Gospel* in July 1901 and put his Christian reformist ideas to work in the Co-Workers Fraternity, the educational arm of the Cooperative Association of America. Hiram Vrooman then induced him to become a director of the Association in Lewiston, Maine, and edit its newspaper, the *American Cooperator*.[7]

In Maine, unable to rehabilitate a marriage undermined by the Commonwealth experience, Ralph and Irene separated, and Ralph married Hazel Hammond, the daughter of a Commonwealth benefactor.[8] By then, Albertson's enthusiasm for socialism and cooperation had declined. George Littlefield, who had known of Commonwealth, invited him to participate in the Fellowship Farm, a communistic colony in Massachusetts, but Albertson "had had enough" and said no. He relocated to Boston and began to engage in more conventional progressive reform, working for E. A. Filene, the liberal owner of the famous department store.[9]

Hazel was unhappy in Boston, so in 1909 Albertson bought a farm on the Merrimack River in West Newbury, Massachusetts. In a haphazard fashion, and without a specific ideology, "the Farm," as it became known, took on the trappings of an intentional community. Albertson invited Harvard students and Boston reformers regularly. A few stayed permanently, and others filled the house on weekends. Walter Lippmann, then a student, and Lincoln Steffens were the two most prominent visitors, but many others also went on to distinguished careers in the arts and sciences. Not quite a commune, the Farm resembled a weekly salon with much intellectual discussion and creative activity and a little bit of farm work. Arthur Schlesinger Jr. called it a "twentieth-century reenactment of Fruitlands or Brook Farm."[10]

After the suicide of a colleague, Albertson, peripatetic and somewhat of a ladies' man, left Hazel and moved to Greenwich Village in New York. The Farm survived as younger generations kept the community alive. Even today, descendants of Ralph and Hazel live at the Farm and continue to offer the same hospitality to visitors that made it such an attraction in the beginning.

John Chipman, the catalyst for Commonwealth's founding, lived in the community for a few months. He found little of interest to do there and had conflicts with Albertson over the nature of its constitution. In 1899, the Protestant Episcopal Church ordained him as a minister. When he realized that the community was not going to become an ideal Episcopal church, he chose the church over Commonwealth, became a bishop, and relocated to Augusta, Georgia, where he continued to promote cooperation.[11]

After leaving Commonwealth, William Damon and his family joined a brotherhood colony in Virginia. When that did not work out, Damon, committed to education, sailed to the Philippines as a teacher for the U.S. government. Ultimately, he returned to California and the Methodist church.[12]

The idea of success or failure may be moot. The value of such an experiment is considerable but not likely to prove or disprove a particular theory of social organization. Commonwealth was too isolated and narrow in its perspective to prove anything. As one of many communal experiments, each unique, it called attention to alternate ways of living and the need to reform Gilded Age society.[13]

Gibson subscribed to this perspective before leaving Commonwealth. Asked by a minister to explain why brotherhood schemes, such as Brook Farm, failed, Gibson denied that it or any others had failed. Even after their dissolution, many continued to exert influence. In the case of Commonwealth, he called it "a school for the study of brotherhood difficulties and duties" and not a model colony or refuge.[14]

It was an example of people pursuing happiness in a world in which that pursuit by others led to the perpetuation of slums and poverty and the exploitation of labor. Albertson believed that these experiments, no matter how short lived, guided those who wanted to create a world that obliterated the differences between rich and poor.

If happiness was the criterion for success, then the Christian Commonwealth was briefly successful. Despite the hardships and deprivation, reports coming out of Commonwealth indicated joy and pleasure in the company they were keeping and the goal they were seeking. It is unlikely that these people would have been happier somewhere else under ordinary circumstances. They felt a strong sense of fellowship, cooperation, strength, security, independence, and unselfish, noble comradeship. Added to that idealistic vision, they were living outdoors, close to nature, engaged in physical as well as mental labor, and enjoying reasonably good health.

Members were pious and happy and comforted themselves with the belief that what they were doing had some profound social significance. They were not seeking personal gain or spiritual benefits. They loved the world, not themselves. They gave their lives, labor, and property for the love of their brothers and sisters and hopes for society everywhere.

Ultimately, there may not be much social significance to Commonwealth, but members experienced physical, intellectual, and spiritual development. It would be hard to overestimate its benefits to individual participants, and that might have been the best it could accomplish.[15]

The Social Gospel relished their "close contact" with "all sorts and conditions of men." They experienced the "varied phases and many sidedness of human nature." They saw the good side of another man's character by "putting oneself in his place," and learned to appreciate the best in others.[16]

Sue Fay Hinckley reflected on those who stayed and those who did not—"families, single men, tramps, young people, old people, moneyed people, penniless people, refined and ignorant.... None ever came without lovable qualities"—and Commonwealth ministered to them so that "none ever left without having been loved." By bringing their different ways and customs and diverse knowledge and thoughts, they were better than an encyclopedia or a daily paper. They taught valuable lessons.[17]

One unintended consequence of the Christian Commonwealth was its contribution to agricultural diversity in Muscogee County. By rejecting cotton as a cash crop and concentrating on fruit, Commonwealth helped lay the groundwork for what became an important enterprise in the region. Less than two years after Commonwealth's demise, the town of Midland, the nearest railroad stop to Commonwealth, had become the first locality in the county to ship local fruit to the national market. Over a dozen landowners produced profitable crops of peaches, pears, plums, and melons. Midland peaches became famous, and its plums, possibly from Commonwealth's orchards, were the only ones available in the area.[18]

Only a few Commonwealth members left recollections. Damon wrote to Gibson six years after the community's dissolution:

How differently our lives have flowed on from what we thought when we were toiling at Commonwealth to solve the great problem of a Christian Brotherhood put into practical operation before the wondering eyes of skeptical men.

If we had been as wise then as we are now, perhaps we might have succeeded in our undertaking.

And we did succeed in a degree. I have never regretted the efforts we made at that time. It was unselfish and altogether Christian—and I believe we are better and stronger men and women for the experience we then gained.

I still hold, and preach, that Christ was a Socialist, and Christianity is socialism. The world is coming, and not very slowly, into the belief and practice of our ideas. We cannot be held in anything but respect for holding ideas in advance of our time, and which we feel sure that the world must, ere long, approve and adopt.

It would be very pleasant to meet a goodly number of our Commonwealth brotherhood in a reunion. It would certainly revive many pleasant old-time memories. . . .

But we shall doubtless have to defer any such gathering until we cross over the river. Then surely both we and the rest will enter along upon a long and straight career of our pure socialism. And this will be vindication enough.[19]

Years after Commonwealth's demise, Albertson recalled his passion for the community and its ideals as being that of a naïve young man, inexperienced, lacking perspective, and overly religious. Still, he believed it was the most crucial point in his life.[20]

He asked Ida McDermott about her Commonwealth experience. She responded, "It was the finest and grandest experience of our lives. We would not give up what we got in Commonwealth for all the rest of our lives put together. [It] made us what we are—good for something in the world, and good for something to ourselves." Albertson believed that there were many testimonials to that effect: "There are a few people who will look back upon it as the happiest experience of their lives. Their altruism was appealed to more powerfully than ever before, and realized a joy of service and a joy of fellowship elsewhere unknown by them. To those whose labors were unceasing, whose sacrifices were considerable, and for its sake endured persecution and such various hardnesses as are known to men and women in whose hearts the cross is planted, Commonwealth will always stand for holy things."[21]

Not everyone's recollections were positive. Mrs. J. V. Fothergill wrote in 1932, "My experience with the colony was very slight, for while my parents were there during the few years of its existence, . . . and I was there only during vacations—and that time I strove to forget as quickly as possible. It was a wild, impracticable dream of Utopia, which could not possibly succeed."[22] But her memories contradicted what she wrote from the New England Conservatory in 1900: "I keep reading the last number of *The Social Gospel* over and over. . . . If anybody has the least fear that Boston will ever make me the slightest degree less a Commonwealth girl, let her get rid of the idea. For since I am deprived of the Commonwealth atmosphere it seems ten times dearer than ever, and now that I am in the midst of the competitive strife, the living of the Gospel at Commonwealth seems more than ever the noblest and highest thing in all the world."[23]

The Christian Commonwealth had the misfortune of choosing a worn-out parcel of land. From the beginning, their lack of capital weakened them. An indiscriminate admissions policy led to internal dissension. The founding theory of the colony did not account for human characteristics—individuality, personal ambition, selfishness, and differences in talent and temperament. At the same time, one could argue that adverse conditions made a fair trial of the ideology impossible.[24]

Some observers blamed the leaders' lack of "business sense for Commonwealth's failure." Albertson disagreed, acknowledging that some early decisions were poor or overly ambitious, but the fact that they survived four years was evidence that they were doing something right. The administration of business affairs, despite the handicaps of the "open door," poor soil, sickness, lack of capital, and debt, was satisfactory. When the receiver settled community affairs, he was able to pay every dollar of indebtedness and take care of all needy members. That is a testament to a well-managed enterprise.[25]

Others stated that the leaders managed the community well, but the open-door policy made it impossible to survive a system that allowed the poor, the lazy, and the parasitic to come and share equally in all.[26] John Chipman, the son of a founder, wrote, "Reading between the lines of the *Social Gospel* it is easy to see that the colony was plagued by a lot of lazy and thoroughly worthless individuals, that they could not be made to work, and that the leaders of the enterprise were too sincerely Christian to expel them. This would seem to be one of the main causes that contributed to the failure of the Commonwealth. This conjecture coincides with what I remember of my father's statements concerning the enterprise."[27]

Albertson did not disagree but explained that the difficulty was not the open door but imparting the open-door spirit. Without that, there was no point in forming a colony. "It was the spirit of the open door—the spirit that gave its all to everybody—that was the one excuse for the enterprise."[28]

Even supporters thought Commonwealth was doomed to fail. Despite that, John Gavit believed that the movement it represented would be "one of the mother roots of Cooperative Commonwealth" in the twentieth century. W. A. Ross, the Columbus resident and friend of Commonwealth, but never a member, agreed that Commonwealth had failed, but thought its "experience would serve as a guiding star or a danger signal to others that follow."[29]

But was it a failure? Or is living out one's ideals a satisfactory end in itself? After her 1899 visit to Commonwealth, Jane Addams thought so:

> We had the curious sensation that while the experiment was obviously coming to an end, in the midst of its privations it yet embodies the peace of mind which comes to him who insists upon the logic of life—whether it is reasonable or not—the fanatic's joy in seeing his own formula translated into action. When we reached Columbus the commonplace Southern town of workaday men and women, . . . its ordered streets, divided into those of the rich and those of the poor, seemed much more unreal to us than the struggling colony we left behind. . . . When conscience does become the dictator of the daily life of a group of men, it forces our admiration as no other modern spectacle has the power to do. It seemed but a mere incident that this group should have lost sight of the facts of life in their earnest endeavor to put to the test the things of the spirit.[30]

Graham Taylor agreed:

> A more pathetically heroic adventure of faith than that which at least outwardly failed in the attempt to establish The Christian Commonwealth in Georgia, we know not of. Those may criticize or sneer . . . but the brave men and women who dared to fail may issue their challenge to those who come after them in the words in which Bunyan puts into the mouth of Mr. Valiant-For-Truth as he answered his summons: "My sword I give to him that shall succeed me in my pilgrimage and my courage and skill to him that can get it, my marks and scars I carry with me to be a witness for me that I have fought His battles."[31]

NOTES

✦ ✦ ✦

ABBREVIATIONS

CN	*Coming Nation*
FDP	Frances Davis Papers
GDH	George D. Herron
GHG	George Howard Gibson
GHQ	*Georgia Historical Quarterly*
HDL	Henry Demarest Lloyd
RA	Ralph Albertson
SG	*Social Gospel*

Citations to some archives and newspapers, as well as to articles appearing in the *Social Gospel*, are generally given solely in the notes, provided in full on first reference. All other citations are provided in full in the bibliography.

CHAPTER I. AWAKENED AND INSPIRED

1. Chipman, "Proposition"; Frederick, *Knights of the Golden Rule*, 169; White and Hopkins, *Social Gospel*, 150–51, 176.

2. Chipman, "Proposition"; Acts 4:32; RA, "Christian Commonwealth," TMs, FDP, 2; RA, "Christian Commonwealth in Georgia," 127.

3. John Chipman, "An Appeal to the Church of God. By One of Her Sons," *SG*, Feb. 1898, 9–10.

4. Jobes, "Is Communism Practicable?"; Chipman, "Mr. Chipman's Reply"; Arnold, "Is It Practicable?"; W. Harper, "Communistic Societies Unwise."

5. George D. Herron, "The Economics of the Monastery," *SG*, Feb. 1899, 30–32.

6. Dombrowski, *Early Days of Christian Socialism*, 135–37.

7. RA, "Christian Commonwealth," TMs, FDP, 11.

8. Fogarty, *All Things New*, 1–3, 9; Oved, *Two Hundred Years*, 6, 12; Spann, *Brotherly Tomorrows*, 177, 226.

9. William Edmonds, review of *The New Economy* by Laurence Gronlund, *SG*, Jan. 1899, 32–33.

10. Advertisement for *The Dawn, New Republic*, 20 Nov. 1892, 4, and 5 Dec. 1890, 2; GHG, untitled, *Wealth Makers*, 18 Oct. 1894, 4; GHG, "Interesting Symposium," 2; White and Hopkins, *Social Gospel*, 26–30, 129, 168–71; Dressner, "William Dwight Porter Bliss's Christian Socialism"; Gladden, "Eight-Hour Problem."

11. GHG to the editor, *Alliance-Independent*, 27 Apr. 1893; GHG to HDL, 6 Dec. 1895, HDL Papers, Wisconsin Historical Society, Madison; Pollack, *Populist Response to Industrial America*, 20–21.

12. GHG, review of *Differences* by Harvey White, *SG*, Jan. 1900, 32–33; GHG, review of *The City Wilderness: A Settlement Study by Residents and Associates of the South End House*, edited by Robert A. Woods, *SG*, Mar. 1899, 31–32.

13. *Alliance-Independent*, 5 Oct. 1893; RA, "Christian Commonwealth," TMs, FDP, 11; GHG, "Christian Commonwealth," *Commons*, 4.

14. Walker, "George Howard Gibson," 554; GHG, "Salutatory," 4.

15. Walker, "George Howard Gibson," 553–72; *Alliance-Independent*, 28 Dec. 1893, 1 Aug. 1895, 11 Apr. 1895; GHG, "The Social Need," *SG*, Feb. 1898, 4–5; GHG, "Business Excludes Brotherhood," *SG*, Feb. 1898, 13.

16. Frederick, *Knights of the Golden Rule*, 170; Walker, "George Howard Gibson," 553–72; Dombrowski, *Early Days of Christian Socialism*, 132–70; Quint, *Forging of American Socialism*, 103–41; GHG, "The New Redemption," *SG*, Mar. 1898, 30–31; GHG, "Christian Commonwealth," *Commons*, 5; Fogarty, *Dictionary*, 40; GHG, review of *Socialism and the Social Movement in the Nineteenth Century* by Werner Sombart, *SG*, Mar. 1899, 30–31.

17. Destler, *Henry Demarest Lloyd*, 380–81; Walker, "George Howard Gibson," 558–60; Dombrowski, *Early Days of Christian Socialism*, 132; Quint, *Forging of American Socialism*, 131–32; *Wealth Makers*, 15 Aug. 1895, 29.

18. Walker, "George Howard Gibson," 555–67; *Wealth Makers*, 17 Jan. 1895; *Alliance-Independent*, 15 Feb. 1894; *Nebraska Independent* (Lincoln), 16 Jan. 1896.

19. GHG to HDL, 10 Dec. 1894, HDL Papers; Pollack, *Populist Response to Industrial America*, 138.

20. GHG, "Christian Commonwealth," *Commons*, 4–5; *Alliance-Independent*, 15 Feb. 1895; *Wealth Makers*, 8 Nov. 1894.

21. GHG, "Faith and Philosophy," *SG*, Sept. 1898, 19. GHG, "Christian Commonwealth," *Commons*, 4–5; Walker, "George Howard Gibson," 553–72.

22. *Wealth Makers*, 18 Apr. 1895, Feb.-Apr. 1895.

23. *Nebraska Independent* (Lincoln), 16 Jan. 1896; "Colony Notes," *CN*, 4 Dec. 1897.

24. GHG, "Communism Again."

25. GHG, "Social Need," 4; GHG, "A Hundred Fold in This Life," *SG*, Oct. 1898, 6–7; William T. Brown, "The Folly and Immorality of the Charity System," *SG*, Dec. 1899, 3–8.

26. "Current Topics," *SG*, Dec. 1898, 19; Brown, "Folly and Immorality," 3–8.

27. GHG, "Communism Again," 643.

28. GDH to HDL, 13 Jan. 1896, Annie L. Diggs to HDL, 17 Sept. 1895, 27 Sept. 1895, HDL to Mrs. Diggs, 23 Sept. 1895, GHG to HDL, 6 Dec. 1895, HDL to GHG, 18 Dec. 1895, GDH to HDL, 13 Jan. 1896, Julius Wayland to HDL, Letters 1894–1895, HDL Papers; HDL, "No Mean City," in HDL, *Mazzini and Other Essays*, 201–32; Caro Lloyd, *Henry Demarest Lloyd*, 2:53–60, 65, 67; Frederick, *Knights of the Golden Rule*, 59–60, 169–70.

29. Dombrowski, *Early Days of Christian Socialism*, 132, 135; Quint, *Forging of American Socialism*, 131–32; Destler, *Henry Demarest Lloyd*, 380–81; Walker, "George Howard Gibson," 559; GDH to HDL, 7 Jan. 1896; GHG to HDL, 13 Jan. 1896; GHG to HDL, 15 Jan. 1896; GHG to HDL, 25 Jan. 1896, GHG to HDL, 8 Feb. 1896, HDL Papers.

30. Anthony, *Fifty Years of Methodism*, 306. On Damon, see "The Christian Commonwealth: Colony Notes," *SG*, Apr. 1898, 23; RA, "Christian Commonwealth," TMs, FDP, 10; RA, *Thy Cloak Also*, 93. *Thy Cloak Also* is an unpublished novel that is an account of Albertson's own life and the basis for Malcolm Ross's *The Man Who Lived Backward*.

31. Wright, *Bulletin of the Department of Labor*, 639; RA, "Reminiscences"; "The Christian Commonwealth," *SG*, Apr. 1898, 22; Andersen, *Race and Politics*, 96; Fried, *Socialism in America*, 341.

32. RA, "Reminiscences," 26, 64; Appelbaum, *St. Francis of America*; RA, "Christian Commonwealth," TMs, FDP, 36; GDH, "Christ's Economic of Distribution," *SG*, Feb. 1898, 6–9; *SG*, Nov. 1898, 17; Alston, *Tolstoy and His Disciples*, 123–24; Frederick, *Knights of the Golden Rule*, 170.

33. *SG*, Feb. 1898, 12–13.

34. RA, "Journal," 8, 13, 17–18, 22–23; "A Right Life," *SG*, Oct. 1898, 4; "A Social Faith," *SG*, Feb. 1899, 11.

35. RA, "Journal," 25; RA, "Reminiscences," 77; RA, "Christian Commonwealth," TMs, FDP, 2; RA, "Christian Commonwealth in Georgia," 126; RA, *Thy Cloak Also*.

36. RA, "Adullam," *SG*, Jan. 1899, 7–9.

37. RA, *Thy Cloak Also*, 65–66.

38. RA, "Christian Commonwealth," TMs, FDP, 2; RA, "Christian Commonwealth in Georgia," 126; RA, *Thy Cloak Also*, 93–94.

39. RA, "The Social Problem," *SG*, May 1899, 7–10; William T. Brown, "The Social Ideal," *SG*, May 1899, 3–7.

40. RA, "Reminiscences," 76; GDH, "Christ's Economic of Distribution," 7; Frederick, *Knights of the Golden Rule*, 170; Hopkins, *Rise of the Social Gospel*, 196; Alston, *Tolstoy and His Disciples*, 124.

41. S. H. Comings, "Christian Political Economy," *SG*, Feb. 1898, 10; RA, "Theories and a Life," *SG*, Sept. 1899, 24–25; RA, "Christian Commonwealth," TMs, FDP, 1; RA, "Reminiscences," 76.

42. RA, "Common Property"; RA, "Christianizing Property," 10–11; RA, "Reminiscences," 78; Dombrowski, *Early Days of Christian Socialism*, 134; Woodall, "Our Town";

RA, "Selfish Socialism"; Fish, "Christian Commonwealth Colony," 214. The only two extant letters between Albertson and Gibson are from April and May 1904. See GHG to RA, 19 Apr. 1904, 10 May 1904, RA Papers, Manuscripts and Archives, Yale University, New Haven, Conn.; RA, "Journal," 29; RA, "Christian Commonwealth," TMs, FDP, 2; RA, "Christian Commonwealth in Georgia," 126; RA, *Thy Cloak Also*, chap. 27.

43. GHG, "Christian Commonwealth," *Commons*, 5; "The Christian Commonwealth," *SG*, Aug. 1899, 29; RA, "Autobiography, 1936," TMs 44; RA, "Christian Commonwealth in Georgia," 125.

44. *CN*, 8 Feb. 1896, 14 Mar. 1896.

45. GHG, "Christian Commonwealth," *Commons*, 5; *Kingdom*, June 1896.

46. RA, "Selfish Socialism," 226; RA, "Common Property," 338–39; RA, "Social Incarnation"; RA, "New Evangelism"; RA, "Christian Commonwealth," *The Kingdom*; RA, "Christian Commonwealth," TMs, FDP, 1; *CN*, 16 May 1896; "To Reform Industrial Evils," *Daily Inter Ocean* (Chicago), 26 July 1896, 9; Dombrowski, *Early Days of Christian Socialism*, 132–43; Timothy Miller, *Quest for Utopia*, 9–10; Oved, *Two Hundred Years*, 275–77; Sutton, *Communal Utopias*, 144.

47. RA, "Common Property."

48. GHG, "Communism Again," 643; RA, "The Social Ideal," *SG*, Feb. 1898, 6; RA, "Barriers," *SG*, Aug. 1898, 7.

49. "A Brotherhood Organization," *SG*, Feb. 1898, 21; *Christian Commonwealth*, 1; *Columbus Enquirer-Sun*, 20 Dec. 1896; RA, "Survey of Mutualistic Communities," 425.

50. *Christian Commonwealth*, 1; *SG*, Mar. 1900; Hopkins, *Rise of the Social Gospel*, 196.

51. "How We Organize," *SG*, Feb. 1898, 24; RA, "The Christian Commonwealth," *SG*, Feb. 1898, 15; GHG, "The Law and the Gospel," *SG*, May 1899, 12–13; White and Hopkins, *Social Gospel*, 151.

52. GHG, "Why Commonwealth Failed," 5; RA, "Saving the World," *SG*, July 1898, 5.

53. "The Cause of Cooperation," *CN*, 8 Aug. 1896; "Business Matters," *SG*, Sept. 1898, 26; Brundage, *Socialist Utopia*, 17; Brundage, "Utopian Frontier in the New South"; *CN*, 14 Apr. 1900; *Columbus Enquirer-Sun*, 8 Feb. 1898.

54. *Columbus Sunday Herald*, 14 May 1899; "Colony Notes," *SG*, May 1899, 26.

55. "Business Matters," *SG*, Sept. 1898, 26; GHG, "Christian Commonwealth," *Commons*, 6; *Commonwealth Details*, 3, 6; RA, "Christian Commonwealth," TMs, FDP, 2–3; Elliot and Dean, "Commonwealth, Georgia," 2.

56. *Columbus Enquirer-Sun*, 24 Nov. 1896; "Letter from the Christian Commonwealth," *CN*, 11 June 1898; "Business Matters," *SG*, Sept. 1898, 26; "Colony Notes," *SG*, Jan. 1899, 26; RA, "Reminiscences," 87; RA, "Christian Commonwealth in Georgia," 127; RA, "Fifty Years After"; "The Citizen," *SG*, Feb. 1901, 28.

57. "A Brotherhood Organization," *SG*, Feb. 1898, 21; "Colony Notes," *SG*, Sept. 1899, 27; RA, "Christian Commonwealth," TMs, FDP, 2–3, 23; "Business Matters," *SG*, Sept. 1898, 26; *Columbus Enquirer-Sun*, 24 Nov. 1896.

58. RA, "Reminiscences," 87; "Commonwealth Possibilities," *SG*, Mar. 1899, 22; *Columbus Enquirer-Sun*, 26 Nov. 1896; RA, "Christian Commonwealth," TMs, FDP, 3.

59. *Columbus Enquirer-Sun*, 17 Dec. 1896; "A Brotherhood Organization," *SG*, Feb. 1898, 21; GHG, "Christian Commonwealth, of Commonwealth," 300.

60. *Columbus Enquirer-Sun*, 17 Dec. 1896, 20 Dec. 1896, 24 Dec. 1896, 31 Dec. 1898; RA, "The Assistant Cook," *SG*, Aug. 1899, 24.

61. *Columbus Enquirer-Sun*, 20 Dec. 1896; *Commonwealth Details*, 3.

62. *Columbus Enquirer-Sun*, 17 Dec. 1896, 18 Dec. 1896, 24 Dec. 1896; "Colony Notes," *SG*, June 1898, 25; RA, *Reminiscences*, 89.

63. *Columbus Enquirer-Sun*, 18 Dec. 1896, 20 Dec. 1896, 24 Dec. 1896, 29 Dec. 1896; *Commonwealth Details*, 3; GHG, "Christian Commonwealth, of Commonwealth," 299; RA, "Journal," 29.

64. *Columbus Enquirer-Sun*, 24 Dec. 1896, 29 Dec. 1896; "A Diary," *SG*, Feb. 1900, 31; RA, "Reminiscences," 89.

65. *Columbus Enquirer-Sun*, 20 Dec. 1896, 24 Dec. 1896, 27 July 1897, 22 Aug. 1897.

66. RA, "Christian Commonwealth," TMs, FDP, 21–22.

67. *Columbus Enquirer-Sun*, 20 Dec. 1896, 23 Sept. 1897, 30 Oct. 1897; "A Descriptive Note," *SG*, Mar. 1900, 22.

68. *Columbus Enquirer-Sun*, 30 Oct. 1897; White and Hopkins, *Social Gospel*, 151, 177; Hopkins, *Rise of the Social Gospel*, 196; Alston, *Tolstoy and His Disciples*, 150; Handy, "George D. Herron."

69. GHG, "Christian Commonwealth, of Commonwealth," 300–301.

CHAPTER 2. THE LAW OF LOVE

1. RA, "Christian Commonwealth," *Kingdom*.

2. "A Brotherhood Organization," *SG*, Feb. 1898, 21.

3. RA, "Social Incarnation."

4. "Colony Notes," *CN*, 13 Mar. 1897.

5. RA, "Christian Commonwealth," TMs, FDP, 7; GHG, "Christian Commonwealth," *Commons*, 6; "The Assistant Cook," *SG*, June 1900, 19.

6. "A Brotherhood Organization," *SG*, Feb. 1898, 21; *Commonwealth Details*, 11; Sutton, *Communal Utopias*, 144.

7. RA, "The Assistant Cook," *SG*, Feb. 1900, 27.

8. "How We Organize," SG, Feb. 1898, 23; RA, "Reminiscences"; *Columbus Enquirer-Sun*, 31 Dec. 1898.

9. RA, "The Peacemakers," *SG*, Mar. 1899, 8–9; RA, *Social Incarnation*, 6, 40; Dombrowski, *Early Days of Christian Socialism*, 139.

10. "Announcement," *SG*, Feb. 1898, 3; RA, "Christian Commonwealth," TMs, FDP, 54–55.

11. *Commonwealth Details*, 3.

12. RA, *Social Incarnation*, 40–41.

13. James P. Kelley, "Concerning Waste," *SG*, Aug. 1899, 7–8; RA, "Reminiscences," 89.

14. RA, "Christian Commonwealth," TMs, FDP.

15. RA, "Christian Commonwealth," TMs, FDP; "The Old Gentleman," *SG*, Apr. 1899, 13; RA, "Survey of Mutualistic Communities," 425.

16. RA, "The Assistant Cook," *SG*, Sept. 1899, 24; RA, "Christian Commonwealth in Georgia," 125.

17. Appelbaum, *St. Francis of America*, 1–2, 11, 23, 37.

18. Sue Fay Hinckley, "Diary," quoted in Dombrowski, *Early Days of Christian Socialism*, 144.

19. "The Assistant Cook," *SG*, June 1900, 20–21; RA, "Christian Commonwealth in Georgia," 126.

20. RA, "Christian Commonwealth," TMs, FDP, 25; *Kingdom*, 11 Sept. 1896; *SG*, Feb. 1898, 16.

21. RA, "Theories and a Life," *SG*, Sept. 1899, 25; S. E. F[ay], "Equality and Unlikeness," *SG*, Nov. 1898, 22; RA, "Christian Commonwealth," TMs, FDP, 28; GHG, "Christian Commonwealth," *Commons*, 6–7.

22. S. E. F[ay], "Equality and Unlikeness," *SG*, Nov. 1898, 21–22.

23. RA, *The Christian Commonwealth*, quoted in Dombrowski, *Early Days of Christian Socialism*, 142.

24. RA, "Theories and a Life," *SG*, Sept. 1899, 25; *Commonwealth Details*, 11; "Colony Notes," *SG*, July 1898, 27; RA, "Christian Commonwealth," TMs, FDP, 7–8, 51; RA, "Christian Commonwealth in Georgia," 131.

25. RA, "Christian Commonwealth" TMs, FDP, 7; "A Diary," *SG*, Feb. 1900, 31.

26. RA, "A Better Christianity," *SG*, May 1900, 7–8.

27. GHG, "The Church of the Kingdom," *SG*, July 1899, 3–6; GHG, "Business Excludes Brotherhood," *SG*, Feb. 1898, 11–13; GHG, "Why Commonwealth Failed," 6.

28. Edgar L. Morse, letter to *Social Gospel*, "Notes of Progress," July 1899, 30–31.

29. "The Church of the Kingdom," *SG*, Aug. 1899, 13–16.

30. RA, "The Message of Commonwealth," *SG*, Feb. 1900, 4; Dombrowski, *Early Days of Christian Socialism*, 140.

31. RA, "Christian Altruism and Its Message to the Churches," *SG*, June 1901, 3–4.

32. RA, "A Divine Social Drama, *SG*, Aug. 1899, 3; "The Assistant Cook," *SG*, Mar. 1900, 18–19; RA, *Social Incarnation*, 10–11, 16–17; Dombrowski, *Early Days of Christian Socialism*, 140.

33. RA, "A Divine Social Drama," 4; RA, *Social Incarnation*, 11–12; RA, "The Social Ideal," *SG*, Feb. 1898, 5–6.

34. RA, "Christian Commonwealth," TMs, FDP, 8, 29; "Colony Notes," *SG*, June 1898, 24; GHG, "Letter from the Christian Commonwealth."

35. RA, "Christian Commonwealth," TMs, FDP, 9, 26; Dombrowski, *Early Days of Christian Socialism*, 150.

36. "The Christian Commonwealth: Colony Notes," *SG*, Mar. 1898, 21; Hinckley, "Diary," quoted in Dombrowski, *Early Days of Christian Socialism*, 157; "The Assistant Cook," *SG*, Sept. 1899, 22; RA, "Christian Commonwealth," TMs, FDP, 9, 23; "Questions and Answers," *SG*, Aug. 1898, 22; RA, "Christian Commonwealth in Georgia," 132.

37. "Colony Notes," *SG*, Sept. 1898, 28; Nevins and Albertson, "Reminiscences of Ralph Albertson," 87; "Colony Notes," *SG*, July 1899, 25.

38. "Colony Notes," *SG*, Aug. 1899, 29.

39. *Commonwealth Details*, 11.

CHAPTER 3. HOW WE ORGANIZE

1. *Columbus Enquirer-Sun*, 17 Dec. 1896.

2. *Christian Commonwealth*, 1; *SG*, Mar. 1900; *Columbus Enquirer-Sun*, 20 Dec. 1896; "A Brotherhood Organization," *SG*, Feb. 1898, 21; RA, "Survey of Mutualistic Communities," 425; "Colony Notes," *SG*, Feb. 1899, 24; "Colony Notes," *SG*, Sept. 1898, 28.

3. *Columbus Enquirer-Sun*, 27 Mar. 1898; "The Christian Commonwealth: Colony Notes," *SG*, Mar. 1898, 21.

4. GHG, "Christian Commonwealth, of Commonwealth," 303.

5. *SG*, Feb. 1898, 13; GHG, "Christian Commonwealth," *Commons*, 6.

6. *Commonwealth Details*, 11; Sue Fay Hinckley, "Diary," quoted in Dombrowski, *Early Days of Christian Socialism*, 153; "The Christian Commonwealth: Colony Notes," *SG*, Mar. 1898, 21; GHG, "Christian Commonwealth, of Commonwealth," 302.

7. *Columbus Sunday Herald*, 27 Mar. 1898; GHG, "Christian Commonwealth," *Commons*, 6; *SG*, May 1898, 22.

8. "How We Organize," *SG*, Feb. 1898, 23; RA, "Christian Commonwealth," TMs, FDP, 4; Dombrowski, *Early Days of Christian Socialism*, 147.

9. "A Brotherhood Organization," *SG*, Feb. 1898, 21; "A Descriptive Note," *SG*, Mar. 1900, 22; *Commonwealth Details*, 11; GHG, "Christian Commonwealth, of Commonwealth," 300; J. C., "Our Recent Trouble," *SG*, July 1899, 23; GHG, "In the Light of Experience," *SG*, Jan. 1900, 9, 11; "A Descriptive Note," *SG*, Mar. 1900, 22.

10. "The Constitution," *SG*, Jan. 1899, 23; "How We Organize," *SG*, Feb. 1898, 24; RA, "Christian Commonwealth in Georgia"; *Columbus Enquirer-Sun*, 21 May 1898; RA, "A General Letter to the Members of the Christian Commonwealth," *SG*, May 1898, 22–23; GHG, "Christian Commonwealth," *Commons*, 10.

11. *CN*, 22 Apr. 1899; RA, "Christian Commonwealth," TMs, FDP, 23; RA, "Survey of Mutualistic Communities," 415; Kent, "Cooperative Communities," 616.

12. "Colony Notes," *SG*, Dec. 1898, 27; "Colony Notes," *SG*, Feb. 1900, 32.

13. Brundage, *Socialist Utopia*, 16.

14. *Columbus Enquirer-Sun*, 17 Dec. 1896; "Business Matters," *SG*, Sept. 1898, 26–27; "Colony Notes," *SG*, Aug. 1898, 25–26.

15. *Columbus Enquirer-Sun*, 27 Mar. 1898; "Editorial Paragraphs," *SG*, Apr. 1899, 11; "A Brotherhood Organization," *SG*, Feb. 1898, 22; Kent, "Cooperative Communities," 612–16.

16. "Commonwealth Colony Notes," *SG*, Feb. 1898, 24–25; *Columbus Enquirer-Sun*, 5 Feb. 1899; "Colony Notes," *SG*, Feb. 1899, 25–26; "Colony Notes," *SG*, Mar. 1899, 26.

17. "The Constitution," *SG*, Jan. 1899, 23; "Colony Notes," *SG*, Dec. 1898, 27; "Colony Notes," *SG*, Feb. 1900, 32.

18. "By-Laws," *SG*, Jan. 1899, 24.

19. J. C., "A Lawsuit," *SG*, July 1899, 23; "Colony Notes," *SG*, Oct. 1898, 28; "By-Laws," *SG*, Jan. 1899, 24.

20. *Columbus Enquirer-Sun*, 7 June 1899, 14 May 1898.

21. RA, "A General Letter to the Members of the Christian Commonwealth," *SG*, May 1898, 22.

22. "The Charter," *SG*, Dec. 1898, 23–24; *SG*, Dec. 1898, 24–25.

23. GHG, "Christian Commonwealth," *Commons*, 6; Charter Record Book I, Muscogee County Superior Court, 227–29; "Constitution of the Christian Commonwealth of Muscogee County, Georgia," 5; *SG*, Jan. 1899, 22–25; *Commonwealth Details*, 11; "Our Commonwealth Politics," *SG*, Jan. 1899, 21; *Columbus Enquirer-Sun*, 31 Dec. 1898; RA, "Christian Commonwealth," TMs, FDP, 4.

24. "The Constitution," *SG*, Jan. 1899, 22; "By-Laws," *SG*, Jan. 1899, 24.

25. "Colony Notes," *SG*, July 1899, 25.

26. RA, "Christian Commonwealth," TMs, FDP, 25; "The Constitution," *SG*, Jan. 1899, 22–25; "A Descriptive Note," *SG*, Mar. 1900, 22; RA, "Christian Commonwealth," TMs, FDP, 5, 23.

27. *Columbus Enquirer-Sun*, 27 Mar. 1898, 21 May 1898; RA, "Christian Commonwealth," TMs, FDP, 31.

28. RA, "Christian Commonwealth," TMs, FDP, 30–31.

29. "A Brotherhood Organization," *SG*, Feb. 1898, 21; GHG, "Christian Commonwealth," *Commons*, 6; *Commonwealth Details*, 11; RA, "Christian Commonwealth," TMs, FDP, 5; "Our Commonwealth Politics," *SG*, Jan. 1899, 21–22.

30. "A Brotherhood Organization," *SG*, Feb. 1898, 21; GHG, "Christian Commonwealth," *Commons*, 6; S. F. H., "A Meditation," *SG*, Mar. 1900, 23; RA, "Christian Commonwealth," TMs, FDP, 5, 23; "Colony Notes," *SG*, Nov. 1899, 28; "By-Laws," *SG*, Jan. 1899, 24; "Our Commonwealth Politics," *SG*, Jan. 1899, 21; "The Constitution," *SG*, Jan. 1899, 23; "A Descriptive Note," *SG*, Mar. 1900, 22; RA, "Christian Commonwealth," TMs, FDP, 23.

31. RA, "Christian Commonwealth," TMs, FDP, 23, 30; GHG, "Christian Commonwealth," *Commons*, 6; "A Descriptive Note," *SG*, Mar. 1900, 22.

32. "Our Commonwealth Politics," *SG*, Jan. 1899, 21–22; "By-Laws," *SG*, Jan. 1899, 23.

33. RA, "Journal," 29–32; RA, "Christian Commonwealth," TMs, FDP, 11–13; Walker, "George Howard Gibson."

34. Conversation with Louise Mills, 15 June 1994, West Newbury, Mass.

35. RA, "Christian Commonwealth," TMs, FDP, 11–13; *Columbus Enquirer-Sun*, 24 May 1899, 31 May 1899; "Colony Notes," *SG*, Nov. 1899, 28.

36. "Colony Notes," *SG*, Sept. 1898, 27; RA, "Reminiscences," 89; *Columbus Enquirer-Sun*, 31 Dec. 1898; RA, "Christian Commonwealth," TMs, FDP, 12; "Colony Notes," *SG*, Nov. 1898, 24.

37. RA, "Christian Commonwealth," TMs, FDP, 3, 16, 35; Jule Talmadge, "The Ideal," *SG*, June 1898, 17; "Colony Notes," *SG*, Mar. 1899, 26; "Colony Notes," *SG*, Feb. 1899, 25; *Columbus Enquirer-Sun*, 5 Feb. 1899.

38. RA, "Christian Commonwealth," TMs, FDP, 15; "Colony Notes," *SG*, Dec. 1898, 27; "Colony Notes," *SG*, Mar. 1899, 26.

39. "Colony Notes," *SG*, Mar. 1899, 26; RA, "Christian Commonwealth," TMs, FDP, 6, 39–40.

40. RA, "Christian Commonwealth," TMs, FDP, 12; "Colony Notes," *SG*, Nov. 1898, 24; *SG*, Jan. 1901, 3.

41. "Colony Notes," *SG*, Mar. 1899, 26; *Commonwealth Details*, 11; GHG, "Christian Commonwealth, of Commonwealth," 301; "Colony Notes," *SG*, June 1900, 23.

42. "By-Laws," *SG*, Jan. 1899, 24; "Our Commonwealth Politics," *SG*, Jan. 1899, 22; "Colony Notes," *SG*, Mar. 1899, 26; RA, "Christian Commonwealth," TMs, FDP, 13–14.

43. "By-Laws," *SG*, Jan. 1899, 24; "Colony Notes," *SG*, Mar. 1899, 26.

44. "Letter from the Christian Commonwealth," *CN*, 11 June 1898; "By-Laws," *SG*, Jan. 1899, 24; "Colony Notes," *SG*, Mar. 1899, 26; RA, "Christian Commonwealth," TMs, FDP, 10, 17; "Colony Notes," *SG*, Nov. 1898, 25; "Colony Notes," *SG*, Feb. 1899, 25; RA, *Thy Cloak Also*, 93.

45. "Our Commonwealth Politics," *SG*, Jan. 1899, 22; "By-Laws," *SG*, Jan. 1899, 24.

46. "Our Commonwealth Politics," *SG*, Jan. 1899, 22; RA, "Christian Commonwealth," TMs, FDP, 9.

47. "Colony Notes," *SG*, June 1898, 25; "Colony Notes," *SG*, Aug. 1898, 24; RA, "Reminiscences," 89; RA, "Christian Commonwealth in Georgia," 131–32; GHG, "Christian Commonwealth, of Commonwealth," 304.

48. "A Call for Volunteers," *SG*, Aug. 1899, 25–26.

49. "A Business Proposition," *SG*, Oct. 1898, 25–26; GHG, "Similia Similibus Curantur," *SG*, Mar. 1899, 9–11.

50. *Columbus Enquirer-Sun*, 31 Dec. 1898; "Our Present Needs," *SG*, Feb. 1898, 28; "The Charter," *SG*, Dec. 1898, 24; "Colony Notes," *SG*, Oct. 1898, 29; GHG, "Christian Commonwealth," *Commons*, 6.

51. "How We Organize," *SG*, Feb. 1898, 23; "Colony Notes," *SG*, Aug. 1898, 26; "Notes of Progress," *SG*, May 1899, 30–31.

52. Chipman, "Doing Christ's Work," *SG*, Sept. 1898, 6–7.

53. "A New Colony Proposed," *SG*, Oct. 1898, 26–27.

54. "Colony Notes," *SG*, Dec. 1898, 26–27.

55. "Colony Notes," *SG*, July 1898, 27; Nevins and Albertson, "Reminiscences of

Ralph Albertson," 40; N. O. Nelson, "Notes of Village Leclaire," *SG*, July 1899, 27–29; "April at Commonwealth," *SG*, May 1900, 30; D. T. Hinckley, "Village Leclaire," *SG*, Jan. 1901, 3–9.

56. "Notes of Progress," *SG*, Apr. 1899, 27; "New Cooperative Colony," *CN*, 2 Sept. 1899.

57. *Columbus Enquirer-Sun*, 27 Mar. 1898; "Colony Notes," *SG*, Nov. 1898, 25; "Colony Notes," *SG*, Feb. 1899, 25.

58. "Notes of Progress," *SG*, May 1899, 30; Oneida Community Collection, Syracuse University Library, Syracuse, N.Y.; "The Assistant Cook," *SG*, Mar. 1900, 19.

59. "Colony Notes," *SG*, July 1899, 26.

60. RA, "Christian Commonwealth," TMs, FDP, 4–5.

61. GHG, "The Economics of Love," *SG*, Jan. 1899, 5–7; "Colony Notes," *SG*, Nov. 1898, 25.

62. "The Christian Commonwealth," *SG*, Nov. 1898, 22; "Colony Notes," *SG*, July 1898, 25, Feb. 1898, 24; Elliot and Dean, "Commonwealth, Georgia," 7; RA, "The Assistant Cook," *SG*, Aug. 1899, 24; "Colony Notes," *SG*, June 1898, 25; "Colony Notes," *SG*, Jan. 1899, 26.

CHAPTER 4. BROTHERHOOD LABOR

1. GHG, "Christian Commonwealth, of Commonwealth," 302; GHG, "Why Commonwealth Failed," 6; RA, "Christian Altruism and Its Message to the Churches," *SG*, June 1901, 7.

2. "A Brotherhood Organization," *SG*, Feb. 1898, 23; "Commonwealth Colony Notes," *SG*, Feb. 1898, 24; "Letter from the Christian Commonwealth," *CN*, 11 June 1898.

3. *Columbus Enquirer-Sun*, 24 Nov. 1896; "Colony Notes," *SG*, Dec. 1898, 26; *Commonwealth Details*, 3; "A Descriptive Note," *SG*, Mar. 1900, 22; RA, "Christian Commonwealth," TMs, FDP, 24; "Colony Notes," *SG*, Nov. 1898, 25; "Colony Notes," *SG*, Mar. 1899, 26.

4. "Colony Notes," *SG*, July 1898, 27; *Commonwealth Details*, 3; "Colony Notes," *SG*, Dec. 1899, 26; "Thirty Days," *SG*, Mar. 1900, 21; "Our Present Needs," *SG*, Feb. 1898, 26; "Colony Notes," *SG*, May 1898, 25; RA, "Christian Commonwealth," TMs, FDP, 8–9.

5. *Columbus Enquirer-Sun*, 27 July 1897, 23 Sept. 1897, 30 Oct. 1897, 7 Nov. 1900; *SG*, Apr. 1898, 22–25; "Business Matters," *SG*, Sept. 1898, 26; GHG, "Christian Commonwealth," *Commons*, 6; W. A. Ross, Receiver to William T. Harvey and Wm. Henry Harvey, 20 Apr. 1901, Muscogee County Deed Book "NN," 278–80; Elliot and Dean, "Commonwealth, Georgia," 3.

6. *Columbus Enquirer-Sun*, 27 Mar. 1898; "Business Matters," *SG*, Sept. 1898, 26; GHG, "Christian Commonwealth," *Commons*, 6; *Commonwealth Details*, 3; RA, "Christian Commonwealth," TMs, FDP, 9; "The Christian Commonwealth," *SG*, Nov. 1898, 22.

7. *Columbus Enquirer-Sun*, 16 Dec. 1897, 31 Dec. 1898, 24 Nov. 1896; GHG, "Letter

from the Christian Commonwealth"; "Colony Notes," *SG*, Sept. 1898, 27; GHG, "Christian Commonwealth," *Commons*, 6; Brundage, *Socialist Utopia*, 17.

8. RA, "Christian Commonwealth," TMs, FDP, 6, 20.

9. "The Assistant Cook," *SG*, June 1900, 20.

10. RA, "Christian Commonwealth," TMs, FDP, 26–27.

11. "Questions and Answers," *SG*, Aug. 1898, 22–23.

12. "The Assistant Cook," *SG*, Sept. 1899, 22; "Colony Notes," *SG*, Nov. 1899, 28; RA, "Christian Commonwealth," TMs, FDP, 28; Timothy Miller, *Quest for Utopia*, 10.

13. "Questions and Answers," *SG*, Aug. 1898, 22.

14. "Colony Notes," *SG*, Oct. 1898, 28; "The By-Laws," *SG*, Jan. 1899, 23.

15. "By-Laws," *SG*, Jan. 1899, 23; RA, "Christian Commonwealth," TMs, FDP, 27.

16. RA, "The Assistant Cook," *SG*, Aug. 1899, 23–24; "Colony Notes," *SG*, Sept. 1898, 27; "Colony Notes," *SG*, Mar. 1899, 26; RA, "Christian Commonwealth," TMs, FDP, 36–37.

17. RA, "Christian Commonwealth," TMs, FDP, 37.

18. RA, "The Assistant Cook," *SG*, Aug. 1899, 23.

19. "Colony Notes," *SG*, July 1898, 24.

20. "Colony Notes," *SG*, June 1898, 23; "Colony Notes," *SG*, Aug. 1898, 25; "Business Matters," *SG*, Sept. 1898, 26.

21. "Commonwealth Colony Notes," *SG*, Feb. 1898, 24; *Columbus Enquirer-Sun*, 31 Dec. 1898; GHG, "Christian Commonwealth," *Commons*, 6; "Business Matters," *SG*, Sept. 1898, 26; *Commonwealth Details*, 3.

22. "Colony Notes," *SG*, May 1898, 25.

23. "Colony Notes," *SG*, Aug. 1898, 25–26; "Business Matters," *SG*, Sept. 1898, 26; GHG, "Christian Commonwealth," *Commons*, 6; *Commonwealth Details*, 3; GHG, "Christian Commonwealth, of Commonwealth," 303.

24. RA, "Christian Commonwealth," TMs, FDP, 17; "Colony Notes," *SG*, Mar. 1899, 26; "Colony Notes," *SG*, May 1898, 25, July 1898, 26, Feb. 1899, 23; *Columbus Enquirer-Sun*, 5 Feb. 1899, 7 Dec. 1898; "Colony Notes," *SG*, Mar. 1899, 26; "Colony Notes," *SG*, Sept. 1898, 27–28; "Colony Notes," *SG*, Dec. 1898, 26; "Colony Notes," *SG*, Aug. 1899, 26.

25. *Columbus Enquirer-Sun*, 20 Dec. 1896; "Colony Notes," *SG*, June 1898, 23; "The Assistant Cook," *SG*, Sept. 1899, 22; RA, "Christian Commonwealth," TMs, FDP, 20; GHG, "Christian Commonwealth," *Commons*, 6; "Colony Notes," *SG*, Feb. 1900, 32.

26. "The Assistant Cook," *SG*, Sept. 1899, 22; "Colony Notes," *SG*, Aug. 1899, 20, 22.

27. *Columbus Enquirer-Sun*, 20 Dec. 1896; [RA], "The Citizen," *SG*, July 1901, 21; "Colony Notes," *SG*, June 1898, 23; "Colony Notes," *SG*, Nov. 1898, 24–25; "Colony Notes," *SG*, Jan. 1899, 27–28.

28. "Colony Notes," *SG*, July 1898, 26.

29. "Colony Notes," *SG*, Feb. 1899, 24; "Colony Notes," *SG*, Sept. 1898, 28.

30. "Business Matters," *SG*, Sept. 1898, 26; *Commonwealth Details*, 5; "Colony Notes," *SG*, Nov. 1898, 25; "Colony Notes," *SG*, Feb. 1900, 32.

31. "Current Topics," *SG*, Nov. 1898, 24; *Columbus Enquirer-Sun*, 7 Dec. 1898; "Colony Notes," *SG*, Dec. 1898, 26; *Commonwealth Details*, 3; "Colony Notes," *SG*, Aug. 1898, 26; "Business Matters," *SG*, Sept. 1898, 26–27; "Colony Notes," *SG*, Nov. 1898, 24–25; "Colony Notes," *SG*, July 1898, 26.

32. "Commonwealth Colony Notes," *SG*, Feb. 1898, 25; RA, "Christian Commonwealth," TMs, FDP, 10, 17.

33. "Colony Notes," *SG*, Aug. 1898, 25, Oct. 1898, 27.

34. "Colony Notes," *SG*, Aug. 1898, 25; "Colony Notes," *SG*, Oct. 1899, 31; "Colony Notes," *SG*, Sept. 1898, 28.

35. "Colony Notes," *SG*, Aug. 1898, 25; "Business Matters," *SG*, Sept. 1898, 26; *Commonwealth Details*, 3; "Around the World," *CN*, 22 Apr. 1899; *SG*, Feb. 1899, 36; "Colony Notes," *SG*, Mar. 1899, 24, 36; "Colony Notes," *SG*, Apr. 1899, 24; RA, "Reminiscences," 89.

36. "Colony Notes," *SG*, Nov. 1898, 25; "Colony Notes," *SG*, Jan. 1899, 27; *Columbus Enquirer-Sun*, 5 Feb. 1899; "Colony Notes," *SG*, Feb. 1899, 25.

37. "Colony Notes," *SG*, June 1898, 24; *Columbus Enquirer-Sun*, 5 Feb. 1899; "Business Matters," *SG*, Sept. 1898, 25–26; "Colony Notes," *SG*, Feb. 1899, 23, 25; "Colony Notes," *SG*, Mar. 1899, 26.

38. "Colony Notes," *SG*, Feb. 1899, 23; "Colony Notes," *SG*, Mar. 1899, 25–26; "Colony Notes," *SG*, July 1899, 25; *SG*, Aug. 1899, 28.

39. "Around the World," *CN*, 22 Apr. 1899; "Colony Notes," *SG*, Mar. 1899, 23, 25–26; *Columbus Enquirer-Sun*, 3 Mar. 1899, 9 Mar. 1899, 31 Mar. 1899; "Colony Notes," *SG*, Apr. 1899, 22, 24.

40. "Colony Notes," *SG*, Apr. 1899, 23; *Columbus Sunday Herald*, 14 May 1899; "Colony Notes," *SG*, May 1899, 28.

41. "Colony Notes," *SG*, July 1899, 24–25; "Colony Notes," *SG*, Aug. 1899, 26.

42. *Sunday Herald*, 2 Apr. 1899; *Commonwealth Details*, 7, 11; "Commonwealth Possibilities," *SG*, Mar. 1899, 22; "Colony Notes," *SG*, Mar. 1899, 25.

43. "Colony Notes," *SG*, Aug. 1899, 27.

44. "Colony Notes," *SG*, Sept. 1899, 26; "Colony Notes," *SG*, Oct. 1899, 30; GHG, "Christian Commonwealth, of Commonwealth," 303.

45. "Colony Notes," *SG*, Oct. 1899, 31; "The Diary," *SG*, Feb. 1900, 29.

46. *Commonwealth Details*, 11; "Colony Notes," *SG*, Oct. 1899, 31; "Colony Notes," *SG*, Nov. 1899, 28.

47. *Commonwealth Details*, 5; "Colony Notes," *SG*, Oct. 1898, 27; "Colony Notes," *SG*, Aug. 1899, 26, 28; "Thirty Days," *SG*, Mar. 1900, 21.

48. "Colony Notes," *SG*, Dec. 1898, 27; "Colony Notes," *SG*, Jan. 1899, 27; "Colony Notes," *SG*, Mar. 1899, 25; *Columbus Enquirer-Sun*, 3 Mar. 1899; "Colony Notes," *SG*, Apr. 1899, 23.

49. "Colony Notes," *SG*, Apr. 1898, 23; RA, "Christian Commonwealth," TMs, FDP, 19; Dombrowski, *Early Days of Christian Socialism*, 151.

50. "Colony Notes," *SG*, June 1898, 23; "A Diary," *SG*, Feb. 1900, 31; "The Assistant Cook," *SG*, Mar. 1900, 18.

51. "Colony Notes," *SG*, June 1898, 24–25; "Colony Notes," *SG*, Sept. 1898, 27; "Colony Notes," *SG*, Mar. 1899, 26; "The Assistant Cook," *SG*, Sept. 1899, 22; "Colony Notes," *SG*, Feb. 1900, 32.

52. "Colony Notes," *SG*, June 1898, 23; *Sunday Herald*, 2 Apr. 1899; "Around the World," *CN*, 22 Apr. 1899.

53. "Colony Notes," *SG*, June 1898, 23; RA, "Christian Commonwealth," TMs, FDP, 7, 19.

54. "The Assistant Cook," *SG*, Aug. 1899, 23; "The Assistant Cook," *SG*, June 1900, 20.

55. RA, "The Assistant Cook," *SG*, Aug. 1899, 25.

56. "Colony Notes," *SG*, Aug. 1899, 26, 28.

57. "Colony Notes," *SG*, Dec. 1899, 26; "Thirty Days," *SG*, Mar. 1900, 20; *Retail Coalman* (Chicago), Apr. 1915.

58. "Colony Notes," *SG*, Oct. 1898, 28; "The By-Laws," *SG*, Jan. 1899, 23–24.

59. "A Diary," *SG*, Feb. 1900, 30; "Thirty Days," *SG*, Mar. 1900, 20.

60. "Death of Mrs. S. H. Comings," *SG*, Jan. 1899, 25.

61. *Commonwealth Details*, 7, 9; "A Descriptive Note," *SG*, Mar. 1900, 22; RA, "Christian Commonwealth," TMs, FDP, 22, 24; RA, "Reminiscences," 89.

62. "Colony Notes," *SG*, Jan. 1899, 28; *Columbus Enquirer-Sun*, 4 Jan. 1899, 5 Feb. 1899, 3 Mar. 1899; "Colony Notes," *SG*, Feb. 1899, 23, 25; "Colony Notes," *SG*, Mar. 1899, 25–26, Apr. 1899, 24.

63. "Colony Notes," *SG*, Nov. 1898, 24; "Colony Notes," *SG*, Mar. 1899, 26; *Columbus Enquirer-Sun*, 31 Mar. 1899; "Colony Notes," *SG*, Apr. 1899, 23–24.

64. GHG, "An Hundred Fold in This Life," *SG*, Oct. 1898, 7.

65. *Columbus Enquirer-Sun*, 4 Jan. 1899; *Commonwealth Details*, 5; "Colony Notes," *SG*, Sept. 1898, 27; "A Descriptive Note," *SG*, Mar. 1900, 22.

66. "Colony Notes," *SG*, June 1898, 25; "Colony Notes," *SG*, Jan. 1899, 25.

67. S. M. Jones, "Letters," *SG*, May 1901, 12–13; Dombrowski, *Early Days of Christian Socialism*, 137.

68. "Colony Notes," *SG*, Mar. 1899, 24–25; *Columbus Enquirer-Sun*, 4 Jan. 1899, 3 Mar. 1899; "Around the World," *CN*, 22 Apr. 1899; "Colony Notes," *SG*, Aug. 1899, 29; *Commonwealth Details*, 7; "Colony Notes," *SG*, Feb. 1899, 24; "Colony Notes," *SG*, Apr. 1899, 24.

69. "The Christian Commonwealth," *SG*, Oct. 1899, 30.

70. "A Diary," *SG*, Feb. 1900, 31.

71. "Colony Notes," *SG*, June 1898, 24–25; "Colony Notes," *SG*, Mar. 1899, 26; "Colony Notes," *SG*, Feb. 1900, 32.

72. "Colony Notes," *SG*, Apr. 1899, 24; "A Descriptive Note," *SG*, Mar. 1900; RA, "Christian Commonwealth," TMs, FDP, 24.

73. "A Descriptive Note," *SG*, Mar. 1900, 22.

74. "Colony Notes," *SG*, Jan. 1899, 26; *Columbus Enquirer-Sun*, 4 Jan. 1899; "A Business Proposition," *SG*, Oct. 1898, 25–26.

75. "Colony Notes," *SG*, Oct. 1898, 27–28; *SG*, Nov. 1898, 23, 25; "Colony Notes," *SG*, Mar. 1899, 26.

76. "Business Matters," *SG*, Sept. 1898, 26; RA, "Christian Commonwealth," TMs, FDP, 2; N. O. Nelson to GHG, 22 January 1898, printed in *SG*, Feb. 1898, 27.

77. "Colony Notes," *SG*, Oct. 1898, 27–28; *SG*, Nov. 1898, 23; "Colony Notes," *SG*, Mar. 1899, 26; "Outside Brotherhood Help Proposed," *SG*, Nov. 1898, 23; "Colony Notes," *SG*, Feb. 1899, 24.

78. "Colony Notes," *SG*, Jan. 1899, 25, 27; "Colony Notes," *SG*, Feb. 1899, 24–25; "Colony Notes," *SG*, Mar. 1899, 25; "Colony Notes," *SG*, Apr. 1899, 23.

79. "Colony Notes," *SG*, Oct. 1898, 27; "Outside Brotherhood Help Proposed," *SG*, Nov. 1898, 23; *Columbus Enquirer-Sun*, 7 Dec. 1898; "Colony Notes," *SG*, Dec. 1898, 26; *Commonwealth Details*, 7; "Colony Notes," *SG*, Apr. 1899, 23; "Colony Notes," *SG*, May 1899, 29.

80. "Crash towels" were rugged with a coarse weave, with cotton in a natural state. They most closely resemble modern, inexpensive dish towels.

81. RA, "A Business Proposition," *SG*, Oct. 1898, 27; "Colony Notes," *SG*, Oct. 1898, 27; *SG*, Dec. 1898, 28; "Colony Notes," *SG*, Nov. 1898, 25; *Columbus Enquirer-Sun*, 4 Jan. 1899, 5 Feb. 1899, 3 Mar. 1899, 31 Mar. 1899; "Colony Notes," *SG*, Jan. 1899, 26–27; "Colony Notes," *SG*, Feb. 1899, 23, 36; *Commonwealth Details*, 7; "Colony Notes," *SG*, Mar. 1899, 26; "Colony Notes," *SG*, May 1899, 28; *Atlanta Constitution*, 11 June 1899; RA, "Christian Commonwealth," TMs, FDP, 17.

82. "Colony Notes," *SG*, July 1899, 26; "The Cotton Mill," *SG*, Nov. 1899, 26.

83. "The Cotton Mill," *SG*, Sept. 1899, 25–27; "Colony Notes," *SG*, Dec. 1899, 26; *SG*, Mar. 1900, 23.

84. "The Cotton Mill," *SG*, Sept. 1899, 26–27; "Colony Notes," *SG*, Dec. 1899, 26.

85. "Colony Notes," *SG*, Oct. 1898, 27; "Colony Notes," *SG*, Nov. 1898, 24.

86. "Letter from the Christian Commonwealth," *CN*, 11 June 1898; "Colony Notes," *SG*, Feb. 1899, 24; "Colony Notes," *SG*, May 1899, 29; "Colony Notes," *SG*, Aug. 1899, 28; "Colony Notes," *SG*, Sept. 1899, 26.

87. "Colony Notes," *SG*, Jan. 1899, 28; "Colony Notes," *SG*, Mar. 1899, 26; RA, *Social Incarnation*, 3; GHG, review of RA, *The Social Incarnation, SG*, Jan. 1899, 33–34; *SG*, Apr. 1899, 22; "Colony Notes," *SG*, May 1899, 29.

88. *SG*, Mar. 1898, 35; *Commonwealth Details*, 5, 7; *SG*, Sept. 1898, 32; "Four Books You Ought to Read," *SG*, July 1899, 34; "James P. Kelley," *SG*, Feb. 1900, 24; *SG*, July 1899, 35; GHG, review of *A Love-Lit Path to God* by Hattie C. Flower, *SG*, Nov. 1899, 34; *SG*, Aug. 1899, 35; *SG*, Oct. 1898, 32.

89. Timothy Miller, *Quest for Utopia*, 9; RA, "Christian Commonwealth," TMs, FDP, 8–9; *Columbus Enquirer-Sun*, 27 Mar. 1898.

CHAPTER 5. BROTHERHOOD LIFE

1. "Colony Notes," *SG*, June 1898, 25; "Business Matters," *SG*, Sept. 1898, 26; Sue Fay Hinckley, "Diary," quoted in Dombrowski, *Early Days of Christian Socialism*, 152.

2. "Colony Notes," *SG*, Jan. 1899, 28.

3. "A Descriptive Note," *SG*, Mar. 1900, 22; RA, "Christian Commonwealth," TMs, FDP, 24; "Colony Notes," *SG*, Sept. 1898, 28; "Colony Notes," *SG*, Nov. 1898, 25, June 1898, 23, July 1898, 26, Aug. 1898, 24.

4. RA, "Christian Commonwealth," TMs, FDP, 8–9, 22; *Columbus Enquirer-Sun*, 4 Jan. 1899; "Our Present Needs," *SG*, Feb. 1898, 26.

5. "Colony Notes," *SG*, Nov. 1898, 25; "Colony Notes," *SG*, Jan. 1899, 27; "Christian Commonwealth," *SG*, Nov. 1898, 24; *Commonwealth Details*, 5; *Columbus Sunday Herald*, 2 July 1899; "Colony Notes," *SG*, Feb. 1899, 24.

6. *Columbus Enquirer-Sun*, 31 May 1899, 4 Jan. 1899.

7. RA, "Christian Commonwealth," TMs, FDP, 19–20; "April in Commonwealth," *SG*, May 1900, 31.

8. "Colony Notes," *SG*, Feb. 1899, 24; *Commonwealth Details*, 5, 10; "Colony Notes," *SG*, Mar. 1899, 25; "Colony Notes," *SG*, Apr. 1899, 23; "Colony Notes," *SG*, Aug. 1899, 27.

9. "Around the World," *CN*, 22 Apr. 1899; RA, "Christian Commonwealth in Georgia," 138; Colony Notes," *SG*, Nov. 1899, 137.

10. "Colony Notes," *SG*, Aug. 1899, 26–27; "April at Commonwealth," *SG*, May 1900, 31.

11. James P. Kelley, "The Ideal Life," *SG*, Jan. 1900, 6; Ernest H. Crosby, "The Confessions of a Vegetarian," *SG*, Jan. 1900, 7–9; "A Diary," *SG*, Feb. 1900, 30; Frederick, *Knights of the Golden Rule*, 210.

12. J. Bawden, "Food Reform," *SG*, Jan. 1900, 25–26.

13. "Colony Notes," *SG*, Feb. 1900, 32.

14. "Questions and Answers," *SG*, Aug. 1898, 23; *Commonwealth Details*, 12–13.

15. "Questions and Answers," *SG*, Aug. 1898, 23; "Editorial Paragraphs," *SG*, Dec. 1898, 11–12; "The Assistant Cook," *SG*, Sept. 1899, 23.

16. "Colony Notes," *SG*, June 1898, 24; "A Diary," *SG*, Feb. 1900, 30; "Thirty Days," *SG*, Mar. 1900, 20.

17. "Colony Notes," *SG*, Sept. 1898, 27; "Thirty Days," *SG*, Mar. 1900, 20.

18. RA, "Christian Commonwealth," TMs, FDP, 21; W. C. D[amon], "A Dream," *SG*, Oct. 1898, 22; "Colony Notes," *SG*, Apr. 1899, 23.

19. *Columbus Enquirer-Sun*, 31 Mar. 1899; RA, "Christian Commonwealth," TMs, FDP, 14–15.

20. "Colony Notes," *SG*, May 1899, 27; *Sunday Herald*, 14 May 1899.

21. Reasoner, review of *Civilization, Its Cause and Cure, and Other Essays*, by Edward Carpenter, *SG*, Nov. 1899, 31–32; Frederick, *Knights of the Golden Rule*, 213.

22. GHG, review of *England's Ideal and Other Papers on Social Subjects*, by Edward Carpenter, *SG*, Oct. 1899, 33–34.

23. "A Diary," *SG*, Feb. 1900, 30; "Thirty Days," *SG*, Mar. 1900, 21–22.

24. RA, "Christian Commonwealth," TMs, FDP, 21; "Thirty Days," *SG*, Mar. 1900, 21.

25. "Questions and Answers," *SG*, Aug. 1898, 23; GHG, "Christian Commonwealth," *Commons*, 7.

26. "Colony Notes," *SG*, July 1898, 27; "Colony Notes," *SG*, Sept. 1898, 27; "James P.

Kelley," *SG*, Feb. 1900, 24; RA, "Christian Commonwealth," TMs, FDP, 15; James P. Kelley, "Was John Right?," *SG*, Sept. 1898, 3–4.

27. James P. Kelley, "Another Doctrine of Election," *SG*, Nov. 1899, 5–6.

28. James P. Kelley, "Some Illustrations," *SG*, Nov. 1898, 9.

29. James P. Kelley, "Convictions, and the Courage of Them," *SG*, July 1898, 9–10; Kelley, "The Decadence of Discipline," *SG*, Dec. 1898, 7–8; James P. Kelley, "Self-Culture and Service," *SG*, Oct. 1898, 5–6; James P. Kelley, "The Main Question," *SG*, Sept. 1899, 5–6; RA, "Christian Commonwealth," TMs, FDP, 16.

30. James P. Kelley, "The Ideal Life," *SG*, Jan. 1900, 5–7.

31. "Colony Notes," *SG*, June 1898, 24; "Colony Notes," *SG*, July 1898, 27; "Thirty Days," *SG*, Mar. 1900, 20–21; GHG, "Christian Commonwealth," *Commons*, 7.

32. "Colony Notes," *SG*, Sept. 1898, 28; RA, "Kindness and the Cross," *SG*, Nov. 1898, 10.

33. RA, "Christian Altruism, and Its Message to the Churches," *SG*, June 1901, 6–8; Dombrowski, *Early Days of Christian Socialism*, 154–55.

34. RA, "Christian Commonwealth," TMs, FDP, 11–12; John Chipman, "Appeal to the Church of God," *SG*, Feb. 1898, 9; Chipman, "The Sons of God," *SG*, Dec. 1898, 8–9.

35. John Chipman, "A Call to Repentance," *SG*, July 1898, 10–11.

36. "Colony Notes," *SG*, Jan. 1899, 25; John Chipman, "The Program of Commonwealth," *SG*, May 1899, 14–16.

37. "Colony Notes," *SG*, May 1899, 28; *Sunday Herald*, 14 May 1899; RA, "Christian Commonwealth," TMs, FDP, 12; "Colony Notes," *SG*, Aug. 1899, 29.

38. "Colony Notes," *SG*, Sept. 1899, 27; RA, "Christian Commonwealth," TMs, FDP, 11–12, 21.

39. John Chipman, "A Letter from Brother Chipman," [6 Nov. 1899], *SG*, Dec. 1899, 24–26; RA, "Reminiscences," 90.

40. "Questions and Answers," *SG*, Aug. 1898, 23.

41. GHG, "Christian Commonwealth," *Commons*, 7; GHG, "Christian Commonwealth, of Commonwealth," 301–2.

42. "The Assistant Cook," *SG*, May 1900, 25; RA, "A Commonwealth Sermon," *SG*, Apr. 1900, 25; RA, "Following," *SG*, Sept. 1898, 4–5.

43. Lears, *No Place of Grace*, 96, 98, 109; RA, "Cranks," *SG*, July 1899, 9–11.

44. James P. Kelley, "Meum and Tuum," *SG*, Mar. 1899, 4–7; James P. Kelley, "Education for the New Era," *SG*, May 1900, 8–11.

45. "Colony Notes," *SG*, Oct. 1898, 28; "Literature," review of *In His Steps* by "K," *SG*, Nov. 1898, 29–30; "The Old Gentleman," *SG*, Mar. 1900, 8–9.

46. Jule Talmadge, "The Home," *SG*, Sept. 1898, 12–13.

47. RA, "Reminiscences," 87–88.

48. *Commonwealth Details*, 7, 14; RA, "A Right Life," *SG*, Oct. 1898, 3–4; "The Assistant Cook," *SG*, June 1900, 20.

49. RA, "Christian Commonwealth," TMs, FDP, 20–21, 43–44. In RA's manuscripts, he referred to Brewer as "Pabst." He frequently used false names when criticiz-

ing people, either out of courtesy or to avoid a defamation lawsuit. RA, "Reminis-cences," 88; *Commonwealth Details*, 7; "Colony Notes," *SG*, June 1898, 23; RA, review of *A Mother's Ideals: A Kindergarten Mother's Conception of Family Life*, by Andrea Hofer Proudfoot, *SG*, Mar. 1899, 32–33; *Columbus Enquirer-Sun, 5* Feb. 1899; "Colony Notes," *SG*, Feb. 1899, 24.

50. Jule Talmadge, "The Home," *SG*, Sept. 1898, 12; "Questions and Answers," *SG*, Aug. 1898, 23.

51. *Columbus Enquirer-Sun*, 31 Dec. 1898; "Colony Notes," *SG*, Aug. 1898, 26; *Commonwealth Details*, 14.

52. "Colony Notes," *SG*, Aug. 1899, 29; *Commonwealth Details*, 14; RA, "Christian Commonwealth," TMs, FDP, 20–21, 43–44.

53. Jule Talmadge, "The Home," *SG*, Sept. 1898, 12–13; "Colony Notes," *SG*, June 1898, 23; RA, review of *A Mother's Ideals: A Kindergarten Mother's Conception of Family Life*, by Andrea Hofer Proudfoot, *SG*, Mar. 1899, 32–33.

54. RA, "Christian Commonwealth," TMs, FDP, 38–40.

55. "Questions and Answers," *SG*, Aug. 1898, 22; "Colony Notes," *SG*, Mar. 1899, 24.

56. "Business Matters," *SG*, Sept. 1898, 26–27; "Walking by Faith," *SG*, Nov. 1898, 23.

57. "The Right Relationship League," *SG*, Jan. 1899, 29; "Notes of Progress," *SG*, Feb. 1899, 28–29; "Right Relationship Stores," *SG*, Apr. 1899, 25; Gavit, "Edward Tyler Keyes"; RA, "Reminiscences," 90.

58. "Colony Notes," *SG*, Sept. 1898, 30; "The Right Relationship League," *SG*, Dec. 1898, 3, 28–29; "The Right Relationship League," *SG*, Jan. 1899, 29; "Notes of Progress," *SG*, Jan. 1899, 29; Timothy Miller, *Quest for Utopia*, 120.

59. Samuel M. Jones, "The New Right," *SG*, Feb. 1899, 16–18; *SG*, Mar. 1899, 17; Frederick, *Knights of the Golden Rule*, 242.

60. Gavit, "Edward Tyler Keyes"; "Business Matters," *SG*, Sept. 1898, 26–27; "Colony Notes," *SG*, Nov. 1898, 25; *SG*, Dec. 1898, 21; *Columbus Enquirer-Sun*, 7 Dec. 1898; RA, "Reminiscences," 89; RA, "Christian Commonwealth," TMs, FDP, 2, 34; "Colony Notes," *SG*, Apr. 1899, 24.

61. "Our Chicago Trip," *SG*, Dec. 1898, 21–22; Nevins and Albertson, "Reminiscences of Ralph Albertson," 13–14; Addams, "Visit to Tolstoy," 296, 302; "Settlement Federation," *Commons*, Oct. 1898, 12; "Tolstoyan Visitor," *Commons*, Oct. 1898, 12; "Current Topics," *SG*, Dec. 1898, 19; RA, "Reminiscences," 90; *Commonwealth Details*, 2.

62. "The Beatitudes in Practice," *Commons*, Oct. 1898, 8; "Signs of the Spirit's Presence," *Commons*, Oct. 1898, 8; "Our Chicago Trip," *SG*, Dec. 1898, 21–22.

63. "That Debt," *SG*, Dec. 1898, 21; *Columbus Enquirer-Sun*, 7 Dec. 1898.

64. RA, "A Good Thing," *SG*, Dec. 1898, 5–6.

65. *Columbus Enquirer-Sun*, 20 Dec. 1896, 24 Dec. 1896, 9 Jan. 1898, 17 Aug. 1898; *Commonwealth Details*, 7; RA, "Reminiscences," 89; RA, "Christian Commonwealth in Georgia," 28.

66. "Colony Notes," *SG*, Jan. 1899, 26–27; "Colony Notes," *SG*, Mar. 1899, 26; "Colony Notes," *SG*, Sept. 1899, 26; "Colony Notes," *SG*, Feb. 1900, 32; RA, "Reminiscences," 89;

"Commonwealth Colony Notes," *SG*, Feb. 1898, 24; "A Brotherhood Organization," *SG*, Feb. 1898, 23–24; *Columbus Enquirer-Sun*, 17 Aug. 1898; RA, "Christian Commonwealth," TMs, FDP, 3, 23; *SG*, Mar. 1900; GHG, "Christian Commonwealth," *Commons*, 6.

67. "Editorial Paragraphs," *SG*, Sept. 1898, 10–11.

68. James P. Kelley, "The Decadence of Discipline," *SG*, Dec. 1898, 7; James P. Kelley, "'Is Thy Servant a Dog?,'" *SG*, Apr. 1899, 6–9.

69. *Columbus Enquirer-Sun*, 27 Mar. 1898; "Colony Notes," *SG*, June 1898, 23; "Colony Notes," *SG*, Feb. 1900, 32.

70. "Colony Notes," *SG*, June 1898, 26.

71. *Columbus Enquirer-Sun*, 29 May 1898.

72. "Colony Notes," *SG*, Sept. 1898, 28; "Colony Notes," *SG*, Mar. 1899, 25; "A Brotherhood Organization," *SG*, Feb. 1898, 23; "The Christian Commonwealth: Colony Notes," *SG*, Mar. 1898, 21; *Columbus Enquirer-Sun*, 31 Mar. 1899; "Colony Notes," *SG*, Apr. 1899, 24.

73. GHG, "Christian Commonwealth," *Commons*, 7.

74. *Columbus Enquirer-Sun*, 9 Apr. 1899, 14 June 1899; "Colony Notes," *SG*, July 1899, 25; "Thirty Days," *SG*, Mar. 1900, 21.

75. "Questions and Answers," *SG*, Aug. 1898, 23; *Commonwealth Details*, 14.

76. *Commonwealth Details*, 7; "Colony Notes," *SG*, Jan. 1899, 27; "Colony Notes," *SG*, Mar. 1899, 25; "Colony Notes," *SG*, Sept. 1898, 27; "Colony Notes," *SG*, Oct. 1899, 30; RA, "Christian Commonwealth," TMs, FDP, 10; "Colony Notes," *SG*, Feb. 1900, 32; *SG*, Mar. 1900, 23; "A Brotherhood Organization," *SG*, Feb. 1898, 22; GHG, "Christian Commonwealth," *Commons*, 7.

77. *Columbus Enquirer-Sun*, 20 Dec. 1896; "Colony Notes," *SG*, June 1899, 28.

78. "Our Present Needs," *SG*, Feb. 1898, 28.

79. Ronald C. White Jr., *Liberty and Justice for All*, x, 77–81, 124; "Notes of Progress," *SG*, Apr. 1899, 26; Luker, *Social Gospel in Black and White*, 1, 142.

80. "The Christian Commonwealth: Colony Notes," *SG*, Mar. 1898, 21–22; *Columbus Enquirer-Sun*, 13 Apr. 1898, 29 Apr. 1898.

81. Comings, "Proposals Invited," *SG*, July 1898, 24–26; Comings, "Some Educational Plans," *SG*, Apr. 1898, 10.

82. "Commonwealth School," *SG*, Aug. 1898, 21–22; *Columbus Sunday Herald*, 25 Sept. 1898.

83. *Columbus Sunday Herald*, 25 Sept. 1898; "Colony Notes," *SG*, Dec. 1898, 26; *Columbus Enquirer-Sun*, 7 Dec. 1898.

84. "Thirty Days," *SG*, Mar. 1900, 20; Sutton, *Communal Utopias*, 145; "Colony Notes," *SG*, Oct. 1898, 27; *Commonwealth Details*, 7; "Colony Notes," *SG*, Mar. 1899, 25; "Colony Notes," *SG*, Jan. 1899, 26.

85. *Columbus Enquirer-Sun*, 7 Dec. 1898, 4 Jan. 1899; "Colony Notes," *SG*, Dec. 1898, 26; "Colony Notes," *SG*, Jan. 1899, 27; "Colony Notes," *SG*, Jan. 1900, 26; "A Diary," *SG*, Feb. 1900, 30.

86. "The Old Gentleman," *SG*, Mar. 1899, 13–14; "Colony Notes," *SG*, July 1898, 27; "Colony Notes," *SG*, Nov. 1898, 23–24.

87. "Questions and Answers," *SG*, Aug. 1898, 23; *Commonwealth Details*, 14.

88. GHG, "The Strain of Love," *SG*, Feb. 1899, 21–22.

89. "Thirty Days," *SG*, Mar. 1900, 21; GHG, "The Strain of Love," *SG*, Feb. 1899, 22.

90. "Colony Notes," *SG*, Mar. 1899, 24.

91. Hinckley, "Diary," quoted in Dombrowski, *Early Days of Christian Socialism*, 156.

92. "Colony Notes," *SG*, Sept. 1899, 26; RA, "Christian Commonwealth," TMs, FDP, 16; *SG*, Feb. 1901, 3.

93. "Colony Notes," *SG*, May 1899, 28; *Columbus Sunday Herald*, 14 May 1899.

94. "A Brotherhood Organization," *SG*, Feb. 1898, 22–23; "Colony Notes," *SG*, July 1898, 27; *Commonwealth Details*, 14; "The Christian Commonwealth," *SG*, Oct. 1899, 30; "Colony Notes," *SG*, Jan. 1900, 26; "Thirty Days," *SG*, Mar. 1900, 21.

95. "Colony Notes," *SG*, Dec. 1899, 26.

96. "Colony Notes," *SG*, Aug. 1898, 24, 26; GHG to Leo Tolstoy, 21 Apr. 1899, in Velikanova and Whittaker, *Tolstoy and the USA*, 763–64; "Colony Notes," *SG*, Sept. 1899, 27.

97. "Colony Notes," *SG*, Dec. 1898, 27.

98. "Colony Notes," *SG*, Dec. 1899, 26.

99. "Colony Notes," *SG*, Jan. 1898, 28; *Columbus Enquirer-Sun*, 4 Jan. 1899; GHG, "Christmas at Commonwealth," *SG*, Jan. 1900, 24; "A Diary," *SG*, Feb. 1900, 28.

100. GHG, "Christmas at Commonwealth," *SG*, Jan. 1900, 24; "Colony Notes," *SG*, Jan. 1898, 28, Jan. 1900, 26; *Columbus Enquirer-Sun*, 4 Jan. 1899; "A Diary," *SG*, Feb. 1900, 28; "Colony Notes," *SG*, Feb. 1900, 32.

101. "The Joy of Christmas," *SG*, Dec. 1899, 10; GHG, "Christmas at Commonwealth," *SG*, Jan. 1900, 24–25; "A Diary," *SG*, Feb. 1900, 29.

102. "A Diary," *SG*, Feb. 1900, 29.

CHAPTER 6. THE *SOCIAL GOSPEL*

1. "The Magazine and the Colony," *SG*, June 1900, 24–25; RA, "Christian Commonwealth," TMs, FDP, 3, 9, 18.

2. "Announcement," *SG*, Feb. 1898, 1; "Commonwealth Colony Notes," *SG*, Feb. 1898, 25; "Spread the Social Gospel," *SG*, Feb. 1898, 28; "Colony Notes," *SG*, May 1898, 25; "Colony Notes," *SG*, Dec. 1898, 26; GHG, "Christian Commonwealth, of Commonwealth," 301.

3. Christian, *Tolstoy's Letters*, 565.

4. Letters of 16, 19, 25 June, 7 July 1898, 19 Apr. 1899, box 12, folder "Letters to MLS," Ariadna Tyrkova-Williams Papers, Bakhmeteff Archive, Butler Library, Columbia University, New York; G. H. G., review of *The Romance of the Earth* by A. W. Bickerton, *SG*, Mar. 1900, 32.

5. "Colony Notes," *SG*, June 1898, 25; "Colony Notes," *SG*, Aug. 1898, 24; RA, "Reminiscences," 89; RA, "Christian Commonwealth in Georgia," 131–32.

6. GHG, "Christian Commonwealth, of Commonwealth," 303; Dombrowski, *Early Days of Christian Socialism*, 161, 164; Frederick, *Knights of the Golden Rule*, 170; "James P. Kelley," *SG*, Feb. 1900, 24.

7. "Colony Notes," *SG*, June 1898, 26; RA, "Christian Commonwealth," TMs, FDP, 10–11; S. H. Comings, "Christian Political Economy," *SG*, Feb. 1898, 10; *CN*, 22 Aug. 1896; S. H. Comings, "The Burning Bush," *SG*, July 1898, 11.

8. Benjamin Fay Mills, "What Jesus Taught," *SG*, July 1899, 6–9; Benjamin Fay Mills, "What the Church of the Future Ought to Be," *SG*, Dec. 1898, 16–18; "Notes of Progress," *SG*, Mar. 1899, 28–29.

9. Benjamin Fay Mills, "Heaven and Hell," *SG*, Jan. 1899, 9–10; GHG, "Let God's Kingdom Displace It," *SG*, Sept. 1898, 7–8; *SG*, Nov. 1898, 15.

10. "Notes of Progress," *SG*, Feb. 1899, 26; RA, "Rev. William T. Brown," *SG*, June 1900, 14.

11. William T. Brown, "Commercialism or Brotherhood," *SG*, July 1899, 11–12; William T. Brown, *Kingdom*, 10 Mar. 1898.

12. William T. Brown, "Christ the Emancipator," *SG*, Oct. 1898, 8–11; "Colony Notes," *SG*, Feb. 1899, 25; "Social Ideals," *SG*, May 1899, 3–7.

13. Rev. William T. Brown, "The Appeal of Christianity," *SG*, Oct. 1898, 16–22.

14. William T. Brown, "The Economic Conscience," *SG*, Feb. 1899, 6–9; *SG*, Mar. 1900, 30; *SG*, May 1900, 6.

15. William T. Brown, "The Beginnings of a New Religion," *SG*, Oct. 1899, 9–13.

16. "Colony Notes," *SG*, July 1898, 26; "Publisher's Notes," *SG*, Sept. 1898, 32; *Columbus Enquirer-Sun*, 11 Sept. 1898; "Colony Notes," *SG*, Oct. 1898, 27.

17. "Colony Notes," *SG*, Oct. 1898, 27; *Columbus Enquirer-Sun*, 5 Feb. 1899, 3 Mar. 1899; "Colony Notes," *SG*, Jan. 1899, 25; "Colony Notes," *SG*, Feb. 1899, 24–25; "Around the World," *CN*, 29 Apr. 1899; "Colony Notes," *SG*, Mar. 1899, 24, 26.

18. *Columbus Enquirer-Sun*, 26 Mar. 1899; "Colony Notes," *SG*, Apr. 1899, 23; "Around the World," *CN*, 22 Apr. 1899, 29 Apr. 1899, 27 May 1899; *Columbus Sunday Herald*, 14 May 1899; "Colony Notes," *SG*, May 1899, 26, 28–29.

19. "Colony Notes," *SG*, Dec. 1898, 26; "Colony Notes," *SG*, Apr. 1899, 23; "Colony Notes," *SG*, Sept. 1899, 26; "Colony Notes," *SG*, Aug. 1899, 26.

20. "Around the World," *CN*, 29 Apr. 1899; *Commonwealth Details*, 5; Dombrowski, *Early Days of Christian Socialism*, 157; Alston, *Tolstoy and His Disciples*, 150; "Publishers' Notes," *SG*, May 1898, 24–25; "Topics of the Times," *CN*, 24 June 1899; Frederick, *Knights of the Golden Rule*, 170.

21. GHG to Tolstoy, 22 Feb. 1898, in Velikanova and Whittaker, *Tolstoy and the USA*, 758–59; GHG, "Christian Commonwealth, of Commonwealth," 303; GHG, "The Good News," *SG*, May 1898, 23–24.

22. "Colony Notes," *SG*, Aug. 1898, 24–25; *New York Sun*, 17 Jan. 1899; *Columbus Sunday Herald*, 22 Jan. 1899.

23. *Commons*, Oct. 1898, 13; *SG*, Dec. 1899, 14.

24. *Columbus Enquirer-Sun*, 21 May 1898, 11 Sept. 1898, 26 Mar. 1899, 7 Dec. 1898, 8 June 1900, 17 Sept. 1898.

25. "Colony Notes," *SG*, June 1898, 24.

26. GHG, "The Strain of Love," *SG*, Feb. 1899, 21; "Colony Notes," *SG*, Feb. 1899, 25.

27. *Columbus Enquirer-Sun*, 24 June 1899.

28. "From a Commonwealth Girl," *SG*, Dec. 1898, 23; Dombrowski, *Early Days of Christian Socialism*, 153–54.

29. [RA], "The Assistant Cook," *SG*, Apr. 1900, 24–25; RA, *Thy Cloak Also*, 224–25; "Colony Notes," *SG*, June 1898, 27–28, Aug. 1898, 26, Oct. 1898, 28.

30. "Notes of Progress," *SG*, Feb. 1899, 28; "The Calling of St. Matthew," *SG*, Dec. 1898, 14–15; "Cooperator," "The Need of Doing," *SG*, June 1898, 16–17.

31. "Colony Notes," *SG*, July 1898, 27; G. "Questions and Answers," *SG*, Aug. 1898, 22–23.

32. "Commonwealth Colony Notes," *SG*, Feb. 1898, 25; "Publishers' Notes," *SG*, May 1898, 25.

33. "Colony Notes," *SG*, Aug. 1899, 30.

34. Ibid., 30.

35. "Notes on Progress," *SG*, Apr. 1899, 26; "Cooperative Colonies Abroad," *Brotherhood*, November 1899, 109, in Alston, *Tolstoy and His Disciples*, 266; Dombrowski, *Early Days of Christian Socialism*, 143; "Colony Notes," *SG*, Oct. 1899, 31; "Colony Notes," *SG*, Nov. 1899, 29; "Colony Notes," *SG*, May 1899, 28; "Taken from Letters," *SG*, May 1899, 25; "Colony Notes," *SG*, Aug. 1899, 27–28.

36. "Taken from Letters," *SG*, May 1899, 24–26.

37. "Colony Notes," *SG*, July 1898, 26–27; Agnes Leonard Hill, "In All Labor There Is Profit," *SG*, Sept. 1898, 13; "Taken from Letters," *SG*, May 1899, 24.

38. Hopkins, *Rise of the Social Gospel*; May, *Protestant Churches and Industrial America*; Frederick, *Knights of the Golden Rule*, 170; "The Christian Commonwealth: Colony Notes," *SG*, Mar. 1898, 21; RA, "Christian Commonwealth," TMs, FDP, 18; "Colony Notes," *SG*, Feb. 1899, 25, Jan. 1900, 27, Sept. 1898, 28, June 1898, 25, Aug. 1898, 24.

39. "Taken from Letters," *SG*, May 1899, 24–25; "Colony Notes," *SG*, Sept. 1898, 29.

40. "Colony Notes," *SG*, Aug. 1898, 26.

41. RA, "Following," *SG*, Sept. 1898, 5; RA, "Reminiscences," 68; Enclosure in GHG to Tolstoy, 24 June 1899, in Gosudarstvennyi muzei L. N. Tolstogo, Moscow (hereafter GMT), BL 216/78, in Alston, *Tolstoy and His Disciples*, 150; "Literature," *SG*, Jan. 1899, 34; "Notes of Progress," *SG*, Apr. 1899, 26–27.

42. *SG*, Feb. 1898, 3, 8; "The Quality of Revolution," *SG*, June 1898, 8.

43. "Current Topics," *SG*, Sept. 1898, 22; GDH, "A Question Concerning Social System and Christian Conscience," *SG*, Nov. 1898, 3–6; GHG, "Individual Duty and Responsibility," *SG*, Nov. 1898, 6–9.

44. "Notes of Progress," *SG*, Feb. 1899, 26–27; GDH to Editor *Social Gospel*, 15 Feb. 1899, printed in *SG*, Mar. 1899, 3; "Current Topics," *SG*, July 1899, 20.

45. "Professor Herron's Letter of Resignation," supplement to *SG*, Nov. 1899, 1–4.

46. "The College Faculty Speaks," *SG*, Dec. 1899, 15.

47. "The Trustees Issue a Statement," *SG*, Dec. 1899, 15–16.

48. "Symposium on Professor Herron's Letter of Resignation," *SG*, Dec. 1899, 17–21; Eltweed Pomeroy, "A Belated Symposium Letter," *SG*, Jan. 1900, 17.

49. RA, "Reminiscences," 66; Scudder, "Christian Simplicity," 15–16; *SG*, Aug. 1899, 15; *SG*, Jan. 1900, 30; Frederick, *Knights of the Golden Rule*, 129; Appelbaum, *St. Francis of America*, 40.

50. GHG, review of *Social Ideals of English Letters* by Vida D. Scudder, *SG*, Feb. 1899, 33–34; *SG*, Mar. 1899, 7; Vida D. Scudder, "The New Intuition," *SG*, Mar. 1899, 15–16; *SG*, Apr. 1899, 13.

51. "Social Ethics," *SG*, July 1898, 20–21.

52. Ernest H. Crosby, "The Soul of a People," *SG*, Oct. 1898, 11–12.

53. "Current Topics," *SG*, Sept. 1898, 24–25; "Current Topics," *SG*, Nov. 1898, 19.

54. "Review of Progress," *SG*, July 1898, 28; *SG*, Nov. 1898, 29; *Commonwealth Details*, 14; "Current Topics," *SG*, Feb. 1899, 20.

55. "Notes on Progress," *SG*, Apr. 1899, 27; "Current Topics," *SG*, Mar. 1900, 15.

56. "Notes of Progress," *SG*, Nov. 1899, 30; W. H. Van Ornum, "Only a Part of the Price," *SG*, Nov. 1898, 15; Ernest H. Crosby, "Trusts for the People," *SG*, Mar. 1899, 11–12.

57. "Current Topics," *SG*, Mar. 1899, 18; "Notes of Progress," *SG*, May 1899, 29–30.

58. "Literature," *SG*, Aug. 1898, 31.

59. "Around the World," *CN*, 23 Apr. 1898; *CN*, 28 May 1898; "Review of Progress," *SG*, July 1898, 29; *The Daily News Almanac and Political Register* (Chicago Daily News Company, 1920), 755; "Notes on Progress," *SG*, Nov. 1898, 29; "Notes of Progress," *SG*, Feb. 1899, 34.

60. John Ward Stimson, "The Lesson of John Ruskin," *SG*, Mar. 1900, 9–11; W. E., review of *The Bible References of John Ruskin* by Mary and Ellen Gibbs, *SG*, Dec. 1898, 30–31.

61. GHG, "Letter from the Christian Commonwealth," *CN*, 11 June 1898; *SG*, May 1899, 13; "Colony Notes," *CN*, 23 Apr. 1898; "Notes of Progress," *SG*, Feb. 1899, 29.

62. "Current Topics," *SG*, Sept. 1899, 20, 27; "Kind Words from Our New Neighbors, *CN*, 30 Sept. 1899; "Literature," *SG*, Jan. 1900, 34.

63. "Colony Notes," *SG*, Sept. 1898, 30; "Taken from Letters," *SG*, May 1899, 25.

64. "Literature," *SG*, July 1898, 31.

65. "Notes of Progress," *SG*, Nov. 1899, 30.

66. "'Wainoni'—A Federative Home," *SG*, July 1899, 29–30.

67. Frederic O. MacCartney, "The Religious Value of Cooperation," *SG*, Nov. 1898, 16–17.

68. "Review of Progress," *SG*, Aug. 1898, 29; "Notes of Progress," *SG*, Mar. 1899, 29; "Notes of Progress," *SG*, Apr. 1899, 25; *SG*, May 1899, 30; RA, "A Divine Social Drama," *SG*, Aug. 1899, 3–4; "The Buffalo Conference," *SG*, Aug. 1899, 31–32.

69. "Review of Progress," *SG*, Aug. 1898, 28–29; *Cosmopolitan* 24 (Nov. 1897–Apr. 1898): 100, 224, 333.

70. MOOCs are massive open online courses, which are open access and free for anyone to enroll. MOOCs provide an affordable and flexible way to learn, start a career, and deliver quality educational experiences at scale.

71. "Current Topics," *SG*, July 1899, 19.

72. "Current Topics," *SG*, July 1899, 19–20; "Current Topics," *SG*, Sept. 1899, 20–21; "Notes of Progress," *SG*, Sept. 1899, 29; "Notes of Progress," *SG*, Oct. 1899, 32; "Thomas E. Will, "A College at Your Door," *SG*, Nov. 1899, 19.

73. Thos. E. Will, "The Old and the New in Education," *SG*, Jan. 1900, 3–5.

74. Thomas Elmer Will, "Educate or Perish," *SG*, Feb. 1899, 6–8.

75. Thomas E. Will, "Tendencies towards Socialism," *SG*, Apr. 1900, 3–6.

76. "The Old Gentleman," *SG*, July 1899, 15; "The Old Gentleman," *SG*, July 1898, 12, Oct. 1898, 15, Mar. 1899, 13.

77. "The Old Gentleman," *SG*, Sept. 1898, 11.

78. "The Old Gentleman," *SG*, Dec. 1899, 13–14.

79. "The Old Gentleman," *SG*, Dec. 1898, 13; "The Old Gentleman," *SG*, Sept. 1899, 12.

80. "The Old Gentleman," *SG*, Oct. 1898, 15–16.

81. Luker, *Social Gospel in Black and White*, 143; RA, "Reminiscences," 25.

82. "Current Events," *SG*, May 1898, 20–21.

83. *SG*, June 1898, 18; "Review of Progress," *SG*, July 1898, 29; "Current Topics," *SG*, Mar. 1899, 18.

84. Crosby, "War and Christianity," *SG*, July 1898, 5–6; Frederick, *Knights of the Golden Rule*, 219.

85. "Current Topics," *SG*, July 1898, 23; "Current Topics," *SG*, Sept. 1898, 21, quoting George Kennan in *The Outlook*, 30 July, "Current Topics," *SG*, Sept. 1898, 25.

86. "Current Topics," *SG*, Sept. 1898, 21–22, Oct. 1898, 24.

87. Henry Demarest Lloyd, "What Labor Day Heralds," *SG*, Nov. 1898, 18.

88. "Current Topics," *SG*, Jan. 1899, 18.

89. James P. Kelley, "A Condition, Not a Theory," *SG*, Feb. 1899, 9–10.

90. "Current Topics," *SG*, Mar. 1899, 19–21.

91. "Current Topics," *SG*, Nov. 1898, 19–20.

92. "Current Topics," *SG*, Aug. 1899, 21; "Current Topics," *SG*, Sept. 1899, 19.

93. "Current Topics," *SG*, Feb. 1899, 19–20; "Current Topics," *SG*, Mar. 1899, 18; "Notes of Progress," *SG*, Apr. 1899, 26; "Current Topics," *SG*, Oct. 1899, 25–26; "Current Topics," *SG*, July 1899, 20; "Editorial Paragraphs," *SG*, Nov. 1899, 8–9.

94. "Current Topics," *SG*, July 1899, 20; "Current Topics," *SG*, Mar. 1900, 16.

95. "Current Topics," *SG*, Aug. 1899, 22; "Current Topics," *SG*, May 1900, 23.

96. "Notes on Progress," *SG*, Nov. 1898, 27.

97. "Current Topics," *SG*, May 1899, 21; Dombrowski, *Early Days of Christian Socialism*, 160.

98. "Current Topics," *SG*, Aug. 1899, 22.

99. James P. Kelley, "The Future of This Country," *SG*, June 1899, 15; "Current Topics," *SG*, Sept. 1898, 22–24.

100. "Literature," *SG*, Aug. 1898, 31–32, Nov. 1898, 31.

101. "Colony Notes," *SG*, Sept. 1899, 26; Sue Fay Hinckley, review of *Women and Economics* by Charlotte Perkins Stetson [Gilman], *SG*, Jan. 1899, 31–32.

102. "Literature," *SG*, Aug. 1898, 29–31; "Literature," *SG*, Nov. 1898, 31.

103. "Literature," review of *In His Steps* by "K," *SG*, Nov. 1898, 29–30; "Editorial Paragraphs," *SG*, Aug. 1899, 10; "Current Topics," *SG*, Mar. 1900, 17.

CHAPTER 7. THE OUTSIDE WORLD

1. GHG, "A Sunday Evening Talk," *SG*, June 1898, 21; "Colony Notes," *SG*, July 1899, 25.

2. *Columbus Enquirer-Sun*, 24 Dec. 1896; "Publishers' Notes," *SG*, May 1898, 24; RA, "Christian Commonwealth," TMs, FDP, 3, 23; GHG, "Christian Commonwealth," *Commons*, 6; *Commonwealth Details*, 3; "Colony Notes," *SG*, Jan. 1899, 27; *Record of Appointment of Postmasters*, Post Office Records, National Archives, microfilm 841, roll 24.

3. "Questions and Answers," *SG*, Aug. 1898, 22; "Colony Notes," *SG*, Nov. 1898, 25; "Thirty Days," *SG*, Mar. 1900, 21; *Columbus Enquirer-Sun*, 7 Dec. 1898.

4. "Colony Notes," *SG*, Aug. 1899, 26; "Thirty Days," *SG*, Mar. 1900, 20.

5. RA, "Theories and a Life," *SG*, Sept. 1899, 24; RA, "Christian Commonwealth," TMs, FDP, 32–33; "A Quiet Month," *SG*, Apr. 1900, 30.

6. "Current Topics," *SG*, Jan. 1899, 18; "Current Topics," *SG*, Feb. 1899, 25; X, "The Journal of John Woolman," *SG*, Feb. 1899, 32–33; "The Old Gentleman," *SG*, Mar. 1899, 13.

7. *Columbus Enquirer-Sun*, 20 Dec. 1896; RA, "Christian Commonwealth," TMs, FDP, 32–33; Luker, *Social Gospel in Black and White*; "Cooperative Colonies Abroad," *Brotherhood* 7, no. 7 (November 1899): 109.

8. RA, "The Assistant Cook," *SG*, Feb. 1900, 20: "Thirty Days," *SG*, Mar. 1900, 20–21.

9. "Thirty Days," *SG*, Mar. 1900, 21; "April at Commonwealth," *SG*, May 1900, 30.

10. RA, "Christian Commonwealth," TMs, FDP, 33.

11. "Current Topics," *SG*, Jan. 1899, 20; "Current Topics," *SG*, Sept. 1899, 18; James P. Kelley, "Information Wanted," *SG*, Sept. 1898, 9–10.

12. RA, "Christian Commonwealth," TMs, FDP, 33–34.

13. "Colony Notes," *SG*, Nov. 1898, 25; "Colony Notes," *SG*, Feb. 1899, 24; "A Diary," *SG*, Feb. 1900, 30.

14. RA, "Christian Commonwealth," TMs, FDP, 34; *Columbus Enquirer-Sun*, 9 Mar. 1899.

15. *Columbus Enquirer-Sun*, 22 July 1898, 24 July 1898, 26 July 1898, 28 July 1898.

16. *Columbus Enquirer-Sun*, 29 July 1898, 30 July 1898.

17. *Columbus Sunday Herald*, 24 July 1898, 31 July 1898.

18. "Colony Notes," *SG*, July 1898, 27; *Columbus Sunday Herald*, 30 Dec. 1899; Marie

Marchand Ross, "Icaria," *SG*, Apr. 1901, 3; *Columbus Enquirer-Sun*, 6 May 1898, 12 Mar. 1899, 29 Dec. 1899; "Colony Notes," *SG*, June 1898, 26; "A Diary," *SG*, Feb. 1900, 28–29; "Colony Notes," *SG*, Jan. 1899, 25.

19. *Columbus Enquirer-Sun*, 7 Dec. 1898, 4 Jan. 1899, 5 Feb. 1899, 14 May 1899; *Columbus Sunday Herald*, 30 Dec. 1899.

20. *Columbus Enquirer-Sun*, 11 Sept. 1898, 18 Feb. 1899; "Colony Notes," *SG*, Jan. 1899, 27; *Macon News*, quoted in *Columbus Enquirer-Sun*, 17 Sept. 1898; "Around the World," *CN*, 10 June 1899; "Jackson: A History of Middle Georgia," 4 Mar. 2014, 59–60, www .cityofjacksonga.com/Assets/Files/HistoryofJackson.pdf.

21. "Colony Notes," *SG*, Aug. 1898, 24.

22. S. H. Comings, "Proposals Invited," *SG*, July 1898, 25.

23. *CN*, 18 July 1896; C. L. Brewer, "Is This Scientific Socialism?," *SG*, Feb. 1898, 16–17.

24. "Colony Notes," *SG*, Dec. 1898, 27.

25. "Notes of Progress," *SG*, July 1899, 31; "Notes of Progress," *SG*, Oct. 1899, 33; GHG, "Prosperity Closely Investigated," *SG*, Dec. 1900, 20–22; Tiedje, "People's Hour," 122; Rev. Carl D. Thompson, "The Moral and Economic Basis of Brotherhood," *SG*, Jan. 1900, 14–16.

26. Marxists Internet Archive, "The Socialist Party of America (1897–1905): Document Download Page: 1897 June," www.marxists.org/history/usa/eam/spa/spadown loads-1895-1905.html; Charles E. Beals, ed., *Proceedings of the Second National Peace Congress: Chicago, May 2 to 5, 1909* (Chicago: Peterson, 1909), 6, 170.

27. *Columbus Enquirer-Sun*, 17 Jan. 1899, 28 Jan. 1899, 4 Feb. 1899; "Colony of a Brotherhood," *Morning Star* (Rockford, Ill.), 29 Jan. 1899.

28. *Sunday Herald*, 12 Nov. 1899; "Colony Notes," *SG*, Nov. 1899, 28.

29. "Around the World," *CN*, 21 May 1898; "Christians' Beacon," *CN*, 9 Dec. 1899; "Colony Notes," *CN*, 23 Apr. 1898.

30. *Columbus Enquirer-Sun*, 31 Dec. 1898; *St. Andrew's Cross*, Sept. 1899, 62; review of *Ten Times One Is Ten*, by Edward Everett Hale, *SG*, Mar. 1899, 33; RA, "Christian Commonwealth," TMs, FDP, 35–36; Bolton Hall to P. Sergeyenko, June 1926, box 1, Bolton Hall Papers, New York Public Library.

31. RA, "Christian Commonwealth," TMs, FDP, 36; Gleason, "Main Defect."

32. "Further Comments on the Colony Question," *Kingdom*, 30 Mar. 1899; "Editorial Paragraphs," *SG*, May 1899, 16–17.

33. Bliss, "Self-Serving Colonies Condemned"; *SG*, Apr. 1899, 14–17.

34. GHG, "The Criticism from Mr. Gleason," *SG*, Apr. 1899, 3–6; GHG, "The Preaching and Charity Method," *SG*, Apr. 1899, 20–22; Dombrowski, *Early Days of Christian Socialism*, 146.

35. GHG, review of *Between Caesar and Jesus* by George D. Herron, *SG*, Apr. 1899, 31.

36. Crosby to Tolstoy, 26 July 1897, Tolstoy to Crosby, 21 Aug. 1897, in Velikanova and Whittaker, *Tolstoy and the USA*, 540; Leo Tolstoy to Aylmer Maude, 12 Dec. 1898, in Christian, *Tolstoy's Letters*, 578–79.

37. GHG to Tolstoy, 22 Feb. 1898, in Velikanova and Whittaker, *Tolstoy and the USA*,

758–59; Tolstoy to GHG, 23 Mar. 1898, in Velikanova and Whittaker, *Tolstoy and the USA*, 760–61; "Colony Notes," *SG*, June 1898, 28.

38. "Publishers' Notes," *SG*, May 1898, 24; Alston, *Tolstoy and His Disciples*, 2, 5, 102, 106, 121–22, 128, 264n34, 134.

39. GHG to Tolstoy, 22 Feb. 1898, in Velikanova and Whittaker, *Tolstoy and the USA*, 758–59; Tolstoy to GHG, 23 Mar. 1898, in Velikanova and Whittaker, *Tolstoy and the USA*, 758–61; "Colony Notes," *SG*, June 1898, 28.

40. GHG to Tolstoy, 21 Apr. 1898, in Velikanova and Whittaker, *Tolstoy and the USA*, 763–64.

41. Alston, *Tolstoy and His Disciples*, 134.

42. "Colony Notes," *SG*, Jan. 1899, 29.

43. "The American Colony in Jerusalem," *SG*, Aug. 1899, 32–33.

44. Tolstoy to GHG, 23 Mar. 1898, in Velikanova and Whittaker, *Tolstoy and the USA*, 761.

45. GHG to Tolstoy, 21 Apr. 1898, in Velikanova and Whittaker, *Tolstoy and the USA*, 764.

46. "The Spirit Wrestlers," *SG*, May 1898, 25–26; Alston, *Tolstoy and His Disciples*, 114.

47. "Colony Notes," *SG*, June 1898, 30; "The Emigration of the Doukhobortsi," *SG*, Sept. 1898, 29–30.

48. Tolstoy to Crosby, 30 June 1898, Tolstoy to C. F. Willard, 30 June 1898, in L. N. Tolstoy, *Polnoe Sobranie Sochinenii* pod. obschei red. V. G. Chertkova (Moscow: Gos. izd-vokhudozhestvennoi literatury, 1935-1964), 71, 396-98, in Alston, *Tolstoy and His Disciples*, 114; Tolstoy to Crosby, 12 July 1898, in Velikanova and Whittaker, *Tolstoy and the USA*, 549–50.

49. "Notes of Progress," *SG*, Nov. 1898, 28; "Latest News from the Doukhobortsi," *SG*, Nov. 1898, 26.

50. "The Tolstoy Doukhobortsi Fund," *SG*, Dec. 1898, 29; Ernest H. Crosby, "The Doukhobortsi Again," *SG*, Dec. 1898, 10–11; Crosby to Tolstoy, 23 Jan. 1899, in GMT, TC 211/27, in Alston, *Tolstoy and His Disciples*, 115, 173; Frederick, *Knights of the Golden Rule*, 219.

51. "The Doukhobortsi," *SG*, Jan. 1899, 30–31; "Notes of Progress," *SG*, Feb. 1899, 29; "Notes of Progress," *SG*, Mar. 1899, 29; "Notes of Progress," *SG*, Apr. 1899, 27; "The Doukhobors," *SG*, Aug. 1899, 33.

52. Alston, *Tolstoy and His Disciples*, 106; Crosby, "Wealth of St. Francis"; Crosby, "Trusts and Progress," *SG*, Oct. 1899, 6–8.

53. Crosby to Tolstoy, 15 June 1894, GHG to Tolstoy, 22 Feb. 1898, in Velikanova and Whittaker, *Tolstoy and the USA*, 506-7, 758–59; Ernest Howard Crosby, "Seventieth Birthday of the Grand Old Man of Russia," *SG*, Sept. 1898, 14–19.

54. "Current Topics," *SG*, Dec. 1898, 19–20.

55. Ernest H. Crosby, "War and Christianity," *SG*, July 1898, 5–6; Ernest H. Crosby, "The Soul of a People," *SG*, Oct. 1898, 12; Crosby to Tolstoy, 28 May 1899, in Velikan-

ova and Whittaker, *Tolstoy and the USA*, 560–61; Ernest H. Crosby, "The 'Blessings' of Civilization," *SG*, Sept. 1899, 3–5.

56. Ernest H. Crosby, "The New Freedom," *SG*, Nov. 1898, 13; "Literature," *SG*, Nov. 1898, 31; GHG, review of *Plain Talk in Psalm and Parable* by Ernest H. Crosby, *SG*, Nov. 1899, 32–34.

57. "Notes of Progress," *SG*, Nov. 1898, 27; "Editorial Paragraphs," *SG*, Dec. 1898, 12; Leo Tolstoy to Aylmer Maude, 12 Dec. 1898, in Christian, *Tolstoy's Letters*, 578.

58. Tolstoy to Schmitt, 25 Feb. 1898, *PSS* 71, 295–96, in Alston, *Tolstoy and His Disciples*, 98; Beasley and Bullock, *Russia in Britain*, 61; "Colony Notes," *SG*, June 1898, 28.

59. Alston, *Tolstoy and His Disciples*, 127; *Columbus Enquirer-Sun*, 31 Mar. 1899; "Colony Notes," *SG*, Apr. 1899, 23.

60. Addams, "Visit to Tolstoy," 301; Addams, *Twenty Years at Hull House*, 197–98. Mrs. G. H. Gibson did not remember any of the details of Addams's memoir—one-legged man, nine children, scurvy, migrations of the poor. Letter to Dombrowski, *Early Days of Christian Socialism*, 145n26.

61. Addams, "Visit to Tolstoy," 301; RA, "The Message of Commonwealth," *SG*, Feb. 1900, 4–5; Dombrowski, *Early Days of Christian Socialism*, 146.

62. "Colony Notes," *SG*, Nov. 1898, 25; *CN*, 22 Aug. 1896, 15 Oct. 1898, 20 Nov. 1898; "At Ruskin," *SG*, Jan. 1899, 31; Brundage, *Socialist Utopia*, 8.

63. GHG to Tolstoy, 24 July 1899, in Velikanova and Whittaker, *Tolstoy and the USA*, 767; "Colony Notes," *SG*, Aug. 1899, 28–29; "Colony Notes," *SG*, Sept. 1899, 28; "The Assistant Cook," *SG*, Mar. 1900, 18; Frederick, *Knights of the Golden Rule*, 219.

64. "Colony Notes," *SG*, Aug. 1899, 29; "Colony Notes," *SG*, Sept. 1899, 27.

CHAPTER 8. NONRESISTANCE ABANDONED

1. "Questions and Answers," *SG*, Aug. 1898, 22; *Columbus Enquirer-Sun*, 31 Dec. 1898.

2. RA, "Christian Commonwealth," TMs, FDP, 48–49; "Colony Notes," *SG*, Nov. 1899, 29.

3. *SG*, June 1898, 22–23.

4. RA, "Christian Commonwealth," TMs, FDP, 40.

5. RA, "A Business Proposition," *SG*, Oct. 1898, 27; "Colony Notes," *SG*, Oct. 1898, 27; *SG*, Dec. 1898, 28; *Columbus Enquirer-Sun*, 31 Mar. 1899.

6. RA, "Christian Commonwealth," TMs, FDP, 41.

7. "Business Matters," *SG*, Sept. 1898, 27; *Columbus Enquirer-Sun*, 31 May 1899, 6 June 1899; James P. Kelley, "Asceticism and Philistinism," *SG*, July 1899, 13.

8. RA, "Christian Commonwealth," TMs, FDP, 41; "Colony Notes," *SG*, Sept. 1898, 28; Questel, "Christian Commonwealth Colony," 36.

9. RA, "Christian Commonwealth," TMs, FDP, 41.

10. *Columbus Enquirer-Sun*, 31 May 1899, 6 June 1899, 7 June 1899, 10 June 1899; *Columbus Sunday Herald*, 28 May 1899; "Colony Notes," *SG*, July 1899, 25.

11. RA, "Commonwealth in Retrospect," 7; Questel, "Christian Commonwealth Colony," 39; GHG, "A Lawsuit," *SG*, July 1899, 23.

12. RA, "Christian Commonwealth," TMs, FDP, 41, 43–46.

13. There is no record of a "Tannager" in any source except Albertson's manuscripts. It may be an alias created by Albertson; RA, "Christian Commonwealth," TMs, FDP, 45–46.

14. *Columbus Enquirer-Sun*, 6 June 1899, 7 June 1899, 14 June 1899.

15. "By-Laws," *SG*, Jan. 1899, 24; *Columbus Enquirer-Sun*, 31 May 1899.

16. *Columbus Enquirer-Sun*, 18 May 1899, 7 June 1899; *Columbus Sunday Herald*, 28 May 1899; Elliot and Dean, "Commonwealth, Georgia," 4; There are conflicting accounts of the number of petitioners and the court documents have not been located.

17. *Columbus Enquirer-Sun*, 6 June 1899; *Columbus Sunday Herald*, 28 May 1899.

18. "Colony Notes," *SG*, July 1899, 25; *Columbus Enquirer-Sun*, 18 May 1899, 2 June 1899, 7 June 1899; Elliot and Dean, "Commonwealth, Georgia," 4.

19. *Columbus Enquirer-Sun*, 18 May 1899; *Columbus Sunday Herald*, 28 May 1899; Tolstoy to GHG, 23 Mar. 1898, in Velikanova and Whittaker, *Tolstoy and the USA*, 761; RA, "Reminiscences," 91; RA, "Christian Commonwealth in Georgia," 140–41; RA, "Christian Commonwealth," TMs, FDP, 41.

20. RA, *Thy Cloak Also*, 201–5; Dombrowski, *Early Days of Christian Socialism*, 165–66. Dombrowski refers to *The Passion That Left the Ground*. It was essentially the same text with a different title.

21. *Columbus Sunday Herald*, 28 May 1899.

22. Tolstoy to Crosby, 24 June 1899, in GMT BL217/78, in Alston, *Tolstoy and His Disciples*, 150; "The Christian Commonwealth," *SG*, Aug. 1899, 30; "The Christian Commonwealth," *SG*, Oct. 1899, 27; "The Christian Commonwealth," *SG*, Nov. 1899, 24.

23. "Topics of the Times," *CN*, 17 June 1899, 24 June 1899.

24. *Columbus Enquirer-Sun*, 24 May 1899, 31 May 1899.

25. GHG, "A Lawsuit," *SG*, July 1899, 23; *Columbus Enquirer-Sun*, 18 May 1899, 24 May 1899, 6 June 1899, 7 June 1899, 14 June 1899; Adams, *James A. Dombrowski*, 55.

26. *Columbus Enquirer-Sun*, 7 June 1899, 18 May 1899.

27. *Columbus Enquirer-Sun*, 31 May 1899; *Columbus Sunday Herald*, 28 May 1899.

28. *Columbus Enquirer-Sun*, 2 June 1899, 3 June 1899.

29. *Columbus Enquirer-Sun*, 6 June 1899, 7 June 1899.

30. Fish, "Christian Commonwealth Colony," 222; *Columbus Enquirer-Sun*, 7 June 1899.

31. *Columbus Enquirer-Sun*, 8 June 1899; "Topics of the Times," *CN*, 24 June 1899.

32. *Columbus Enquirer-Sun*, 8 June 1899, 10 June 1899.

33. "Colony Notes," *SG*, July 1899, 25; J. C., "Our Recent Troubles," *SG*, July 1899, 24; G. H. G., "A Lawsuit," *SG*, July 1899, 23.

34. *Columbus Enquirer-Sun*, 7 June 1899, 14 June 1899; "Topics of the Times," *CN*, 24 June 1899.

35. GHG, "Colony Troubles"; G. H. G., "A Lawsuit," *SG*, July 1899, 23.

36. RA, "Christian Commonwealth," TMs, FDP, 41.

37. RA, "A Look Ahead," *SG*, Sept. 1899, 7–8.

38. "Colony Notes," *SG*, Aug. 1899, 27; "The Assistant Cook," *SG*, Sept. 1899, 22.

39. RA, "Christian Commonwealth," TMs, FDP, 47; GHG, "Christian Commonwealth," *Commons*, 7; "The Assistant Cook," *SG*, Sept. 1899, 22–23.

40. GHG, "Christian Commonwealth," *Commons*, 7.

41. J. C., "Our Recent Trouble," *SG*, July 1899, 23–24; "Colony Notes," *SG*, July 1899, 25.

42. *SG*, Dec. 1898), 21; RA, "Reminiscences," 91; RA, "Christian Commonwealth in Georgia," 142.

43. RA, *Thy Cloak Also*, 225–26.

CHAPTER 9. A LOSS OF COURAGE

1. RA, "Christian Commonwealth," TMs, FDP, 47; White and Hopkins, *Social Gospel*, 177; Timothy Miller, *Quest for Utopia*, 10.

2. *SG*, Aug. 1899, 28.

3. "Colony Notes," *SG*, July 1899, 24; "More Interesting Correspondence," *SG*, Jan. 1900, 30.

4. "Colony Notes," *SG*, July 1899, 24, Aug. 1899, 28–29, Nov. 1899, 29; "Thirty Days," *SG*, Mar. 1900, 21.

5. "Colony Notes," *SG*, Nov. 1899, 28; RA, "Reminiscences," 89; John Chipman, "Accepting the Kingdom," *SG*, Aug. 1899, 7.

6. "Colony Notes," *SG*, Dec. 1899, 26.

7. "Colony Notes," *SG*, Nov. 1899, 29; "John Reed McDonald—2019 Inductee," Osborne County Hall of Fame, https://ochf.wordpress.com/category/artist.

8. *Columbus Enquirer-Sun*, 17 June 1899, 7 Sept. 1899, 19 Sept. 1899; "Colony Notes," *SG*, Oct. 1899, 31; "Colony Notes," *SG*, Nov. 1899, 27–29; "Colony Notes," *SG*, Sept. 1899, 26; RA, "Reminiscences," 89; Nevins and Albertson, "Reminiscences of Ralph Albertson," 27; RA, review of *The New Science of Healing, or the Doctrine of the Oneness of All Diseases* by Louis Kuhne, *SG*, July 1899, 33–34.

9. RA, "Christian Commonwealth," TMs, FDP, 49; "Colony Notes," *SG*, Nov. 1899, 28; "Colony Notes," *SG*, Feb. 1900, 32; "Thirty Days," *SG*, Mar. 1900, 20.

10. Derrill Hope, review of *Prisoners of Hope* by Mary Johnston, *SG*, Jan. 1900, 33; "The Social Gospel in the Lord's Prayer," *SG*, Oct. 1899, 16–18.

11. Sue Fay Hinckley, review of *Raphael* by Estelle M. Huril, *SG*, Dec. 1899, 32–33; review of *When Knighthood Was in Flower* by Edwin Caskoden, *SG*, Jan. 1900, 31–32; S. F. H., review of *Higher Life for Working People* by W. Walker Stephens, *SG*, Sept. 1899, 32–33; D. T. Hinckley, review of *Things as They Are* by Bolton Hall, *SG*, Jan. 1900, 31.

12. GHG to Tolstoy, 24 July 1899, in Velikanova and Whittaker, *Tolstoy and the USA*, 766; GHG, "Sell All and Follow Me," *SG*, Aug. 1898, 5.

13. *Columbus Enquirer-Sun*, 17 June 1899, 24 June 1899; RA, "Christian Common-

wealth," TMs, FDP, 10, 18, 22, 47; "A Voice That Is Still," *SG*, July 1899, 24; "Ruth Rules," *SG*, Aug. 1899, 25.

14. "Colony Notes," *SG*, Sept. 1899, 30.

15. "Colony Notes," *SG*, Oct. 1899, 30; "Colony Notes," *SG*, Nov. 1899, 27; "A Diary," *SG*, Feb. 1900, 31; "Thirty Days," *SG*, Mar. 1900, 21; *Columbus Enquirer-Sun*, 19 Sept. 1899; RA, "Reminiscences," 92; RA, "Christian Commonwealth," TMs, FDP, 15.

16. "Colony Notes," *SG*, Sept. 1899, 27; *Columbus Sunday Herald*, 12 Nov. 1899; "Colony Notes," *SG*, Nov. 1899, 28–29.

17. GHG to Tolstoy, 24 July 1899, in Velikanova and Whittaker, *Tolstoy and the USA*, 767; GHG, "An Order of Brothers," *SG*, Sept. 1899, 8–10; GHG, "Why Commonwealth Failed," 6; RA, "Christian Commonwealth," TMs, FDP, 47–48.

18. GHG, "An Order of Brothers. II," *SG*, Oct. 1899, 3–6; *Commonwealth Details*, 14.

19. RA, "Christian Commonwealth," TMs, FDP, 48; GHG to Tolstoy, 5 Oct. 1899, in Velikanova and Whittaker, *Tolstoy and the USA*, 768–69; "Love at Work," *SG*, Oct. 1899, 27–29.

20. "A Letter from Tolstoy," *SG*, Nov. 1899, 15–16; *Sunday Herald*, 12 Nov. 1899.

21. Ernest H. Crosby, "The Suggested New Order of Brothers," *SG*, Nov. 1899, 3–5; "Letters from People Interested in the Proposed Order of Brothers," *SG*, Nov. 1899, 16; Frederick, *Knights of the Golden Rule*, 225.

22. "From a Captain of Industry," *SG*, Nov. 1899, 16.

23. "Letters from People Interested in the Proposed Order of Brothers," *SG*, Nov. 1899, 13–16; G. E. Etherton, "How to Enter into Brotherhood Relations," *SG*, Dec. 1899, 28–29.

24. "More Interesting Correspondence," *SG*, Jan. 1900, 30; GHG, review of *Christ-Like Christianity* by Edward Eels, *SG*, Mar. 1900, 32; G. E. Etherton, "The Ground of Brotherhood Obligation," *SG*, Mar. 1900, 24–28.

25. "Colony Notes," *SG*, Oct. 1899, 31.

26. GHG, "Questions and Suggestions," *SG*, Nov. 1899, 16–17; GHG, "The Way of Escape," *SG*, Nov. 1899, 24–26; "Colony Notes," *SG*, Nov. 1899, 27; Calvin Reasoner, "The Brotherhood Suggestion," *SG*, Dec. 1899, 28; "A Diary," *SG*, Feb. 1900, 30.

27. "Colony Notes," *SG*, Dec. 1899, 27; GHG, "The Christian Jubilee," *SG*, Dec. 1899, 27–28; "The Brother-Love Evangel," *SG*, Dec. 1899, 27; "Colony Notes," *SG*, Jan. 1900, 26–27.

28. "More Interesting Correspondence," *SG*, Jan. 1900, 28–30; [GHG], "A Letter and a Reply," *SG*, Jan. 1900, 28; *SG*, Jan. 1900, 30.

29. GHG, "The Right of Monopoly," *SG*, Mar. 1900, 6–7; GHG, "Just a Personal Talk," *SG*, Feb. 1900, 34.

30. RA, "The Message of Commonwealth," *SG*, Feb. 1900, 3–6.

31. *Commonwealth Details*, 7; *Sunday Herald*, 12 Nov. 1899; RA, "Christian Commonwealth," TMs, FDP, 49; *Columbus Enquirer-Sun*, 19 Sept. 1899; "Colony Notes," *SG*, Oct. 1899, Nov. 1899, 27–28, Dec. 1899, 26; "Colony Notes," *SG*, Jan. 1900, 27.

32. *Sunday Herald*, 12 Nov. 1899; RA, "Christian Commonwealth," TMs, FDP, 3, 6, 47–

49; *Columbus Enquirer-Sun*, 19 Sept. 1899, 23 Sept. 1899, 30 May 1900; "Colony Notes," *SG*, Nov. 1899, 29; "Colony Notes," *SG*, Dec. 1899, 26, Jan. 1900, 26; RA, "Reminiscences," 59.

33. *Fairhope Courier*, Dec. 1899; RA, "Christian Commonwealth," TMs, FDP, 48–49; "Colony Notes," *SG*, Dec. 1899, 27.

34. "Colony Notes," *SG*, Nov. 1899, 27; *Sunday Herald*, 12 Nov. 1899; Albertson, "Christian Commonwealth," TMs, FDP, 49; "Colony Notes," *SG*, Feb. 1900, 33.

35. "Colony Notes," *SG*, Nov. 1899, 27; *Sunday Herald*, 12 Nov. 1899.

36. *Columbus Enquirer-Sun*, 27 Mar. 1898; RA, "Christian Commonwealth," TMs, FDP, 18; GHG, "Christian Commonwealth," *Commons*, 6; Sutton, *Communal Utopias*, 145; "Colony Notes," *SG*, Nov. 1899, 27; *Columbus Sunday Herald*, 12 Nov. 1899.

37. "Colony Notes," *SG*, Dec. 1899, 27, Jan. 1899, 26; "A Diary," *SG*, Feb. 1900, 30; "Thirty Days," *SG*, Mar. 1900, 20; "A Descriptive Note," *SG*, Mar. 1900, 22.

38. RA, "Christian Commonwealth," TMs, FDP, 3, 6, 47–49; *Columbus Enquirer-Sun*, 19 Sept. 1899, 23 Sept. 1899; "Colony Notes," *SG*, Jan. 1900, 26; "The Assistant Cook," *SG*, Jan. 1900, 23–24; "Colony Notes," *SG*, Feb. 1900, 33; "A Diary," *SG*, Feb. 1900, 31.

39. "Colony Notes," *SG*, Jan. 1900, 26–27; "A Diary," *SG*, Feb. 1900, 29–31.

40. "Literature," *SG*, Jan. 1900, 34.

41. "A Diary," *SG*, Feb. 1900, 29; "The Assistant Cook," *SG*, Jan. 1900, 22–23.

42. "A Diary," *SG*, Feb. 1900, 30; "Colony Notes," *SG*, Feb. 1900, 32; GHG, "An Object Lesson," *SG*, May 1900, 21–22; "A Quiet Month," *SG*, Apr. 1900, 29.

43. "Letters from People Interested in the Proposed Order of Brothers," *SG*, Nov. 1899, 16; "April at Commonwealth," *SG*, May 1900, 30; "A General Society Enrollment," *SG*, May 1900, 21; RA, "Reminiscences," 92.

44. GHG, "The Order of Brothers," *SG*, June 1900, 31–32; "A General Society Enrollment," *SG*, June 1900, 32; GHG, "The Inward Conflict," *SG*, Oct. 1900, 15–16; GHG, "Prosperity Closely Investigated," *SG*, Dec. 1900, 22; GHG, *People's Hour and Other Themes*, 43, 45.

45. "April at Commonwealth," *SG*, May 1900, 30; "The Assistant Cook," *SG*, June 1900, 19.

46. RA, "Reminiscences," 92; RA, "Be a Brother," *SG*, Mar. 1900, 28–30.

47. "A Diary," *SG*, Feb. 1900, 31.

48. "The Assistant Cook," *SG*, Jan. 1900, 23–24; "Colony Notes," *SG*, Feb. 1900, 32–33.

49. "A Quiet Month," *SG*, Apr. 1900, 30.

50. "The Assistant Cook," *SG*, Jan. 1900, 23–24; "Colony Notes," *SG*, Feb. 1900, 32.

51. "A Diary," *SG*, Feb. 1900, 29–30; "Thirty Days," *SG*, Mar. 1900, 21.

52. "A Diary," *SG*, Feb. 1900, 29–31; "Colony Notes," *SG*, Feb. 1900, 32–33.

53. "Thirty Days," *SG*, Mar. 1900, 20–22.

54. "A Diary," *SG*, Feb. 1900, 30; "A Quiet Month," *SG*, Apr. 1900, 29; "Thirty Days," *SG*, Mar. 1900, 22.

55. "A Diary," *SG*, Feb. 1900, 30.

56. "April at Commonwealth," *SG*, May 1900, 31.

57. "A Diary," *SG*, Feb. 1900, 29–31; "Thirty Days," *SG*, Mar. 1900, 20–21; *SG*, Mar. 1900, 23; Brundage, *Socialist Utopia*, 50.

58. "Colony Notes," *SG*, Feb. 1900, 32; "Thirty Days," *SG*, Mar. 1900, 20–21.

59. "A Diary," *SG*, Feb. 1900, 29–31; "Colony Notes," *SG*, Feb. 1900, 32.

60. "The Cotton Mill," *SG*, Sept. 1899, 26–27; "Colony Notes," *SG*, Dec. 1899, 26; "A Quiet Month," *SG*, Apr. 1900, 29.

61. "A Quiet Month," *SG*, Apr. 1900, 29.

62. "A Cooperative Coup d'Etat," *CN*, 1 July 1899.

63. "Interesting Letters," *CN*, 29 Aug. 1899.

64. *CN*, 24 Feb. 1900; "A Quiet Month," *SG*, Apr. 1900, 28–29; Merrell and Keyes, "Unite the Colonies."

65. "A Quiet Month," *SG*, Apr. 1900, 28–29; "April at Commonwealth," *SG*, May 1900, 31.

66. "The Assistant Cook," *SG*, June 1900, 19–20.

67. "Colony Notes," *CN*, 9 June 1900; "The Social Gospel," *SG*, June 1900, 26.

68. Casson, "Truth about Colonies," 3.

69. "A Quiet Month," *SG*, Apr. 1900, 28–30; Naveh and Colletti, *Crown of Thorns*, 111.

70. "A Quiet Month," *SG*, Apr. 1900, 29.

71. "April at Commonwealth," *SG*, May 1900, 30; *SG*, May 1900, passim.

72. Sue Fay Hinckley, "Diary," quoted in Dombrowski, *Early Days of Christian Socialism*, 151.

73. "A Quiet Month," *SG*, Apr. 1900, 30.

74. "April at Commonwealth," *SG*, May 1900, 31.

75. Ibid., 30; "Locals," *SG*, June 1900, 26; "Thirty Days," *SG*, Mar. 1900, 21.

76. "A Quiet Month," *SG*, Apr. 1900, 30.

77. "April at Commonwealth," *SG*, May 1900, 30–31.

78. *Columbus Enquirer-Sun*, 31 May 1900, 17 June 1900.

79. *Commonwealth Details*, 11; "Still at Commonwealth," *SG*, June 1900, 24; "Locals," *SG*, June 1900, 26.

80. "The Assistant Cook," *SG*, June 1900, 21; "A Statement," *SG*, June 1900, 23; "The Social Gospel," *SG*, June 1900, 26; *Columbus Enquirer-Sun*, 31 May 1900; "Locals," *SG*, June 1900, 26; RA, "Christian Commonwealth," TMs, FDP, 50.

81. "The Assistant Cook," *SG*, June 1900, 22.

82. *CN*, 14 Apr. 1900; RA, "Reminiscences," 68; Timothy Miller, *Quest for Utopia*, 10–11; Otohiko Okugawa, "Annotated List of Communal and Utopian Societies, 1787–1919," in Fogarty, *Dictionary*, 225–26.

83. "The Magazine and the Colony," *SG*, June 1900, 25–26; *Columbus Daily-Enquirer*, 24 July 1900.

84. *Columbus Enquirer-Sun*, 8 June 1900; RA, "Christian Commonwealth," TMs, FDP, 3, 18, 50.

85. "A Statement," *SG*, June 1900, 23.

86. *Columbus Enquirer-Sun*, 8 June 1900; "The Assistant Cook," *SG*, June 1900, 22;

"The Social Gospel," *SG*, June 1900, 26; RA, "Christian Commonwealth," TMs, FDP, 3, 15, 18, 50; "A Magazine of Christian Altruism," *SG*, Aug. 1900, 42; *SG*, Dec. 1900, 31.

87. Sue Fay Hinckley, conversation with Dombrowski, in Dombrowski, *Early Days of Christian Socialism*, 153.

88. "Still at Commonwealth," *SG*, June 1900, 24; "The Social Gospel," *SG*, June 1900, 26; "Locals," *SG*, June 1900, 26.

89. *Columbus Enquirer-Sun*, 13 Oct. 1903; RA, "Christian Commonwealth," TMs, FDP, 50; Dombrowski, *Early Days of Christian Socialism*, 166n61; Leon de Brabant to RA, 24 Sept. 1904, folder 58, box 1, MS1752, Yale University Library, New Haven, Conn.

90. *Columbus Enquirer-Sun*, 29 July 1900; *Appeal to Reason*, 18 Aug. 1900, 4.

91. W. A. Ross, Receiver to William T. Harvey and Wm. Henry Harvey, 20 Apr. 1901, Muscogee County Deed Book "NN," 278–80; *Columbus Daily-Enquirer*, 29 July 1900.

92. *Columbus Enquirer-Sun*, 7 Nov. 1900; W. A. Ross, Receiver to William T. Harvey and Wm. Henry Harvey, 20 Apr. 1901, Muscogee County Deed Book "NN," 278–80; *Columbus Daily Enquirer*, 2 Dec. 1900.

93. W. A. Ross, Receiver to William T. Harvey and Wm. Henry Harvey, 20 Apr. 1901, Muscogee County Deed Book "NN," 278–80; Leon de Brabant to Albertson, 24 Sept. 1904 and 30 Dec. 1904, folder 58, box 1, MS1752, Yale University Library; Elliot and Dean, "Commonwealth, Georgia," 15; *Columbus Ledger*, 30 Mar. 1903; *Columbus Enquirer-Sun*, 13 Oct. 1903.

94. *Columbus Enquirer-Sun*, 7 Nov. 1900, 6 Dec. 1900, 19 Dec. 1900, 24 Jan. 1901, 11 June 1901; Timothy Miller, *Quest for Utopia*, 10.

95. *Columbus Enquirer-Sun*, 24 Jan. 1901, 29 July 1900, 11 June 1901.

96. "Publisher's Notes," *SG*, Jan. 1901; *Columbus Enquirer-Sun*, 11 June 1901, 28 Jan. 1902; Albertson, "Reminiscences," 92; RA, "Christian Commonwealth," TMs, FDP, 2, 50.

97. *Columbus Enquirer-Sun*, 11 June 1901, 28 Jan. 1902; RA, "Christian Commonwealth," TMs, FDP, 2, 50.

98. Pierson, "Dream Which Proved Baseless," 226.

99. Elliot and Dean, "Commonwealth, Georgia," 26.

100. Gill, *School of the Americas*.

CHAPTER 10. IN RETROSPECT

1. White and Hopkins, *Social Gospel*, 176.

2. RA, "Christian Commonwealth," TMs, FDP 3, 25.

3. Timothy Miller, *Quest for Utopia*, 9.

4. GHG, "Why Commonwealth Failed," 5–6.

5. RA, "Reminiscences," 58, 92; RA, "Commonwealth in Retrospect," 7–8; "The Assistant Cook," *SG*, June 1900, 21; RA, "Christian Commonwealth," TMs, FDP, 51.

6. *SG*, Apr. 1901, 48; RA, "Christian Altruism and Its Message to the Churches," *SG*, June 1901, 3–9.

7. Destler, *Henry Demarest Lloyd*, 397–98.

8. GHG to RA, 10 May 1904; Alexander Kent to RA, 6 June 1904; untitled poem, folder 43, box 5, MS1752, Manuscripts and Archives, Yale University Library.

9. RA, "Reminiscences," 72; Timothy Miller, *Quest for Utopia*, 107–8.

10. Arthur Schlesinger Jr., "Foreword," in Frances Davis, *Fearful Innocence*, ix–xii; Timothy Miller, *Quest for Utopia*, 119.

11. "Colony Notes," *SG*, Sept. 1899, 27; RA, "Christian Commonwealth," TMs, FDP, 8, 31.

12. *Columbus Enquirer-Sun*, 2 Aug. 1901; RA, "Christian Commonwealth," TMs, FDP, 8.

13. RA, "Christian Commonwealth," TMs, FDP, 52.

14. GHG, "In the Light of Experience," *SG*, Jan. 1900, 9–11.

15. RA, "Christian Commonwealth," TMs, FDP, 53–56.

16. *SG*, Mar. 1900, 22.

17. S. F. H., "A Meditation," *SG*, Mar. 1900, 23.

18. *Columbus Enquirer-Sun*, 2 June 1901.

19. Damon to GHG, ca. Dec. 1907, in Dombrowski, *Early Days of Christian Socialism*, 168–69.

20. RA, "Christian Commonwealth," TMs, FDP, 8; RA, "Reminiscences."

21. RA, "Christian Commonwealth," TMs, FDP, 8; RA, "Commonwealth in Retrospect," 8.

22. Mrs. J. V. Fothergill to Dombrowski, 19 Oct. 1932, in Dombrowski, *Early Days of Christian Socialism*, 168.

23. "Colony Notes," *SG*, June 1898, 25.

24. *Columbus Enquirer-Sun*, 28 Jan. 1902.

25. Kent, "Cooperative Communities," 616; Dombrowski, *Early Days of Christian Socialism*, 167; RA, "Christian Commonwealth," TMs, FDP, 53–54.

26. Bushee, "Communistic Societies," 652.

27. John Chipman, Letter to Dombrowski, 16 Nov. 1932, in Dombrowski, *Early Days of Christian Socialism*, 167.

28. RA, "Commonwealth in Retrospect," 7.

29. Gavit, "Edward Tyler Keyes"; W. A. Ross, "The Growth of Right Principle," *SG*, Nov. 1900, 23–24.

30. Addams, "Visit to Tolstoy," 301–2; Addams, *Twenty Years at Hull House*, 198–99.

31. Graham Taylor, "Editorial," 1.

BIBLIOGRAPHY

✦ ✦ ✦

Aaron, Daniel. *Men of Good Hope*. New York: Oxford University Press, 1951.

Abell, Aaron Ignatius. *The Urban Impact on American Protestantism, 1865–1900*. Cambridge, Mass.: Harvard University Press, 1943.

Adams, Frank T. *James A. Dombrowski: An American Heretic, 1897–1983*. Knoxville: University of Tennessee Press, 1992.

Addams, Jane. *Twenty Years at Hull House, with Autobiographical Notes*. New York: Macmillan, 1910. Reprint, New American Library, 1961.

———. "A Visit to Tolstoy." *McClure's Magazine* 36 (Jan. 1911): 295–302.

Ahlstrom, Sydney. *A Religious History of the American People*. 1972. Reprint, New Haven, Conn.: Yale University Press, 2004.

Albertson, Ralph. "Autobiography, 1936." TMs, [1936]. Ralph Albertson Papers (MS1752). Yale University Library, New Haven, Conn.

———. "The Christian Commonwealth." *Kingdom*, 2 Apr. 1897.

———. "The Christian Commonwealth." TMs. Frances Davis Papers, 1899–1983. Schlesinger Library, Radcliffe Institute, Harvard University, Cambridge, Mass.

———. "The Christian Commonwealth in Georgia." *Georgia Historical Quarterly* 29 (Sept. 1945): 125–42.

———. "Christianizing Property." *Twentieth Century* 18 (22 May 1897): 10–11.

———. "Common Property." *Kingdom*, 11 Sept. 1896.

———. "Commonwealth in Retrospect." *Commons*, Jan. 1901, 6–8.

———. "Fifty Years After." Ralph Albertson Papers. Manuscripts and Archives, Yale University Library, New Haven, Conn.

———. "Journal." The "Farm" Papers, West Newbury, Mass.

———. "New Evangelism." *Kingdom*, 27 Nov. 1896.

———. "Reminiscences." TMs, ca. 1936. Ralph Albertson Papers (MS1752). Yale University Library, New Haven, Conn.

———. "Selfish Socialism." *Kingdom*, 24 July 1896.

———. *The Social Incarnation*. 2nd ed. Commonwealth, Ga.: Christian Commonwealth, 1899.

———. "The Social Incarnation." *Kingdom*, 16 Oct. 1896.

———. "Some Suggestions for a Christian Criminology." *Kingdom*, 6 Sept. 1895.

——. "A Survey of Mutualistic Communities in America." *Iowa Journal of History and Politics* 34 (Oct. 1936): 375–444.

——. *Thy Cloak Also.* 1947(?). TMs. Ralph Albertson Papers, (MS1752). Manuscripts and Archives, Yale University Library, New Haven, Conn.

Alliance-Independent (Lincoln, Nebr.). 1892–95.

Alston, Charlotte. *Russia's Greatest Enemy: Harold Williams and the Russian Revolutions.* London: Tauris Academic Studies, 2007.

——. *Tolstoy and His Disciples: The History of a Radical International Movement.* London: I. B. Tauris, 2014.

Alyea, Paul E., and Blanche R. Alyea. *Fairhope, 1894–1954: The Story of a Single Tax Colony.* University: University of Alabama Press, 1956.

American Fabian (New York). May 1898–Dec. 1899.

American Peace Society. "Editorial Notes." *Advocate of Peace* 60, no. 11 (1898):253–54.

Andersen, Eric. *Race and Politics in North Carolina, 1872–1901.* Baton Rouge: Louisiana State University Press, 1980.

Anthony, C. V. *Fifty Years of Methodism: A History of the Methodist Episcopal Church within the Bounds of the California Annual Conference from 1847 to 1897.* San Francisco: Methodist Book Concern, 1901.

Appeal to Reason (Kansas City, Kans.). 1895–1901.

Appelbaum, Patricia. *St. Francis of America: How a Thirteenth-Century Friar Became America's Most Popular Saint.* Chapel Hill: University of North Carolina Press, 2015.

Arena (Boston). 1896–1901.

Armytage, W. H. G. "J. C. Kenworthy and the Tolstoyan Communities in England." *American Journal of Economics and Sociology* 16 (July 1957): 391–405.

Arnold, J. H. "Is It Practicable?" *Kingdom*, 27 Dec. 1895.

Ayers, Edward L. *The Promise of the New South: Life after Reconstruction.* New York: Oxford University Press, 1992.

Beasley, Rebecca, and Philip Ross Bullock, eds. *Russia in Britain, 1880–1940: From Melodrama to Modernism.* Oxford: Oxford University Press, 2013.

Bederman, Gail. *Manliness and Civilization: A Cultural History of Gender and Race in the United States, 1880–1917.* Chicago: University of Chicago Press, 1995.

Bell, Daniel. *Marxian Socialism in the United States.* Princeton, N.J.: Princeton University Press, 1967.

Bellamy, Edward. *Looking Backward: 2000–1887.* Boston: Ticknor, 1888. Reprint, New York: New American Library, 1960.

Bercovitch, Sacvan. *The Puritan Origins of the American Self.* New Haven, Conn.: Yale University Press, 1975.

Bestor, Arthur. *Backwoods Utopias: The Sectarian and Owenite Phases of Communitarian Socialism, 1663–1829.* Philadelphia: University of Pennsylvania Press, 1950.

Bliss, William D. P. "Self-Serving Colonies Condemned." *Kingdom*, 6 Apr. 1899.

Bolster, Paul D. "Christian Socialism Comes to Georgia: The Christian Commonwealth Colony." *Georgia Review* 26 (Spring 1972): 60–70.

Brundage, W. Fitzhugh. *A Socialist Utopia in the New South: The Ruskin Colonies in Tennessee and Georgia, 1894–1901*. Champaign: University of Illinois Press, 1996.

———. "Utopian Frontier in the New South." Paper presented at the Society for Utopian Studies Conference, St. Louis, Mo.

Buhle, Mari Jo. *Women and American Socialism, 1870–1920*. Urbana: University of Illinois Press, 1981.

Burch, Dinah, ed. *Ruskin and the Dawn of the Modern*. Oxford: Clarendon, 1999.

Bushee, Frederick A. "Communistic Societies in the United States." *Political Science Quarterly* 20 (1905): 625–64.

Butler, Jon. *Awash in a Sea of Faith: Christianizing the American People*. Cambridge, Mass.: Harvard University Press, 1990.

Calhoun, Charles W., ed. *The Gilded Age: Perspectives on the Origins of Modern America*. 2nd ed. New York: Rowman & Littlefield, 2007.

Casson, Herbert N. "The Truth about Colonies." *Appeal to Reason*, 10 Mar. 1900.

Chicago Commons Association. *The Commons*. Chicago, 1897–1905.

Chipman, John. "Mr. Chipman's Reply." *Kingdom*, 27 Dec. 1895.

———. "A Proposition." *Kingdom*, 29 Nov. 1895.

Chmielewski, Wendy E., Louis J. Kern, and Marilyn Klee-Hartzell, eds. *Women in Spiritual and Communitarian Societies in the United States*. Syracuse, N.Y.: Syracuse University Press, 1993.

Christian, R. F., ed. *Tolstoy's Letters, Volume II, 1880–1910*. London: Athlone Press, 1978.

The Christian Commonwealth. Midlands, Ga.: Christian Commonwealth, 1896.

Christian Commonwealth Colony. [Photographs by George Alfred Damon] (ca. 1896–1899). Manuscript Collection 1004. Hargrett Rare Book and Manuscript Library, University of Georgia, Athens.

"The Christian Commonwealth in Georgia." *Outlook* 60 (1898): 635–36.

Clubb, Henry S., ed. "Christian Commonwealth, Ga." *Food, Home and Garden*, n.s., 3, no. 24 (Jan. 1899): 6.

Codman, John Thomas. *Brook Farm Memoirs: Historic and Personal Memoirs*. Boston: Arena, 1894.

Columbus (Ga.) Daily Enquirer. July 1897–1900.

Columbus (Ga.) Enquirer-Sun. Nov. 1896–1903.

Columbus (Ga.) Sunday Herald. Nov. 1896–Dec. 1900.

Coming Age (Boston). 1899–1900.

Coming Nation (Ruskin Commonwealth, Tenn.). 1896–1901.

Commager, Henry S. *The American Mind: An Interpretation of American Thought and Character since the 1880s*. New Haven, Conn.: Yale University Press, 1950.

Commonwealth Details…An Illustrated Account of the Community of Christian Socialists Located at Commonwealth, Georgia. Commonwealth, Ga.: Christian Commonwealth, 1899.

Crosby, Ernest Howard. *Plain Talk in Psalm and Parable*. Boston: Small, Maynard, 1899.

———. "The Wealth of St. Francis: A Study in Transcendental Economics." *Craftsman*, Oct. 1902.

Crunden, Robert M. *Ministers of Reform: The Progressives' Achievement in American Civilization, 1889–1920*. Urbana: University of Illinois Press, 1984.

Curtis, Susan. *A Consuming Faith: The Social Gospel and Modern American Culture*. Baltimore: Johns Hopkins University Press, 1991.

Davis, Allen F. *American Heroine: The Life and Legend of Jane Addams*. New York: Oxford University Press, 1973.

———. *Spearheads for Reform: The Social Settlements and the Progressive Movement, 1890–1914*. New York: Oxford University Press, 1967.

Davis, Frances. *A Fearful Innocence*. Kent, Ohio: Kent State University Press, 1981.

———. Papers, 1899–1983. Schlesinger Library, Radcliffe Institute, Harvard University, Cambridge, Mass.

Degler, Carl N. *In Search of Human Nature: The Decline and Revival of Darwinism in American Social Thought*. New York: Oxford University Press, 1991.

Destler, Chester McArthur. *Henry Demarest Lloyd and the Empire of Reform*. Philadelphia: University of Pennsylvania Press, 1963.

Dombrowski, James. *The Early Days of Christian Socialism in America*. New York: Columbia University Press, 1936.

Dorn, Jacob H. *Washington Gladden: Prophet of the Social Gospel*. Columbus: Ohio State University Press, 1966.

Dressner, Richard B. "William Dwight Porter Bliss's Christian Socialism." *Church History* 47 (Mar. 1978): 66–82.

Edwards, Rebecca. *New Spirits: Americans in the "Gilded Age," 1865–1905*. 2nd ed. New York: Oxford University Press, 2011.

Edwards, Wendy J. Deichmann, and Carolyn De Swarte Gifford, eds. *Gender and the Social Gospel*. Urbana: University of Illinois Press, 2003.

Egbert, Donald D., and Stow Persons, eds. *Socialism and American Life*. 2 vols. Princeton, N.J.: Princeton University Press, 1952.

Elliot, Daniel T., and Tracy M. Dean. "Commonwealth, Georgia." LAMAR Institute Publication Series Report No. 90. Savannah, Ga.: LAMAR Institute, 2007.

Ely, Richard T. *Social Aspects of Christianity and Other Essays*. New York: Thomas Y. Crowell, 1889.

Evans, Christopher H. *The Social Gospel in American Religion: A History*. New York: New York University Press, 2017.

Fairhope (Ala.) Courier. 1898–May 1899.

Fine, Sidney. *Laissez-Faire and the General Welfare State: A Study of Conflict in American Thought, 1865–1901*. Ann Arbor: University of Michigan Press, 1956.

Fish, John O. "The Christian Commonwealth Colony: A Georgia Experiment, 1896–1900." *Georgia Historical Quarterly* 57 (Summer 1973): 213–26.

Flynt, J. Wayne. "Southern Protestantism and Reform, 1890–1920." In *Varieties of Southern Religious Experience*, edited by Samuel S. Hill, 135–57. Baton Rouge: Louisiana State University Press, 1988.

Fogarty, Robert S. *All Things New: American Communes and Utopian Movements, 1860–1914*. Chicago: University of Chicago Press, 1990.

——, ed. *Dictionary of American Communal and Utopian History*. Westport, Conn.: Greenwood, 1980.

Frederick, Peter J. *Knights of the Golden Rule: The Intellectual as Christian Reformer in the 1890s*. Lexington: University Press of Kentucky, 1976.

Fried, Albert, ed. *Socialism in America: From the Shakers to the Third International*. Garden City, N.Y.: Doubleday, 1970.

Gabriel, Ralph Henry. *The Course of American Democratic Thought*. New York: Ronald Press, 1956.

Gavit, John Palmer. "Edward Tyler Keyes: 'A Workman Needeth Not to be Ashamed.'" *Commons* 10 (July 1905): 412–15.

Gibson, George Howard. "Christian Commonwealth." *Commons* 3 (Oct. 1898): 3–7, 10.

——. "The Christian Commonwealth, of Commonwealth, Ga." *Coming Age*, Sept. 1899, 299–304.

——. "Colony Troubles: A Commonwealth View of the Recent Proceedings in the Courts." *Sunday Herald*, 9 July 1899.

——. "Communism Again." *Kingdom*, 17 Jan. 1896.

——. "An Interesting Symposium." *New Republic*, 12 Dec. 1890.

——. "Letter from the Christian Commonwealth." *Coming Nation*, 11 June 1898.

——. *The People's Hour and Other Themes*. Chicago: Englewood, 1909.

——. "Salutatory." *Alliance-Independent*, 5 Oct. 1893, 4.

——. "A Society of Brothers" (Leaflet). Commonwealth, Ga.: Christian Commonwealth, 1898.

——. "Why Commonwealth Failed." *Commons*, Jan. 1901, 5–6.

Gill, Leslie. *School of the Americas: Military Training and Political Violence in America*. Durham, N.C.: Duke University Press, 2004.

Ginger, Ray. *The Bending Cross: A Biography of Eugene Victor Debs*. New Brunswick, N.J.: Rutgers College, 1949.

Gladden, Washington. "The Eight-Hour Problem." *Dawn*, July–Aug. 1890, 137–47.

Gleason, H. W. "The Main Defect in the Cooperative Colony." *Kingdom*, 2 Mar. 1899.

Goodwyn, Lawrence. *The Populist Moment: A Short History of the Agrarian Revolt in America*. New York: Oxford University Press, 1978.

Gorrell, Donald K. *The Age of Social Responsibility: The Social Gospel in the Progressive Era, 1900–1920*. Macon, Ga.: Mercer University Press, 1988.

Grob, Gerald N. *Workers and Utopia: A Study of Ideological Conflict in the American Labor Movement, 1865–1900*. Chicago: Quadrangle, 1968.

Gronlund, Lawrence. *The Cooperative Commonwealth, 1884*. Edited by Stow Persons. Cambridge, Mass.: Belknap, 1965.

Guarneri, Carl J. *The Utopian Alternative: Fourierism in Nineteenth-Century America*. Ithaca, N.Y.: Cornell University Press, 1991.

Hahn, Steven. *The Roots of Southern Populism: Yeoman Farmers and the Transformation of the Georgia Upcountry, 1850–1890*. New York: Oxford University Press, 1983.

Hale, Edward Everett, Jr., ed. *The Life and Letters of Edward Everett Hale*. Boston: Little, Brown, 1917.

Handy, Robert T. "George D. Herron and the Kingdom Movement." *Church History* 19 (June 1950): 97–115.

——. "The Influence of Mazzini on the American Social Gospel." *Journal of Religion* 29 (Apr. 1949): 114–23.

——, ed. *The Social Gospel in America, 1870–1920: Gladden, Ely, Rauschenbusch*. New York: Oxford University Press, 1966.

Hansot, Elisabeth. *Perfection and Progress: Two Modes of Utopian Thought*. Cambridge, Mass.: MIT Press, 1974.

Harper, Keith. *The Quality of Mercy: Southern Baptists and Social Christianity, 1890–1920*. Tuscaloosa: University of Alabama Press, 1996.

Harper, W. "Communistic Societies Unwise." *Kingdom*, 10 Jan. 1896.

Hayden, Dolores. *Seven American Utopias: The Architecture of Communitarian Socialism, 1790–1975*. Cambridge, Mass.: MIT Press, 1976.

Herron, George D. *Between Caesar and Jesus*. New York: Thomas Y. Crowell, 1899.

——. *The Christian Society*. New York: Macmillan, 1894.

——. *The Christian State*. New York: Macmillan, 1895.

——. *The Larger Christ*. Chicago: F. H. Revell, 1891.

——. *The Message of Jesus to Men of Wealth*. New York: Fleming H. Revell, 1891.

——. *The New Redemption: A Call to the Church to Reconstruct Society According to the Gospel of Christ*. New York: Thomas Y. Crowell, 1893.

——. *A Plea for the Gospel*. New York: Macmillan, 1892.

——. *Social Meanings of Religious Experiences*. New York: Thomas Y. Crowell, 1896.

Hill, Mary. *Charlotte Perkins Gilman: The Making of a Radical Feminist, 1860–1896*. Philadelphia: Temple University Press, 1980.

Hinds, William Alfred. *American Communities and Cooperative Colonies*. 2nd rev. ed. Chicago: Charles H. Kerr, 1908. Reprint, Philadelphia: Porcupine Press, 1975.

Hofstadter, Richard. *The Age of Reform: From Bryan to F.D.R.* New York: Vintage, 1955.

——. *Social Darwinism in American Thought*. Rev. ed. Boston: Beacon, 1955.

Hopkins, Charles Howard. *The Rise of the Social Gospel in American Protestantism, 1865–1915*. New Haven, Conn.: Yale University Press, 1940.

Howells, William Dean. *A Traveler from Altruria*. New York: Harper & Brothers, 1894.

Jennings, Chris. *Paradise Now: The Story of American Utopianism*. New York: Random House, 2016.

Jernigan, E. Jay. *Henry Demarest Lloyd*. Boston: Twayne, 1976.

Jobes, Rev. C. S. "Is Communism Practicable?" *Kingdom*, 13 Dec. 1895.

Jones, Jesse Henry. *The Bible Plan for the Abolition of Poverty and the New Political Economy Involved Therein*. Commonwealth, Ga.: Christian Commonwealth, 1900.

Jones, Marnie. *Holy Toledo: Religion and Politics in the Life of "Golden Rule" Jones*. Lexington: University Press of Kentucky, 1998.

Kallman, Theodore. "The Pilgrimage of Ralph Albertson." *Communal Societies* 26 (Aug. 2006): 79–98.

———. "The Pilgrimage of Ralph Albertson (1866–1951): Modern American Liberalism and the Pursuit of Happiness." Ph.D. dissertation, Georgia State University, Atlanta, 1997.

Kanter, Rosabeth. *Commitment and Community: Communes and Utopias in Sociological Perspective*. Cambridge, Mass.: Harvard University Press, 1972.

Kasson, John F. *Civilizing the Machine: Technology and Republican Values in America, 1776–1900*. New York: Grossman, 1976.

Katscher, Leopold. "Owen's Topolobampo Colony, Mexico." *American Journal of Sociology* 12 (Sept. 1906): 145–75.

Kent, Rev. Alexander. "Cooperative Communities in the United States." *Bulletin of the Department of Labor* 35 (July 1901): 563–646.

Kessler, Carol Farley. *Charlotte Perkins Gilman: Her Progress toward Utopia with Selected Writings*. Syracuse, N.Y.: Syracuse University Press, 1995.

Keston, Seymour. *Utopian Episodes: Daily Life in Experimental Colonies Dedicated to Changing the World*. Syracuse, N.Y.: Syracuse University Press, 1993.

Kingdom (Minneapolis). 1895–99.

Klaw, Spencer. *Without Sin: The Rise and Fall of the Oneida Community*. New York: Penguin, 1993.

K'Meyer, Tracy. *Interracialism and Christianity in the Postwar South: The Story of Koinonia Farm*. Charlottesville: University of Virginia Press, 1997.

Knight, Louise W. *Citizen: Jane Addams and the Struggle for Democracy*. Chicago: University of Chicago Press, 2005.

Lasch, Christopher. *The New Radicalism in America, 1889–1963: The Intellectual as a Social Type*. New York: Knopf, 1965.

Laslett, John H. M., and Seymour Martin Lipset, eds. *Failure of a Dream? Essays in the History of American Socialism*. Rev. ed. Berkeley: University of California Press, 1974.

Lears, T. J. Jackson. *No Place of Grace: Antimodernism and the Transformation of American Culture, 1880–1920*. New York: Pantheon, 1981.

LeWarne, Charles. "Labor and Communitarianism, 1880–1900." *Labor History* 16 (1975): 393–407.

———. *Utopias on Puget Sound*. Seattle: University of Washington Press, 1975.

Link, Arthur, and Richard L. McCormick. *Progressivism*. Arlington Heights, Ill.: Harlan Davidson, 1983.

Lloyd, Caro. *Henry Demarest Lloyd, 1847–1903: A Biography*. 2 vols. New York: Putnam's, 1912.

Lloyd, Henry Demarest. *Mazzini and Other Essays*. New York: Putnam's, 1910.

———. Papers. Wisconsin Historical Society, Madison.

———. *Wealth against Commonwealth*. New York: Harper & Brothers, 1894.

Luker, Ralph E. "Liberal Theology and Social Conservatism: A Southern Tradition, 1840–1920." *Church History* 50 (June 1981): 193–204.

———. "The Social Gospel and the Failure of Racial Reform, 1877–1898." *Church History* 46 (Mar. 1977): 80–99.

——. *The Social Gospel in Black and White: American Racial Reform, 1885–1912.* Chapel Hill: University of North Carolina Press, 1991.

Mann, Arthur. *Yankee Reformers in the Urban Age.* New York: Harper & Row, 1966.

Manuel, Frank, and P. Fritzie Manuel. *Utopian Thought in the Western World.* Cambridge, Mass.: Harvard University Press, 1979.

Marks, Steven Gary. *How Russia Shaped the Modern World: From Art to Anti-Semitism.* Princeton, N.J.: Princeton University Press, 2003.

Matthews, Shailer. "The Development of Social Christianity in America during the Past Twenty-Five Years." *Journal of Religion* 7 (July 1927): 376–86.

——. *The Social Teaching of Jesus: An Essay in Christian Sociology.* London: Macmillan, 1897.

Maude, Aylmer. *Life of Tolstoy: First Fifty Years.* London: Constable, 1917.

——. *Peculiar People: The Doukhobors.* New York: Funk & Wagnalls, 1904.

May, Henry F. *Protestant Churches and Industrial America.* New York: Harper, 1967.

McGerr, Michael. *A Fierce Discontent: The Rise and Fall of the Progressive Movement in America, 1870–1920.* 2003. Reprint, Oxford: Oxford University Press, 2005.

McKanan, Dan. *Prophetic Encounters: Religion and the American Radical Tradition.* Boston: Beacon, 2012.

McKeogh, Colm. *Tolstoy's Pacifism.* Amherst, N.Y.: Cambria Press, 2009.

McMath, Robert C., Jr. *American Populism: A Social History, 1877–1898.* New York: Hill & Wang, 1992.

McQuaid, Kim. "Businessman as Social Innovator: N. O. Nelson, Promoter of Garden Cities and Consumer Cooperatives." *American Journal of Economics and Sociology* 34 (Oct. 1975): 411–22.

Merrell, John B., and E. T. Keyes. "Unite the Colonies." *Coming Nation,* 19 May 1900.

Miller, Perry, ed. *American Thought: Civil War to World War I.* New York: Rinehart, 1954.

Miller, Timothy. *Following in His Steps: A Biography of Charles M. Sheldon.* Knoxville: University of Tennessee Press, 1987.

——. *The Quest for Utopia in Twentieth-Century America, Volume 1: 1900–1960.* Syracuse, N.Y.: Syracuse University Press, 1998.

Mixed Stocks (Chicago). 1898–99. Edited by Edward T. Keyes.

Moorhead, James H. "The Erosion of Postmillennialism in American Religious Thought, 1865–1925." *Church History* 53 (1984): 61–77.

Morris, Adam. *American Messiahs: False Prophets of a Damned Nation.* New York: Liveright, 2019.

Mumford, Lewis. *The Story of Utopias.* New York: Boni and Liveright, 1922.

Muncy, Raymond Lee. *Sex and Marriage in Utopian Communities: 19th-Century America.* Bloomington: Indiana University Press, 1973.

Naveh, Eyal J., and Lucio Colletti. *Crown of Thorns.* New York: New York University Press, 1992.

Nevins, Allen, and Dean Albertson, eds. "The Reminiscences of Ralph Albertson." Columbia University Oral History Collection, pt. 2, no. 3 (5 Apr. 1950).

Niebuhr, H. R. *The Kingdom of God in America*. 1937. Reprint, Middletown, Conn.: Wesleyan University Press, 1988.

Niklason, F. "Henry George: Social Gospeller." *American Quarterly* 22 (Fall 1970): 445–58.

Nordhoff, Charles. *The Communistic Societies of the United States: From Personal Visit and Observation*. 1875. Reprint, New York: Dover, 1966.

Noyes, John Humphrey. *History of American Socialisms*. 1870. Reprint, New York: Dover, 1966.

Nye, Russell B. *Midwestern Progressive Politics: A Historical Study of Its Origins and Development, 1870–1958*. New York: Harper & Row, 1959.

Oneida Community Collection. Syracuse University, Syracuse, N.Y.

Oved, Yaacov. *Two Hundred Years of American Communes*. 1988; Reprint, New Brunswick, N.J.: Transaction, 1993.

Parrington, Vernon Louis, Jr. *American Dreams: A Study of American Utopias*. 2nd ed. New York: Russell & Russell, 1964.

Paulson, Ross. *Radicalism and Reform: The Vrooman Family and American Social Thought, 1837–1937*. Lexington: University Press of Kentucky, 1968.

Phillips, Paul T. *A Kingdom on Earth: Anglo-American Social Christianity, 1880–1940*. University Park: Pennsylvania State University Press. 1996.

Pierson, Arthur T., ed. "A Dream Which Proved Baseless." *Missionary Review of the World*, Mar. 1901.

Pitzer, Donald E., ed. *America's Communal Utopias*. Chapel Hill: University of North Carolina Press, 1997.

Pollack, Norman. *The Populist Response to Industrial America: Midwestern Populist Thought*. New York: Norton, 1962.

Prettyman, Gib. "Gilded Age Utopias of Incorporation." *Utopian Studies* 1 (2001): 19–40.

Quandt, Jean B. *From the Small Town to the Great Community: The Social Thought of Progressive Intellectuals*. New Brunswick, N.J.: Rutgers University Press, 1970.

Questel, Lynn K. "The Christian Commonwealth Colony." M.A. thesis, University of Georgia, Athens, 1982.

Quint, Howard. *The Forging of American Socialism: Origins of the Modern Movement*. Columbia: University of South Carolina Press, 1953.

Ram's Horn (Chicago). 1898–May 1899.

Ray, Randall Jordan. *The Law of Love: The Christian Commonwealth Colony, A Utopian Experiment*. M.A. thesis, Auburn University, 2013.

Resek, Carl, ed. *The Progressives*. New York: Bobbs-Merrill, 1967.

Rodgers, Daniel T. *Atlantic Crossings*. Cambridge, Mass.: Harvard University Press, 1998.

———. "In Search of Progressivism." *Reviews in American History* 10 (Dec. 1982): 113–32.

Roemer, Kenneth M. *The Obsolete Necessity: America in Utopian Writings, 1888–1900*. Kent, Ohio: Kent State University Press, 1976.

Rohrlich, Ruby, ed. *Women in Search of Utopia*. New York: Schocken Books, 1984.

Rooney, Charles J., Jr. *Dreams and Visions: A Study of American Utopias, 1865–1917*. Westport, Conn.: Greenwood, 1985.

Ross, Malcolm. *The Man Who Lived Backward*. New York: Farrar, Straus, 1950.

Sabatier, Paul. *The Road to Assisi: The Essential Biography of St. Francis*. 1894. Reprint, Brewster, Mass.: Paraclete Press, 2003.

Salvatore, Nick. *Eugene v. Debs: Citizen and Socialist*. 2nd ed. Champaign: University of Illinois Press, 2007.

Sanford, Charles L. *The Quest for Paradise: Europe and the American Moral Imagination*. Urbana: University of Illinois Press, 1961.

Scudder, Vida Dutton. "Christian Simplicity." *Publications of the Christian Social Union* 52 (15 Aug. 1898): 1–16.

——. *Social Ideals in English Letters*. Boston: Houghton Mifflin, 1898.

Sheldon, Charles. *In His Steps: What Would Jesus Do?* Chicago: Chicago Advance, 1896.

Smith, Gary Scott. *Salvation: Social Christianity and America, 1880–1925*. Lanham, Md.: Rowman & Littlefield, 2000.

Social Gospel (Commonwealth, Ga.). Feb. 1898–July 1901.

Spann, Edward K. *Brotherly Tomorrows: Movements for a Cooperative Society in America, 1820–1920*. New York: Columbia University Press, 1989.

Stedman, Murray S., Jr. "'Democracy'" in American Communal and Socialist Literature." *Journal of the History of Ideas* 12 (Jan. 1951): 147–54.

Stein, Stephen J. *Communities of Dissent: A History of Alternative Religions in America*. New York: Oxford University Press, 2003.

Sutton, Robert P. *Communal Utopias and the American Experience: Religious Communities, 1732–2000*. Westport, Conn.: Praeger, 2003.

Swift, Morrison. "Altruria in California." *Overland Monthly*, June 1897, 643–45.

Taylor, Barbara. *Eve and the New Jerusalem: Socialism and Feminism in the Nineteenth Century*. New York: Pantheon, 1983.

Taylor, Graham. "Editorial." *Commons*, Jan. 1901.

Thies, Clifford F. "The Success of American Communes." *Southern Economic Journal* 67 (July 2000): 186–99.

Thomas, John L. *Alternative America: Henry George, Edward Bellamy, Henry Demarest Lloyd and the Adversary Tradition*. Cambridge, Mass.: MIT Press, 1976.

Tichi, Cecelia. *Shifting Gears: Technology, Literature, Culture in Modernist America*. Chapel Hill: University of North Carolina Press, 1987.

Tiedje, Michelle D. "The People's Hour and the Social Gospel: George Howard Gibson's Gilded Age Search for an Organization of the Kingdom of God." M.A. thesis, University of Nebraska at Lincoln, 2010.

Tolstoy, Leo. *The Kingdom of God Is within You*. 1894. Reprint, New York: Dover, 2006.

——, ed. *Leo Tolstoy: Complete Collected Works in 90 Volumes*. Academic Anniversary ed., vol. 71. Moscow: Public Art, 1954.

Trachtenberg, Alan. *The Incorporation of America: Culture and Society in the Gilded Age*. New York: Hill & Wang, 1982.

Tuveson, Ernest. *Millennium and Utopia: A Study of the Background of the Idea of Progress*. Berkeley: University of California Press, 1949.

"Utopian Societies." In *World History: The Modern Era*. 15 May 2007. www.world history.abc-clio.com.

Velikanova, Natalia, and Robert T. Whittaker, eds. *Tolstoy and the USA*. Moscow: IMLI RAN, 2004.

Veysey, Laurence. *The Communal Experience: Anarchist and Mystical Counter-Cultures in America*. New York: Harper & Row, 1973.

Visser 't Hooft, Willem A. *The Background of the Social Gospel in America*. 1928. Reprint, St. Louis: Bethany Press, 1963.

Vrooman, Anne L. *Silver Text Bible Lessons: A Sociological Interpretation of the Bible from Genesis to Joshua*. St. Louis: Walter Vrooman, 1898.

Wachtell, Cynthia. "Ernest Howard Crosby's Swords and Plowshares: A Lost Anti-imperialism, Anti-militarism, and Anti-war Classic." *South Central Review* 30 (Spring 2013): 133–54.

Wagner, Jon. "Sexuality and Gender Roles in Utopian Communities: A Critical Survey of Scholarly Work." *Communal Societies* 6 (1985): 172–88.

———. "Success in Intentional Communities: The Problem of Evaluation." *Communal Societies* 5 (1985): 89–100.

Walker, Robert. *Reform in America: The Continuing Frontier*. Lexington: University Press of Kentucky, 1985.

Walker, Samuel. "George Howard Gibson: Christian Socialist among the Populists." *Nebraska History* 55 (Dec. 1974): 548–72.

Ware, Norman. *The Labor Movement in the United States, 1860–1895*. Gloucester, Mass.: Peter Smith, 1959.

Wealth Makers (Lincoln, Nebr.). 1894–95.

Webber, Everett. *Escape to Utopia: The Communal Movement in America*. New York: Hastings House, 1959.

Week's Work (Springfield, Ohio). Mar.–Sept. 1894.

Weimer, Mark. "The William Hinds *American Communities* Collection." *Communal Societies* 7 (1987): 95–103.

Weinstein, James. *The Corporate Ideal in the Liberal State, 1900–1918*. Boston: Beacon, 1968.

Weisbrod, Carol. *The Boundaries of Utopia*. New York: Pantheon, 1980.

White, Morton G. *Social Thought in America: The Revolt Against Formalism*. London: Oxford University Press, 1976.

White, Ronald C., Jr. *Liberty and Justice for All: Racial Reform and the Social Gospel (1877–1925)*. San Francisco: Harper & Row, 1990.

White, Ronald C., Jr., and C. Howard Hopkins. *The Social Gospel: Religion and Reform in Changing America*. Philadelphia: Temple University Press, 1976.

Whittaker, Robert. "Tolstoy's American Disciple: Letters to Ernest Howard Crosby, 1894–1906." *Triquarterly*, no. 98 (Winter 1996/1997): 210–51.

Wiebe, Robert H. *The Search for Order, 1877–1920*. New York: Hill & Wang, 1967.

"Willard Colony." In *Appleton's Annual Cyclopedia,* 3rd series, vol. 1, 533–36. New York: D. Appleton, 1897.

Woodall, W. C. "Our Town." *Columbus (Ga.) Ledger-Enquirer,* 17 Aug. 1969.

Woodward, C. Vann. *Origins of the New South, 1877–1913.* Baton Rouge: Louisiana State University Press, 1951.

———. *The Strange Career of Jim Crow.* 2nd rev. ed. New York: Oxford University Press, 1966.

———. *Tom Watson: Agrarian Rebel.* 1938. Reprint, New York: Oxford University Press, 1963.

Wright, Carroll D. *Bulletin of the Department of Labor.* Vol. 6. Washington, D.C.: Government Printing Office, 1901.

Yount, David. *America's Spiritual Utopias: The Quest for Heaven on Earth.* Westport, Conn.: Praeger, 2008.

INDEX

✦ ✦ ✦

CPSIA information can be obtained
at www.ICGtesting.com
Printed in the USA
LVHW111257020621
689143LV00003B/126